86814728S

Mobilizing Democracy

D0139622

THEMES IN GLOBAL SOCIAL CHANGE

Christopher Chase-Dunn, Series Editor

Mobilizing Democracy

Globalization and Citizen Protest

PAUL ALMEIDA

RARITAN VALLEY COMMUNITY COLLEGE
EVELYN S. FIELD LIBRARY

Johns Hopkins University Press

BALTIMORE

© 2014 Johns Hopkins University Press
All rights reserved. Published 2014
Printed in the United States of America on acid-free paper
9 8 7 6 5 4 3 2 1

Johns Hopkins University Press
2715 North Charles Street
Baltimore, Maryland 21218-4363
www.press.jhu.edu

Library of Congress Cataloging-in-Publication Data

Almeida, Paul, 1968–
    Mobilizing democracy : globalization and citizen protest /
Paul Almeida.
        pages cm. — (Themes in global social change)
    Includes bibliographical references and index.
    ISBN-13: 978-1-4214-1408-9 (hardcover : alk. paper)
    ISBN-13: 978-1-4214-1409-6 (pbk. : alk. paper)
    ISBN-13: 978-1-4214-1410-2 (electronic)
    ISBN-10: 1-4214-1408-2 (hardcover : alk. paper)
    ISBN-10: 1-4214-1409-0 (pbk. : alk. paper)
    ISBN 10: 1-4214-1410-4 (electronic)
    1. Social movements—Central America.   2. Protest movements—
Central America.   3. Globalization—Social aspects—Central
America.   4. Central America—Economic policy—Social aspects.
5. Central America—Politics and government—1979–.   I. Title.
    HM881.A396 2014
    303.48'4—dc23   2013043576

A catalog record for this book is available from the British Library.

*Special discounts are available for bulk purchases of this book. For more
information, please contact Special Sales at 410-516-6936 or
specialsales@press.jhu.edu.*

Johns Hopkins University Press uses environmentally friendly book
materials, including recycled text paper that is composed of at least
30 percent post-consumer waste, whenever possible.

For Patsy and Andrea

Contents

Figures and Tables

TABLES

Acknowledgments

In the late 1990s and early 2000s, as I was finishing my doctoral dissertation on popular movements in El Salvador during the 1960s and 1970s and trying to understand how sustained mass mobilization was even possible under authoritarian military regimes, a new type of protest seemed to be emerging in a relatively more democratic context. As I attempted to follow events as they unfolded, a clear pattern emerged: major outbreaks of protests were occurring over similar issues in multiple Central American countries. These conflicts usually centered on some type of public infrastructure privatization. Later in the 2000s, the Central American Free Trade Agreement was added to the list of polarizing issues. In order to take on the daunting task of documenting these protest campaigns across six countries, I sought out the assistance of dozens of individuals and institutions. First and foremost, I am eternally indebted to my graduate school supervisor, Linda Brewster Stearns, whose countless hours with me can never be reciprocated. I thank her for showing me the tools of the trade; a student of sociology could not ask for more. I am so fortunate that our paths crossed and she invited me to work with her.

In El Salvador, I benefited from the assistance of Roxana Delgado, including our collaborative work on the role of the women's movement in the campaigns against health care privatization. Also, I value my lifelong friendship with Andrés Ortiz. Luis Armando González allowed me access to the newspaper and periodical archives in the former Center for Research and Research Assistance (CIDAI) in the Universidad Centroamericana "José Simeón Cañas" and always found time to engage in discussions of Salvadoran politics. I am deeply indebted to the doctors in the Salvadoran Social Security Institute Union (SIMETRISSS) and the health care workers union (STISSS) who took time from their medical obligations to be interviewed and to share valuable archival materials from the protest campaigns. I also appreciate the support of Wilfredo Berrios on understanding the history of telecommunications privatization and the assistance of the Coordinator of Salvadoran Workers Unions (CSTS) for information on organized labor's view of the Central American Free Trade Agreement. I also thank Manlio Argueta, the director of the National Library, for allowing me daily access to the newspaper archives in the basement of the downtown building and for his extremely helpful staff. Professor Carlos Lara from the University of El Salvador invited me to give talks at the three-day-long Social Movements Forum, in May 2011, where many of the ideas in chapters 3 and 4 of this book were presented and received critical feedback from conference attendees.

I received a Fulbright Scholar Award for 2008–2009, which allowed me to carry out dozens of interviews in Central America during my sabbatical year. I was based at the Institute for Social Research (IIS) at the University of Costa Rica. My fellow social scientists and students in the Institute and the sociology department made for a particularly stimulating year. I thank the IIS director, Carlos Sandoval, for making such a welcoming space. I am also indebted to Ciska Raventos for sharing her office with me and many inspirational conversations about social movements. The chairs of the Sociology Department, Mayra Achío Tacsan and Asdrúbal Alvarado, also welcomed me in the university. Allen Cordero at the Facultad Latinoamericana de Ciencias Sociales (FLACSO) and the University of Costa Rica has continued to be a close colleague and spent dozens of hours educating me about Costa Rican and Central American social movements. His specialized knowledge of the region has guided me throughout my research, and I thank him for organizing multiple academic and public panels on social movements in Central America and inviting me to participate. I also appreciate my longtime friendship with George Garcia and his sharing of contacts and deep knowledge of Costa Rican history and politics.

A high point of my Fulbright fellowship involved a "road trip" from the University of Costa Rica to the University of El Salvador in November 2008 for the Eleventh Conference of the Central American Sociological Association (ACAS). I traveled in an international caravan in University of Costa Rica minibuses with about two dozen faculty and sociology undergraduate students. I was so impressed with the resources the public university system of Costa Rica had placed in sending students and faculty to this international conference. I learned much about Central American politics from a variety of perspectives during this trip and regional conference. I also thank the many activists, politicians, and labor leaders I interviewed in Costa Rica for providing me with insights into struggles from the 1970s to the 2000s, including members of the telecommunication and electrical power unions (FIT-ICE/ASDEICE); the public sector employees association (ANEP); the coordinator of unions and teachers associations (CUSIMA); the militant public workers federation of the late 1970s (FENATRAP); the university staff union (SINDEU); Frente Amplio, PVP, and PAC political parties; the National Front for Struggle against CAFTA (FNL); the Federation of University Students (FEUCR); the Pastoral Social; and the Movimiento Cultural.

In Panama, I benefited from interviews with participants and leaders in CO-CINA, FRENADESSO, CONUSI, and SUNTRACS. I thank Olmedo Beluche for spending time and sharing information with me at the University of Panama. Paul Cordoba also provided special assistance. In Nicaragua, I am always appreciative of Wilmar Cuarezma and his support. I thank the National Workers Front (FNT) for providing interviews and sharing archival materials. I also benefited from discussions with the National Network in Defense of Consumers (RNDC) and the Masaya Consumers Defense Organization, as well as their sharing of precious archival materials and press clippings. In Honduras, I received special support from the Sociology Department in the National Autonomous University, the Friedrich Ebert Foundation, and the Honduran Documentation Center. I appreciate the time individuals in MUCA, FOMH, FNRP, CODEMUH, and the UD took to be interviewed. In Guatemala, I thank Simona Yagenova and Edmundo Urrutia at FLACSO for arranging a special conference on Central American social movements in the fall of 2010 and inviting me to participate.

At Texas A&M University my colleagues were always a source of inspiration. I enjoyed my long conversations and professional advice from Harland Prechel, Sam Cohn, Dudley Poston, and Mark Fossett. I also appreciate the support of Nancy Plankey-Videla, Jane Sell, Rob Mackin, and Zulema Valdez. Several short-term field research grants from Texas A&M allowed me to travel every summer to Central America between 2002 and 2007. At the University of California, Merced, I thank my departmental chair, Nella Van Dyke, whose scheduling flexibility permitted me the time to finish this manuscript. I am also a beneficiary of a University of California Academic Senate Faculty Grant that assisted in the completion of this research. Over the past ten years, this project has also tapped into the labors of several undergraduate and graduate research assistants, including Augusto Cuarezma, Jocelyn Delgado, Brenda Faulkner, Allison Garrett, Kyle Ja Hyouk Koo, Luis Larrea, Dina Martínez, Carolina Molina, María Mora, Jay O'Neal, Aaron Pinnick, Anna Schoendorfer, and

Erica Walker. I am especially grateful to Andrew Zumkehr in Environmental Engineering for his assistance with map construction. I also benefited from the assistance and friendship of fellow Latin Americanist colleagues María Inclán and Bill Robinson.

I received valuable feedback on different stages of this project from public presentations I gave to sociology faculty and graduate students at Stanford, Texas A&M, Tulane, and uc Merced. Critical commentary was also provided by students and faculty at a host of educational institutions in Central America from presentations I made at the Universidad Centroamericana (uca) (coordinated by Luis Serra) Managua (2002), University of El Salvador (2004) (organized Candelaria Navas and Pablo Castro), flacso Guatemala (2010), the University of Costa Rica (2007–2009), and the Universidad Especializada de Las Américas (udelas) (facilitated by Alfredo Castillero) in Panama City (2009). I also received important responses at presentations at meetings of the American Sociological Association, Latin American Studies Association, the Political Economy of the World System Conference, and a special international workshop on Democracy and Social Movements organized by Bert Klandermans and Cornelius van Stralen held at the Federal University of Minas Gerais (ufmg) in Belo Horizonte, Brazil in November 2009.

I would also like to share my deep appreciation to Glenn Perkins, my copy editor for Johns Hopkins University Press. I want to express my gratitude to Suzanne Flinchbaugh, my editor at the Press, for her enthusiasm for the project at an early stage and her patience with my turnaround times from reviewer revisions. I also appreciate the assistance of Catherine Goldstead and Andre Barnett at the Press in moving my manuscript through the final stages of production and design. The reader for the manuscript also provided constructive criticisms and insights that have improved the final version. In an academic world so pressing on time and commitments, the reader proved extremely generous in offering such thoughtful comments and changes to the work. Chris Chase-Dunn, the series editor, has also been encouraging about this project since its inception. I admire Chris's career-long dual commitment to cutting-edge scholarship and progressive social change.

My immediate family and in-laws have always offered support and relief as well as my friend Mike McMillan. My brother and sister-in-law, Dave and Jenn, contributed early to my career from dissertation field research, to always being only a phone call away. Finally, I thank my partner, Andrea, for all her support and assistance as we both balance our academic careers.

Abbreviations

ALBA	Alternativa Bolivariana para los Pueblos de Nuestra América (Alternative Bolivarian Alliance)
ARENA	Alianza Republicana Nacionalista (Nationalist Republican Alliance, El Salvador)
CAFTA	Central American Free Trade Agreement
CCN	Comité Cívico Nacional (National Civic Committee, Costa Rica)
CNRP	Coordinadora Nacional de Resistencia Popular (National Popular Resistance Coordinator, Honduras)
CONATO	Consejo Nacional de Trabajadores Organizados (National Council of Organized Workers, Panama)
CSS	Caja de Seguro Social (Social Security Bureau, Panama)
DINADECO	Dirección Nacional de Desarrollo Comunal (National Directorate of Community Development, Costa Rica)
FMLN	Farabundo Martí National Liberation Front (Frente Farabundo Martí para la Liberación Nacional, El Salvador)
FNRP	Frente Nacional de Resistencia Popular (National Front of Popular Resistance, Honduras)
FNT	Frente Nacional de Trabajadores (National Workers Front, Nicaragua)
FOM	Frente de Organizaciones Magisteriales (Front of Teachers Organizations, Costa Rica)
FRENADESSO	Frente Nacional por la Defensa de la Seguridad Social (National Front in Defense of Social Security, Panama)
FSLN	Frente Sandinista de la Liberación Nacional (Sandinista National Liberation Front, Nicaragua)

ICE	Instituto Costarricense de Electricidad (Costa Rican Electricity Institute, Costa Rica)
IMF	International Monetary Fund
MICSP	Movimiento Indígena, Campesino, Sindical y Popular (Indigenous, Peasant, Union, and Popular Movement, Guatemala)
MONADESO	Movimiento Nacional por la Defensa de la Soberanía (National Movement in Defense of Sovereignty, Panama)
MPR-12	Moviemiento Popular de Resistencia 12 de Octubre (October 12 Popular Resistance Movement, El Salvador)
NGO	nongovernmental organization
PAC	Partido de Acción Ciudadana (Citizens Action Party, Costa Rica)
PLN	Partido Liberación Nacional (National Liberation Party, Costa Rica)
PVP	Partido Vanguardia Popular (Popular Vanguard Party, Costa Rica)
RNDC	Red Nacional de Defensa de los Consumidores (National Network in Defense of Consumers, Nicaragua)
SAP	Structural Adjustment Program
SUNTRACS	Sindicato Único Nacional de Trabajadores de la Industria de la Construcción y Similares (National Union of Workers of Construction and Similar Industries, Panama)

Mobilizing Democracy

1

Introduction

Globalization and Citizen Protest

More than a decade into the new millennium, battles continue to rage in the global South over the direction of economic change. Even after the great worldwide recession of 2008–2009, social conflict over the ongoing implementation of orthodox free market reforms and economic liberalization produced the following three major social conflicts:

1. On October 4, 2012, Guatemalan citizens launched a national day of protest against the high consumer electricity rates charged by transnational energy firms that took over the country's power distribution after privatization in the late 1990s. At a strategic roadblock and protest on the Pan-American Highway in Totonicapán, soldiers opened fire and killed six indigenous peasants and injured scores of others.

2. On October 20, 2012, the Panamanian National Assembly voted to privatize lands in the Colón Free Trade Zone at the Atlantic entrance of the Panama Canal. The legislative action set off a string of riots in Colón, nationwide protests, roadblocks, and strikes by students, indigenous peoples, construction workers, teachers, and the Frente Amplio opposition party. After a week of sustained social conflict, during which security forces killed five protesters, the National Congress and pro-business President Ricardo Martinelli canceled plans for the sell-off of public lands.

3. From May 4 to 6, 2011, the Honduran government hosted an international forum in the nation's second-largest city, San Pedro Sula, with the participation of 1,500 businesspeople from 55 countries. The forum was entitled, "Honduras Is Open for Business." The cosmopolitan

event was an attempt to attract foreign capital back into the country. Honduras had experienced a rapid decline in external investment following a series of boycotts and sanctions from the international community following the 2009 military coup that ousted President Manuel Zelaya. The main Honduran multisectoral resistance movement to the coup, the Frente Nacional de Resistencia Popular (FNRP), organized major street marches and demonstrations against the Open for Business Forum because it viewed the meetings as a new round of transnational penetration and access to natural resources at bargain rates. On May 6, the final day of the forum, security forces and police used armored vehicles to crush a student-led demonstration in front of the public university of San Pedro Sula at the same time that the Second National Conference of Honduran Sociology was taking place. Several students and a reporter were seriously injured. Police fired tear gas into the autonomous public university while dozens of demonstrators were arrested. I myself ingested the tear gas, and experienced fellow conference participants had to provide me with bottled water to clear the toxic fumes from my watering eyes.

These are examples of the types of battles detailed in the pages that follow. Over the past two decades, a wave of popular struggle gathered strength against a new round of global capitalist integration as market reforms swept across the developing world. The anti-neoliberal oppositional mobilizations replaced the revolutionary and armed struggles of the past against military and authoritarian regimes. The leaders of the new resistance employ largely nonviolent, but often disruptive, tactics and strategies to oppose the threats of privatization, free trade, and the withdrawal of state commitments to social citizenship via an expanding welfare state. In particular, this study focuses on subnational mobilization opposing unwanted economic changes associated with neoliberal globalization. These three examples of protest campaigns also offer insight into the multiple protagonists leading the oppositional coalitions such as labor-based associations, students, teachers, indigenous groups, nongovernmental organizations (NGOs), women's groups, and left-leaning political parties.

Opposition to Globalization

The recent nonviolent mass mobilizations in Brazil, North Africa, and the Middle East; the austerity protests and general strikes in Bulgaria, Greece,

Portugal, Spain, and Italy; the students in Chile demanding the renationalization of public education; the Occupy Wall Street movement; and the decade-long upsurge in social movement activity throughout Latin America all demonstrate that global economic processes (such as international food prices, government debt or fiscal crises, mass unemployment, distorted concentrations of wealth, and public-sector privatization policies) are associated with heightened levels of collective action and even regime change. At the same time, we know relatively little about how these "national revolts" against globalization vary and bubble up from below at the local level. This work centers on the patterning of subnational opposition to economic liberalization in the global South—why some localities revolt while others remain quiescent. In addition, I explore the cross-national differences in the composition of the coalitions opposing free market reforms and the capacity of civil society to establish enduring multisectoral alliances.

Just as the South American nations of Argentina, Bolivia, Brazil, Ecuador, Paraguay, Peru, and Venezuela experienced massive demonstrations and protest activity over the past decade (Roberts 2008; Silva 2009), so too has Central America. The largest protest campaigns have involved issues related to globalization: economic liberalization, privatization, and regional free trade. In Costa Rica between 2003 and 2007, labor unions, universities, environmental groups, opposition political parties, and NGOs organized several mass street demonstrations and strikes in opposition to the Central American Free Trade Agreement (CAFTA). Some of the rallies reached up to 150,000 participants, making them the largest mobilizations in modern Costa Rican history. In El Salvador in late 2002 and early 2003, doctors and health-care workers joined in an alliance with NGOs to sustain a campaign against the privatization of the public hospital system. The campaign endured for nearly ten months and represented one of the largest campaigns against privatization in Latin America, with street demonstrations (the famous *marchas blancas*) mobilizing up to 3% of the entire Salvadoran population. Over the past fifteen years, similar types of mass demonstrations have occurred in Guatemala, Honduras, Nicaragua, and Panama. This work compares all six Central American countries and reconstructs the largest campaigns against economic globalization.

While much attention was given to Central America during the 1980s, as the Cold War drew to a close and the region was embroiled in violent conflicts, scholarship lags in analyses of the region in the contemporary era of globalization. Most of the recent studies on Central America focus on the rise of transnational street gangs (Cruz 2011), immigration dynamics (Menjívar 2000), and agricultural restructuring (Enríquez 2010). We lack systematic studies of the recent political mobilization in the isthmus (for exceptions, see Chase-Dunn, Amaro, and Jonas 2001; W. Robinson 2003; Martín Álvarez 2005; Burrell and Moodie 2013). The mobilizations are critical to document and explain for several reasons. For one, some theories of political democratization predict that mobilization will decrease with the onset of democracy, as more political parties and other institutionalized actors enter the political scene (Hipsher 1996; Oxhorn 1996). By the early 1990s, regional experts characterized Central America as "pacified" with the demobilization of the historic revolutionary struggles (Dunkerley 1994). Nonetheless, in every country on the isthmus, we observe an increase in street politics and protest campaigns in the 2000s, even as formal democracy and polyarchy (W. Robinson 1996) deepened. Additionally, the groups involved in the popular movement activities—NGOs, militants of opposition political parties, and new social movements based on ecological, gender, consumer, or other collective identities—typically benefit from democratization. Finally, much of the Latin American left has abandoned armed revolution and opted for electoral strategies to seek structural, and even revolutionary, change via the ballot box (Foran 2005; Levitsky and Roberts 2011).

Threats associated with deepening global economic integration and declining state commitments to social welfare have driven the unexpected upsurge in mass mobilization (Almeida 2007). These conditions of declining commitments of states to social welfare are widespread in the early twenty-first century (Chase-Dunn 2006; Evans and Sewell 2013; Mann 2013). Meanwhile, almost half of Central America's 40 million inhabitants live near or below the local poverty line. Large majorities attempt to scrape out a living in the informal sector as street vendors, domestic workers, and rural and urban day laborers. Hundreds of thousands of other Central American citizens are forced to make the harrowing trek to the United States in search of employment. The highly disputed forms of economic development that international financial institutions and local elites encourage produce social outcomes that affect the life chances for the citizens of the region in terms of household economic survival and the likelihood of improvements in employment, health, and education (Vreeland 2007; McMichael 2012).

Figure 1.1 illustrates the growing and crippling external debt faced by Central American states since the 1980s, offering a concise context for the constrained political and economic options available for policy makers in this

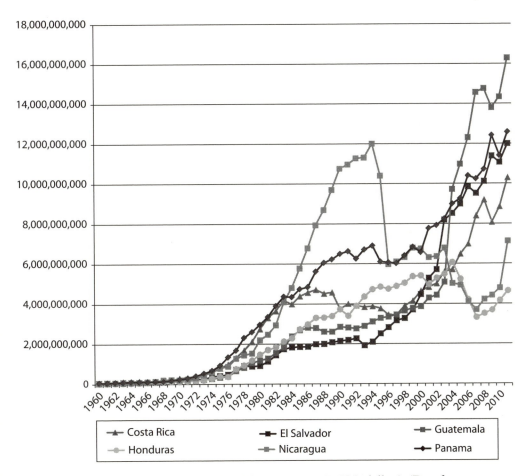

Figure 1.1. Central American foreign debt, 1960–2011 (in U.S. dollars). (Data from World Bank and Interamerican Development Bank.)

world region. After a period of sustained economic growth in the 1960s, governments borrowed heavily in the 1970s to continue state modernization and infrastructural expansion. The foreign borrowing reached a crisis point by the early 1980s as world commodity prices plummeted for Central American agricultural exports and interest rates increased on the original loans (Bulmer-Thomas 1987). By the mid-1980s, government cutbacks in social spending and basic subsidies triggered the first major outbreaks of popular unrest in the region against neoliberal reforms. However, with a lack of democracy in most countries, only Costa Rica, and to a lesser extent Panama, experienced sustained campaigns against the first generation of structural adjustment agreements. During the 1990s, the International Monetary Fund (IMF), World Bank, and Inter-American Development Bank renegotiated foreign debts in each country. By the 2000s, as the foreign debt problem continued to worsen, the international financial institutions (IFIs) began to pressure for the privatization of the basic economic and social infrastructure of Central American states, including health care, public utilities, ports, and natural resources (Haglund 2010). They also pushed for the implementation of free trade agreements. In Honduras and Nicaragua alone, the World Bank and IMF began to initiate debt relief and forgiveness as part of the Heavily Indebted Poor Countries (HIPC) initiative, under the condition that these countries would continue privatization programs. Hence, in exchange for massive debt relief, the IFIs stipulated the outsourcing of publicly administered electrical power and water and aqueduct systems to multinational utility corporations that do not harbor national loyalties or welfare-state type commitments to social citizenship whereby satisfying basic needs is a high priority.

Unlike in the 1980s, however, this time the IFIs attempted to implement these second-generation neoliberal reforms in a context of greater democratic space in the region. A new generation of activists, NGOs, rural cooperatives, school-teachers, labor unions, public health professionals, students, indigenous peoples, environmentalists, women's groups, and opposition political parties were ready to galvanize substantial portions of the population to resist policy changes they perceived would leave the middle and working classes in a less desirable economic situation with the selling off of the national patrimony and other economic liberalization policies. This fundamental cleavage of social citizenship rights versus free market reforms provides the central axis of societal conflict detailed in the pages that follow.

Protest Campaigns

I have organized the book around the theme of protest campaigns. Protest campaigns operate as shorter-term acts of collective defiance rather than as longer-term social movements. Campaigns focus on a particular policy and usually disassemble when that policy is implemented or overturned (such as a price hike, privatization, free-trade treaty, or passage of a labor flexibility law).[1] Opposition groups or temporary alliances often piece together campaigns with a unifying set of slogans and specified goals, such as the annulment of the unwanted economic policy (e.g., no privatization, no price hike, no free trade agreement). Actual mobilization in the developing world typically takes the form of a protest campaign. Most anti-neoliberal campaign participants and organizers employ nonviolent methods of struggle, which at times may turn aggressive or disruptive, even violent. However, previous characterizations of protests as "IMF riots" or "free market riots" (Walton and Seddon 1994) do not adequately capture the nature of most present-day campaigns. Much of this pathbreaking (and prescient) earlier literature investigated the outbreak of mass discontent against the debt crisis in the late 1970s and early 1980s in the global South, when many regimes had yet to shed their authoritarian legacies and practices.

Contemporary protest campaigns in Latin America (and elsewhere in the global South) are more often nonviolent than riots and frequently occur in relatively more democratic contexts than the first wave of austerity protest in the early 1980s. The current mobilizations involve calculated medium and long term strategies with the use of tactics such as strikes, rallies, marches, boycotts, sit-ins, and traffic obstruction. Protest campaigns tend to be relatively less spontaneous than riots, with much more coordination over the course of the struggle (sometimes in concert with opposition political parties). When violence does occur, as in the examples at the opening of this chapter, it usually derives from governmental crackdowns.[2]

Protest campaigns provide an appropriate empirical level of analysis to observe essential processes of social-movement-type activity (e.g., intensity of protest, repertoires employed, territorial variation of opposition, composition and breadth of protest coalition, and relative level of success). Campaigns also offer credible corroboration of organized citizen resistance to neoliberalism beyond less direct indicators, such as public opinion polls, elections, or the exaggerated claims of partisan leaders in fiery speeches and writings. Systematic empirical reconstruction of protest campaigns against neoliberal policies affords the best evidence possible that ordinary people are using valuable time and extremely limited resources to mobilize collectively against perceived harmful economic programs associated with globalization and transnational capital.

The following chapters examine the largest protest campaigns in six Central American countries between 1980 and 2013. In each nation, I emphasize variations at the subnational level that lead to mobilizations against globalization on a national scale. These mobilizations are built from broad oppositional alliances that I refer to as *multisectoral coalitions*. Chapter 2 provides a theoretical overview on the central forces driving protest campaign activity across localities in the global South and offers a conceptual framework for understanding the staying power of state and community infrastructures once they are put into place. The process of democratization lowers the costs and risks of building long-term organizational structures at the local level. The ongoing threats of economic liberalization provide incentives for community members to mobilize with their available organizational assets and work jointly in building multisectoral coalitions. Localities with more extensive state and community infrastructures will be more likely to coordinate collective action. At the national level, resistance to unpopular economic liberalization policies has a greater chance of emerging when broad oppositional coalitions are already in existence.

Chapter 3 spotlights the crucial case of Costa Rica. There, the opposition party alliances with protest campaigns against earlier waves of globalization (with the arrival of transnational fruit and mining companies in a context of democratization in the 1930s and 1970s) were critical as an organizing example for later protests, such as the early 1980s debt crisis mobilizations that set the standard for the rest of the region. The Costa Rican protests act as a kind of first experiment or "prototypical" mobilization. Costa Rican democracy and popular mobilization in the 1980s offer a lens to observe the future of Central and South America (and perhaps the global South in general). The anti-neoliberal demonstrations and coalitions appear similar to other Latin American countries in the following decades. In the chapter, I also examine the protest campaign against the third major structural adjustment program (SAP III, 1995), the "Combo" campaign against power and telecommunications privatization (2000), and the historic campaign against the Central American Free Trade Agreement (CAFTA) (2003–2007)—the largest in the region. In chapter 4 the focus turns to El Salvador, where I reconstruct the telecommunications and health care privatization campaigns (1994–2003) and the anti-CAFTA mobilizations (2003–2008).

Chapter 5 explores popular struggles in Panama. I map out the 1986 and 1995 strikes against labor flexibility laws, mobilizations against water privatization in 1998, campaigns against social security privatization and restructuring (2003 and 2005), and the wave of strikes in 2010, protesting labor flexibility laws, which was headed by indigenous groups working on the banana plantations in Bocas del Toro province. In chapter 6, I analyze Nicaragua and the popular unrest of the 1990s against the neoliberal restoration after the revolutionary 1980s. I also review campaigns against water privatization and consumer price increases in water, electricity, and transportation (2000–2006), as subsidies were cut to make payments on the foreign debt. Chapter 7 addresses major campaigns against globalization in Guatemala and Honduras. In Guatemala, I examine two massive mobilizations against an IMF-imposed sales tax hike (2001 and 2004) and the anti-CAFTA campaign in 2005–2006. In Honduras, I investigate the campaigns against structural adjustment in the early 1990s, and public-sector privatization and free trade in the 2000s, and how those previous campaigns provided the organizational basis for the massive and unprecedented mobilizations against the military coup d'état between 2009 and 2011. Chapter 8 offers a final summary that compares these struggles across nation-states. Even as these campaigns share commonalities in terms of when we would expect anti-neoliberal contention to surface, there are significant cross-national differences in the composition of the coalitions resisting the globalization-induced changes. Many of the national variations in the makeup of the oppositional coalitions are rooted in the state-led development trajectories of nation-states in the twentieth century in the pre-globalization era.

In terms of methodology, I document the largest mass mobilizations in this world region over the past thirty years. I have collected original data on over 4,000 protest events within campaigns resisting globalization in Central America from multiple local news sources. In several anti-neoliberal protest campaigns I have disaggregated national-level mobilizations into their regional distributions in order to examine the patterning of local-level variation within countries based on the geocoding of the protest events down to the municipal level. In several campaigns, I explain which regions and counties joined the globalization-induced campaigns and which localities failed to mobilize. I have given special attention to multisectoral coalitions and local infrastructures in terms of administrative offices, transportation arteries, local public-sector labor unions, NGOs, oppositional political parties, and the strategic experience of mobilizing against previous neoliberal reform measures. In addition, I carried out 40 interviews with key leaders in the struggles covered. In sum, this study demonstrates the dynamics of local mass mobilization in the developing world in the era of globalization. Its wider objective is to contribute to our collective understanding of the groups "on the ground" mobilizing at the subnational level in response to macro-globalization processes and push scholarship beyond the highly aggregated large-sample global-data-set studies of collective protest to a more fine-grained approach of the contested process of global social change within and between nations.

2

A Theory of Local Opposition to Globalization

As nations in the developing world gradually and unevenly abandoned state-led development strategies in the late twentieth century, replacing them with free market reforms and new transnational linkages to the world economy, the transition spawned major campaigns of popular unrest. This chapter offers a framework for understanding the conditions under which communities in the global South mobilize against neoliberal forms of globalization. Giving analytical attention to the combined processes of democratization, economic threat, and the availability of state and community infrastructures reveals the motivations and patterning of resistance to globalization by opposition groups. The particular state-led development histories of each country also shape the composition of the multisectoral coalitions confronting economic liberalization across national contexts. The ability of groups in civil society to form such broad coalitions may determine the level of opposition they can achieve in campaigns challenging the direction of global economic change.

Globalization in the Developing World

Scholars define globalization as the increasing economic and cultural integration of nation-states (J. Meyer et al. 1997; Sklair 2006: 60–61). Much of the literature on social movements and globalization has focused on activities in the global North (L. Wood 2012), such as the growth of transnational social movements in the early twenty-first century (Tarrow 2005; Smith 2008). The studies of contention in the global North largely focus on transnational mobilizing structures and how organizers have used new communications technologies to coordinate campaigns against elite financial and political institutions such as the International Monetary Fund, World Bank, G-8, and the World

Economic Forum (Smith and Weist 2012; L. Wood 2012). We know less about the mobilizations against economic liberalization in the global South (Von Bulow 2011).[1] Much more social conflict over issues related to globalization takes place in peripheral and newly industrialized countries than in advanced capitalist democracies (Podobnik 2005), especially as the global South increasingly participates in transnational advocacy organizations (Smith and Weist 2012). In addition, after religious and ethnic strife, economic globalization drives some of the largest mobilizations in the developing world (Almeida 2010a). Indeed, teams of regional scholars are beginning to document these struggles in a series of volumes on collective action in Asia (Broadbent and Brockman 2011), Africa (Dwyer and Zeilig 2012), and Latin America (López Maya 1999; Eckstein and Wickham-Crowley 2003; Johnston and Almeida 2006; Stahler-Sholk, Vanden and Kuecker 2008; Modonesi and Rebón 2011; Silva 2013; Almeida and Cordero 2014).

Since the 1980s, campaigns against economic liberalization in the global South have led to major outbreaks of social unrest, including the toppling of governments via mass mobilization (Silva 2009; Goldstone 2011). Moreover, opposition political parties in democratic states have successfully converted the mass discontent and popular mobilizations against market reforms into electoral triumphs at the local and national levels of government (Levitsky and Roberts 2011; Roberts 2014). Yet even with dozens of journalistic and scholarly accounts of the major mobilizations in the developing world, we know much less about the local variation in these social conflicts. How do mobilizing agents build up these revolts from the local grassroots into sustained, national-level campaigns?

Increasingly, scholars recognize that analyzing how global processes impinge on local conditions offers a promising new line of inquiry (Babones 2006). Historical sociologists call for methodologies that allow for empirical studies of globalization penetrating down to the subnational level. Saskia Sassen (2007: 4) contends, "Conceiving of globalization not simply in terms of interdependence and global institutions but also as inhabiting the national opens up a vast and largely unaddressed research agenda." From this vantage we can examine how globalization affects popular protest and social movement activity within nation-states, even down to the local level. Javier Auyero (2001) characterizes community level battles over globalization as "glocal contention," whereby global economic conditions converge with local contexts to produce collective action unevenly across a national territory. Large-scale macro-economic processes driving structural adjustment and social exclusion are interpreted at the community level by collective actors as a "moral politics" (Auyero 2006). This study builds on the "glocalization" literature by demonstrating how establishing state, administrative, and organizational infrastructures at the community level can be used to resist unwanted changes brought about by deepening economic liberalization. When communities take advantage of democratization and their own organizational and strategic capital, they can appropriate these structures for a variety of mobilization tasks.

Democratization

The third wave of global democratization began to take shape in the late 1970s (Huntington 1991; Markoff 1996). By the early 1990s, much of Latin America had transitioned to democratic forms of governance (Hagopian and Mainwaring 2005; Booth and Seligson 2009). However, "a double transition" took place in the region, with democratization coinciding with neoliberalization of the economy (Almeida and Johnston 2006). This twin process of open elections combined with free markets proved to be explosive in several Latin American states resulting in higher levels of mass mobilization (Arce and Bellinger 2007). Relatively open polities have allowed more groups to form organizations and associations (Tilly and Wood 2012), including a wide variety of nongovernmental organizations and new social movements (Johnston, Laraña, and Gusfield 1994). Even traditional civil society associations (such as labor unions, public-sector associations, and rural cooperatives) have perceived the less repressive environment and relatively more accessible state institutions as an invitation to renewed rounds of popular mobilization (Tarrow 1994). Democratic social structures influence the political orientations of opposition groups (Walder 2009), channeling them into more nonviolent forms of collective action.

Newly organized challengers can more easily take advantage of existing institutions and state infrastructures for sustained campaigns under conditions of democratization. Even polyarchic regimes tightly controlled by rotating economic elites (W. Robinson 1996) are more susceptible to enduring protests campaigns than states that rule exclusively by repressive force. The economic elite under polyarchy is more apt to implement aggressive neoliberal measures that cause the kinds of economic-based threats that fuel mass collective action. Furthermore, conditions of democratization permit opposition political parties to mobilize alongside civil society groups in order to expand their base of appeal and future electoral fortunes. These coalitions transform into potent alliances when they incorporate multiple sectors within civil society. Such mobilizing tasks are much more difficult under highly authoritarian and nondemocratic regimes (Brockett 2005; Earl 2011; Johnston 2011).

Economic Threats

A core component of neoliberal policy making in the global South involves dismantling large parts of the public sector and implementing economic reform and austerity measures. The international debt crisis of the early 1980s forced developing countries to open their economies to greater external economic influence. When international financial institutions stepped in to renegotiate debts owed by poorer countries to commercial banks and governments in the global North, they arranged conditionality loans and secured structural adjustment agreements (Green 2003; Vreeland 2007). During the 1980s, the first phase of structural adjustment reforms largely focused on reducing import tariffs, devaluing national currencies, controlling inflation, and reducing expenditures in the public sector (Walton and Seddon 1994; Green 2003). Indeed, David Harvey claims that by 1982 the IMF and World Bank had become "centres for the propagation and enforcement of 'free market fundamentalism' and neoliberal orthodoxy. In return for debt rescheduling, indebted countries were required to implement institutional reforms, such as cuts in welfare expenditures, more flexible labour market laws, and privatization" (2005: 29).

The 1990s ushered in a second wave of economic reforms and structural adjustment in a further attempt to jump-start feeble economies—with public-sector privatization playing a central role. Between 1988 and 1994, lesser-developed countries (LDCs) privatized over three thousand public entities (Babb 2005). The second round of reform was driven not only by the debt crisis but also by the institutionalization of economic liberalization measures in elite economic-policy-making circles in world society (Meyer, Drori, and Hwang 2006; Weyland 2006) and supported by the increasing density of neoliberal economists in executive bureaucracies (Markoff and Montecinos 1993). In other words, implementing free market reforms became the accepted way of managing national economies in the post–Cold War era (Fourcade-Gourinchas and Babb 2002). These "second-generation" reforms centered on privatization of public-sector services and utilities such as health care, pension systems, water administration, telecommunications, port management, electricity distribution, and natural resource endowments (Green 2003; Kaufman and Nelson 2005). In the 1990s, Latin America accounted for 55 percent of all privatization revenues in the global South (Chong and López de Silanes 2005: 5).

Table 2.1   Economic liberalization policies that have induced protest campaigns

1980–1994	1995–2013
End of food subsidies, resulting in price increases in basic foods (wheat, corn, rice, cooking oil, etc.)	Privatization of public infrastructure (social security, health systems, pensions, water and sewage administration, electricity, ports, telecommunications, natural resources)
Price increases in transportation, housing, and clothing	Labor flexibility laws
Stabilization policies that freeze wages and lay off public-sector workers	Pension system reform (increase in payroll contributions and age of retirement; transfer of funds to private bank accounts)
Privatization of state-run companies and manufacturing	Free trade treaties

The second-generation measures occurred in the context of greater democratization in the developing world (Markoff 2006), especially in Latin America, where civil society was developing the capacity to express sustained opposition to government economic policies that stripped away benefits gained in the earlier period of state-led development (Roberts 2008). Before the turn to postneoliberal governments at the end of the first decade of the twenty-first century (Macdonald and Ruckert 2009), the international financial institutions had transformed most developing countries into "neoliberal states." Harvey defines such regimes as, "a state apparatus whose fundamental mission was to facilitate conditions for profitable capital accumulation on the part of both domestic and foreign capital" (2005: 7). The types of economic liberalization policies implemented by the neoliberal state that have generated widespread discontent in the global South over the past thirty-five years are summarized in table 2.1. The policies, discussed in detail in the following chapters, affect the economic well-being of citizens across the global South. These austerity measures and economic strategies shape consumption levels, income distribution, and access to education, health, and vital services that are often not captured by standard indicators of economic growth (Stiglitz, Sen, and Fitoussi 2010).

In the developing world, some of the largest protest campaigns since the 1990s have been associated with government attempts to privatize key natural resources, public services, and utilities. Even scholarship that highlights public support for economic liberalization measures (in terms of more consumer choice and access to a greater variety of goods and services) acknowledges that privatization of the public infrastructure remains highly unpopular, especially in Latin America (Baker 2009; Flores Macías 2012). These kinds of public sentiments provide a more favorable context for efficacious mobilization. One of the largest social movements on the South American continent, the movement of unemployed workers (*los piqueteros*) in Argentina, originated from communities in the privatized petroleum industries (Svampa and Pereyra 2003). Peru erupted in large-scale regional protests and riots when authorities attempted to privatize the state-run power system in Arequipa in 2002 (Arce 2008). In the early 2000s, both Paraguay and Uruguay experienced major campaigns against privatization. The water and gas wars over privatization in Bolivia involved organized popular mobilizations (and dozens of roadblocks) that overthrew two presidents and brought a left-leaning government to power at the end of 2005 (Postero 2007).

Several other types of neoliberal policies also induce mass unrest in the global South, including free trade, labor flexibility laws, pension reform, wage freezes and mass layoffs in the public sector, and regressive sales taxes (see table 2.1). They form a family of policies linked directly to the debt crisis and economic globalization as governments attempt a range of strategies to oblige multilateral lenders, tighten domestic spending, and open up to foreign investment and international markets. Beyond Latin America, we observe mass mobilization over these policies in Asia, Africa, and southern Europe (Almeida 2010a). China has experienced several rounds of labor protests over the privatization of state-owned firms and the workers' corresponding pensions, the largest mobilizations registered in the past twenty years over any issue or grievance (Lee 2007; Chen 2012). South Korean students, opposition political parties, farmers, and labor unions united in several campaigns against free-trade treaties between 2006 and 2011. Notable mass mobilizations over privatization have also occurred repeatedly in India and South Africa between 2000 and 2013.

Between 2011 and 2013, southern Europe erupted into austerity protests in Portugal, Greece, and Spain, with several general strikes and mass mobilizations against government cutbacks, mass layoffs, and labor flexibility laws linked to external debts. In addition, a renewed wave of food price protests spread across the developing world between 2007 and 2011, partially caused by the reduction of price subsidies on foodstuffs and basic grains by neoliberal governments (Patel and McMichael 2009). Several of these cost-of-living and food protests occurred in countries that experienced the Arab Spring uprisings of 2011, such as Bahrain, Egypt, Tunisia, Syria, Jordan, and Yemen (Bush 2010). By early 2013, the global wave of anti-neoliberal protest had stretched into Eastern Europe, as Bulgarian citizens in dozens of cities demonstrated against high electricity prices charged by transnational energy firms that monopolized regional markets following privatization. The Bulgarian popular uprising led to the resignation of the government by late February. Similar mass mobilizations erupted in Kosovo over privatization and electricity price hikes in late 2012 and 2013, while Brazil experienced its largest outpouring of protests in twenty years in mid-2013 that began as demonstrations over price increases in public transportation led by the Movimiento Passe Livre (Free Pass Movement) and later labor union protest and strikes over the selling off of the country's massive offshore oil reserve (the Libra oil field) in October 2013. The popular unrest over price hikes brought over one million people to the streets in more than a hundred cities (Keck 2013). Similar acts occurred in Mexico following petroleum privatization in 2013 and 2014.

Protesters view austerity, privatization, and rapid price increases as state-attributed economic threats that will make them worse off (Almeida 2003). Economic threats provide a major impetus to collective action, serving as "mobilizing grievances" (Snow and Soule 2009). The original theoretician of threat and popular contention, Charles Tilly, asserts that a "given amount of threat tends to generate more collective action than the 'same' amount of opportunity" (1978: 134–35). The subaltern classes of the global South envision new rounds of social exclusion that will take place following impending neoliberal reforms. As Michael Mann succinctly declares, "Like all economic programs, neoliberalism benefits some more than others and provokes resistance among those it harms" (2013: 132). Shared perceptions of economic threats can also drive multiple groups to form coalitions, generating more potent forms of collective action (McCammon and Van Dyke 2010). Clearly, economic reform policies induced mass protest over the last thirty years with important political outcomes (Silva 2009). However, we know markedly little about which communities are more likely than others to rebel or about the composition of the opposition alliance. In short, these "national" revolts against economic liberalization are built up from dozens of actions at the community level whereby activists and civic leaders appropriate local assets to launch multisectoral collective action campaigns.

State-Led Development

The era from the 1940s to the early 1980s was the high point for state-led development in the global South (W. Robinson 2004). But this phase of economic expansion ended with the Third World debt crisis in the late twentieth century (Walton 1998). Critical globalization scholars view an epochal or transformational shift in global capitalism commencing around 1980 (W. Robinson 2004; Sassen 2008). Although some globalization analysts emphasize the homogeneous nature of economic integration across the developing world (Centeno and Cohen 2010), the manner in which state-led development takes place in the pre-globalization era has important consequences for the patterning of opposition in the contemporary period. Christopher Chase-Dunn contends that "a historical perspective on the latest phase of globalization allows us to see the long-run patterns of interaction between capitalist expansion and the movements of opposition that have tried to protect people from the negative aspects of market forces and exploitation" (2006: 92).

This longer-term framework includes the expansion of the development state between 1940 and 1980, when national governments enlarged bureaucratic administration, educational institutions, social security and health systems, and transportation infrastructures on an unprecedented scale (Segura-Urbiego 2007; Evans and Sewell 2013). Primary and secondary education grew markedly with the building of schools, extending educational access to millions of citizens. National governments established social security institutes to protect workers and their families with health care, pensions and accident insurance. In this period of state-led development, newly erected national highway systems helped integrate national economies beyond the agricultural export enclaves and resource extraction centers such as mines and forests.

Despite having general similarities, developing countries differed in terms of political and economic development strategies in this period. Even though much of the global South embarked on a state-led development path in the mid-twentieth century, national governments did not carry out those plans in the same way, even countries in the same geographical region. These differences have major consequences for the pattern of civil society opposition to economic liberalization in the current period of globalization in each nation. States that built universities in several provinces differ from states that focused postsecondary education in their capital cities. Regimes that democratized earlier allowed a greater role for political parties in the opposition process.

Exclusionary and repressive regimes force oppositional movements to organize themselves through NGOs, where corporatist, populist, and state-centered welfare regimes allow more organizing within state institutions, public-sector unions, and quasi-governmental bodies.

In short, developing countries made major progress in the mid-twentieth century building social and administrative infrastructures, integrating their economies, and expanding welfare-type services at the national level. However, the political-economic governing regimes in each resulted in differing distributions of these infrastructures across local districts, as well as distinctive state-society relationships. These infrastructures set the stage for both the local-level capacity of collective resistance in the global era and the varied composition of that resistance across nation-states. Hence, the histories of state-led development in the global South laid the foundation for the patterning and character of the opposition to economic restructuring in the contemporary age of global integration.

Globalization and Subnational Analysis

Oppositional groups often view the economic restructurings associated with globalization as threats to the social accords reached during the post–World War II period of national economic development. In this era, authoritarian, democratic, and populist-oriented governments provided expanded social services and subsidies to the popular classes (Walton and Seddon 1994). The weakening of these welfare provisions is viewed as harmful to economic well-being, and threat models of collective action predict that it will create more discontent (Van Dyke and Soule 2002; Almeida 2003, 2007). The reduction in welfare provisions increases the costs of inaction by vulnerable groups (Goldstone and Tilly 2001), such as labor and the urban poor, that may see a decline in wages, employment, and access to vital services (Vreeland 2003). Structural adjustment programs that debilitate the welfare state have been linked with more intensive levels of rebellion in cross-national research (Auvinen 1996; Ortiz and Béjar 2013). But we know much less about the conditions associated with local-level variation in opposition to market reforms.

To date, studies of opposition to neoliberalism in the global South tend to aggregate events at the national level (Shefner et al. 2006). These designs work well for large sample cross-national studies in terms of highlighting broad conditions associated with mass mobilization in response to economic liberalization. For instance, Walton and Ragin (1990) find in quantitative cross-national comparisons of austerity protests that IMF pressure (number of loan restructurings), overurbanization, and level of unionization are among the most consistent correlates of intensive rebellion. Auvinen (1996), in a sample of seventy developing countries, also finds political protest related to IMF funding where urbanization and economic development are relatively high. In a large cross-national study (of 131 developing countries between 1981 and 2003) on the impacts of structural adjustment on rebellion and demonstrations of all types, Abouharb and Cingranelli (2007) report a positive influence of IMF and World Bank pressure (length of time under structural adjustment), as well as annual gross domestic product (GDP) and the export of primary commodities. Ortiz and Béjar (2013) find in a cross-national time series sample of 17 Latin American countries between 1980 and 2007 that governments signing an IMF agreement experience an increase in the number of protest events, especially riots and strikes.

The above cross-national studies, using different time periods and samples of developing countries, all concur that key causal dimensions, such as overurbanization, GDP, and economic development, serve as general proxies for the kinds of resources and "organizational infrastructures" (Walton and Seddon 1994: 45) that likely come into play in inducing protest campaigns and rebellions but are difficult to capture with highly aggregated cross-national data. Analyzing subnational opposition to economic liberalization allows for a more fine-grained analysis of community structures and strategic resources where the mobilization process actually occurs.

Infrastructures Supporting Protest Campaigns

Analysts need to classify more precisely the local assets inside a community that are most likely to be converted into collective action in the developing world. In order to better understand the timing and distribution of collective action, it is necessary to discern which types of administrative, physical, social, and organizational properties are more favorable for common people to appropriate locally and engage in social-movement-type activities. A local infrastructure perspective assists by specifying the baseline conditions under which mass mobilization emerges in some localities and not in others. To further partition the kinds of assets that may generate collective action in response to globalization processes, I define different types of state and community infrastructures. Localities differ in their levels of state and community structures, with important consequences for assembling collective challenges (Edwards and McCarthy 2004). In addition, developing countries have varied histories in terms of the distribution of particular types of state and community infrastructures.

State infrastructures are physical and organizational units national governments construct to sustain ongoing economic and administrative activities. State infrastructures were originally developed in the pre-globalization era with different national contexts shaping their distribution. Community infrastructures include locally operating social organizations that may be used for collective action campaigns (Andrews 2004). Such organizations connect at times to national and international networks such as political parties or transnational nonprofit organizations and international nongovernmental organizations (Smith and Weist 2012), but their local activities are most consequential for community-level mobilization.

State Infrastructures

Localities vary in the extensiveness of state created infrastructures. Those locally anchored political, cultural, and physical components of the state that assist in most efficiently mobilizing people to reach target audiences act as strategic assets. Three types of state infrastructure that facilitate collective action in the global South are administrative infrastructure, transportation infrastructure, and higher educational infrastructure.

Administrative Infrastructure

The modern state serves as a major target and arbiter for social movement demands (Jenkins and Klandermans 1995a; Amenta and Young 1999; Johnston 2011). Local government offices provide one means of institutional access for groups to express their grievances to state managers and public officials (Inclán 2008). Such administrative outposts are largely concentrated in provincial capital towns and cities that house regional public administration offices and services (Silva 2009). This uneven geographical distribution provides fewer opportunities for aggrieved communities to mobilize protest events in more isolated villages, regions, and towns (Boudreau 1996). For example, in the Brazilian mass unrest over transport fares in mid-2013, the first places to witness demonstrations were the state capitals.

Transportation Infrastructure

Transportation routes offer protesters a place to gather and apply disruption, or "the seizure of space . . . as a means of exerting pressure on people outside that space" (Tilly 1986: 376). In Latin America, opposition groups from northern Mexico to southern Argentina routinely apply the road blockade as a major protest tactic in their opposition to economic liberalization measures. The Confederación de Nacionalidades Indígenas del Ecuador (CONAIE), a confederation of the nation's indigenous peasant organizations, has shut down the country on multiple occasions between 1990 and the 2000s through the use of barricades on the country's major highways, including a successful campaign to halt a free trade agreement in the spring of 2006.

Similar blockade actions occurred in Argentina throughout the late 1990s and early 2000s, led by the unemployed workers movement. By 2002, at the height of the country's debt crisis, there were over 2,000 roadblocks per year. In the concluding chapter of his comparative study of protest over economic reforms in six South American countries, Eduardo Silva (2009: 271) found that "the roadblock emerged as the most novel form of struggle during our episodes of anti-neoliberal contention." Xi Chen (2012) reports the roadbock as a major form of protest in China against the free market reforms in the 1990s and early 2000s by workers, pensioners, and small farmers. In addition, communities with major transportation routes attract greater levels of collective action by their strategic worth in drawing the attention of authorities and bystander publics (Zald 1992). In sum, the highway barricade has become one of the most important tactics to cause disruption and to increase a protest campaign's overall leverage with local and national governments.

Higher Education Infrastructure

The era of state-led development unleashed an unprecedented period of university expansion and growth in student enrollments, which has continued to the present (Schofer and Meyer 2005; Weiss, Aspinall, and Thompson 2012). Public universities and their students maintain a long history of opposition to regimes in the developing world, including revolutionary struggles (Wickham-Crowley 1992). University communities (students, faculty, and staff) frequently view aggressive economic liberalization policies as a reversal in the state's commitment to protect economic and social welfare rights for civil society. Students and staff often assist as *brokers* (Diani 2003) by organizing other social sectors, such as nearby communities and high school students. University students in particular benefit from a distinct stage in their life course that provides them with relatively fewer time constraints to dedicate to activism relative to other groups (McAdam 1988). Large concentrations of students residing in the same town or neighborhood also offer favorable ecological conditions for mobilization in comparison to communities that lack universities (Van Dyke 1998; Zhao 2001; Andrews and Biggs 2006). Universities also provide a public space for civil society to congregate and debate national policy issues.

Community Infrastructure

The greater the number of associations and organizations in a community, the more rapidly a campaign of collective action can be mobilized and sustained (Morris 1984; McCammon 2003; Andrews 2004). In their research on neighborhood-level civic activity in Chicago, Robert J. Sampson and his colleagues contend that "episodes of contention tend to develop within established institutions or organizations" (Sampson et al. 2005: 678; see also McAdam 2003). NGOs, labor-based associations, and local chapters of opposition political parties are all vital community-based organizations that may be activated to participate in campaigns against unwanted economic changes.

Nongovernmental Organizations

In the 1990s and 2000s, developing countries witnessed a rapid proliferation in nongovernmental organizations (Bradshaw and Schafer 2000; Drori, Meyer, and Hwang 2006). The missions of NGOs range from community development and public health to antiviolence campaigns. NGOs support many of the new social movements in the global South, such as environmentalism, gender equality, gay rights, and the rights of indigenous minorities. Other types of NGOs support traditional civil society associations such as labor unions and rural cooperatives. In the era of welfare state retrenchment, NGOs offer some of the only organizational forces active in rural, remote, and marginalized communities, providing vital services and maintaining direct contact and trust with local populations. At times, the structures of NGOs may be co-opted for specific social movement campaigns (McCarthy 1987). For example, in South Africa in the early 2000s, groupings of NGOs (the Anti-Privatization Forum and the Soweto Electricity Crisis Committee) coordinated campaigns against the privatization of public utilities and rising consumer prices (Buhlungu 2006). In Guatemala, NGOs engaged in nationwide campaigns in the early 2000s to open up public debate about the Central American Free Trade Agreement and to attempt to stall its implementation (see chapter 7). Many NGOs in the global South benefit from alliances and resources with sympathetic transnational organizations based in the global North such as Oxfam, the Soros Foundation, and the Friedrich Ebert Foundation, among many others (Smith and Wiest 2012).

Conversely, NGOs may serve only the interests of international agencies and governments, acting as local transmitters of neoliberal values and practices; in so doing, they can suppress collective action as an alternative route to social change (Petras and Veltmeyer 2005). NGOs may also be manipulated by local administrators who retain most of the organizational funding to run day-to-day operations and disburse only a small percentage of funds to communities in need. With these two disparate characterizations of NGOs (as a resource for action or as a force for apathy), analysts must consider the state-development history of particular countries to determine the potential of the NGO sector as an ally in protest campaigns. Nations facing especially repressive and exclusionary governments may tend to foster more autonomous and grassroots-types of NGOs that count a long history of using collective action to pressure the state for resources and basic needs. Even with all of the above caveats, the mere existence of a nongovernmental organization in a marginalized community creates the possibility that its structure (in whole or part) may be used in collective action campaigns at some point.

Labor-Based Associations

Between the 1940s and early 1980s, states in the global South established hundreds of public institutions and institutes, ranging from social security and water and energy distribution to food storage and regulation. Economic measures and privatization policies directed at specific state institutions often first mobilize the workers under the impending economic threat. Such public institutes are termed "focal organizations" because privatization policies threaten them the most. Alberto Chong and Florencio López de Silanes (2005) found that labor strikes occurred in 47% of public-sector institutes under the threat of privatization on a global scale and in 66% of public enterprises in Latin America. Hence, we would expect public employees (and their labor associations and unions) to be likely candidates for mobilized opposition to privatization in the institute in question or to economic liberalization processes in general (S. Sandoval 2001).

Collective resistance would more likely surface in those localities where state institutions undergoing imminent privatization are geographically concentrated.

Labor-based groups benefiting from state-led development may be especially critical in campaigns against aggressive welfare state retrenchment and labor flexibility laws. Beverly Silver (2003:18) predicts such cutting back on worker protections with globalization will likely result in Polanyian backlash mobilization by labor unions. In addition, state institutions with multiple locations, such as hospitals and public schools, maintain the potential to mobilize thousands across the territory of a nation. In a systematic study of two cycles of popular contention in Honduras between 1990 and 2005, Eugenio Sosa (2012) found that teachers, health care workers, public employees, and students were the four groups who participated with the most frequency in protest events.

Local Opposition Political Parties

Opposition political parties (those parties outside of executive power) can use unfavorable economic policies to mobilize larger constituencies (Keck 1992; Kriesi 1995). When a majority of public opinion stands against liberalization measures, opposition parties may capitalize on the public's dissatisfaction (Maguire 1995; Stearns and Almeida 2004; Kolb 2007). Political parties remain one of the only coordinated organizational units in the democratizing developing world with branches distributed in several regions within a national territory. Opposition parties not only act in their traditional roles within parliamentary bodies but also are increasingly mobilizing people in the streets in protest campaigns (Goldstone 2003). Similar to other types of social organizations that produce mutual awareness and common identities over a vast territorial space (McCammon 2001), opposition parties unify various groups and supporters in multiple localities across a country. This relationship between protest campaigns and political parties has been referred to as "social movement partyism" (Almeida 2006, 2010b). More specifically, social movement partyism occurs when an opposition party aligns with civil society associations and deploys its organizational membership to engage in mass actions such as street demonstrations, rallies, and blockades. Consequently, the party appears more as a social movement type of entity than a conventional political organization focusing exclusively on legislation within parliament.

This was certainly the case for Bolivia in the early 2000s as the opposition parties Movimiento al Socialismo and Movimiento Indígena Pachakuti mobilized thousands of indigenous peasants, students, and urban workers in protest campaigns in dozens of communities against coca eradication, water privatization, and for the renationalization of natural gas (Van Cott 2005; Yashar 2005). In Ecuador, indigenous activists from the highlands and Amazonia formed the Pachakutik political party and joined forces with public sector unions and 50 other rural and popular organizations in the Social Movement Coordinator. Between the late 1990s and 2000s, Pachakutik simultaneously participated in anti-neoliberal protest campaigns and electoral contests (Becker 2011). At the community level, local chapters of opposition parties often hold weekly meetings and public forums to debate national policy issues such as economic restructuring (Silber 2011). Where nationalist, populist, and left-leaning parties have a local territorial foothold, we would expect more collective resistance to neoliberal reforms.

Strategic Capital

Localities also vary in their strategic capacity to utilize state and community infrastructures in coordinating collective action (Ganz 2009). A community's strategic capital is composed of experiential elements. Past collective actions against unwanted economic policies in a region can add to that community's strategic capital as stockpiles of valuable information and experience in how to launch local mobilization campaigns by exploiting local infrastructural assets. These cognitive resources may be called strategic experience.

Communities with experience in collective dissent would likely have lower startup costs in initiating new rounds of joint action. Routines, templates, and repertoires of mass protest (e.g., barricades, synchronizing roadblocks, specific locales from which to maximize mobilization appeals) familiar to the local population and inscribed in the regional culture may be activated in the face of opportunities or threats (Tilly 1978; Taylor and Van Dyke 2004). These communities act as repositories of collective knowledge about which strategic and organizational elements in their localities are best employed to generate joint action.

Daniel Cress and David Snow (1996: 1095) refer to such experiential information as "strategic support" or the "knowledge that facilitates goal-attainment collective actions, like sit-ins and housing takeovers." In longitudinal and cross-sectional studies, past collective protest is often found to be associated with higher levels of contention (Van Dyke, Dixon, and Carlon 2007; Taylor et al. 2009)—even when actions have occurred in prior decades (Beissinger 2001: 138). At the community level, one would expect that past collective action campaigns against economic liberalization would be strongly associated with current rounds of protest against similar policies. Universities, NGOs, labor associations, political party militants, and community members retain knowledge and routines of past struggles and how to assemble local mobilizations (Taylor and Van Dyke 2004).

Multisectoral Struggle

Organizers will also experience more success in generating large scale collective action if they can piece together a multisectoral coalition. In other words, large-scale mobilization is more likely to be attained by linking groups from multiple sectors of civil society together in common cause. The neoliberal state has created a structural climate whereby traditional social movements (such as labor unions and peasant cooperatives) have been debilitated by years of the debt crisis, austerity, privatization, labor flexibility laws, and global competition. A single labor union is likely too feeble to sustain a national-level campaign. Rural peasant cooperatives have been weakened by government neglect and disinvestment in domestic food production as emphasis is increasingly placed on nontraditional agricultural commodities and export processing plants (W. Robinson 2008; Anner 2011).

One of the only viable means to engage large regions of the national territory in protest campaigns is for multiple sectors to align. Participants may be development NGOs, opposition political parties, labor unions, public-sector employees, educational institutions, and other types of new social movements based on ecology, gender, ethnicity, or human rights. The more of these groups that cooperate, the greater the power in numbers. Indeed, behind the most extensive anti-neoliberal protest campaigns documented in South America over the past two decades, one can usually identify a multisectoral coalition, from the Coordinadora in the Bolivian water wars of 2000 and the Estado Mayor del Pueblo coalition demanding the renationalization of natural gas in 2003 and 2005 to the labor unions, unemployed workers, merchants, and local politicians that constituted the alliance against mass unemployment in the interior provinces of Argentina in the late 1990s (Svampa and Pereyra 2003: 30). Many more multisectoral examples abound: the water privatization conflict in Uruguay (2003–2005) coordinated by the Comisión Nacional en Defensa del Agua y de la Vida (CNDAV), free trade protests in Ecuador (2006) organized by Ecuador Decide, or the multiple campaigns against privatization in Paraguay in the 2000s led by the Frente en Defensa de los Bienes Públicos y Patrimonio Nacional (Riquelme 2004).

In addition, when a diverse cross-section of society defies a particular market-led reform, it provides credible evidence to policy makers the depth of hostility to the measure in question, greatly raising the costs for political and economic elites to continue with its implementation. Furthermore, when the opposition derives from a diversity of groups, simple or traditional co-optation mechanisms of clientelism and patronage will unlikely demobilize the campaign. Multisectoral coalitions also introduce a variety of tactics into a protest campaign based on each participating group's experience. This moves collective action beyond a single repertoire, such as a labor strike in which authorities can focus their social control efforts (Schock 2005). Different patterns of state-led development shape the particular composition of multisectoral coalitions against neoliberal reforms within nation-states. States with a history of populism or social welfare will likely have substantial sectors of the labor movement within a coalition, while exclusive and repressive states may see significant representation from the NGO sector. Most importantly, in terms of timing, we would expect noteworthy campaigns (those occurring across the national territory and generating repeated mobilizations with thousands of participants) to emerge in regions where there are preexisting multisectoral alliances or newly formed ones on the eve of the implementation of the economic reforms.

Figure 2.1 summarizes the global, national, and local conditions that connect to encourage collective resistance to neoliberal forms of capitalism. The core features of state and community infrastructures and strategic capital are summarized in table 2.2, along with their corresponding contributions to

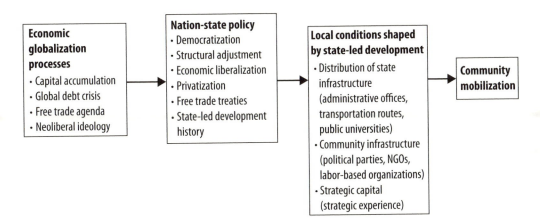

Figure 2.1. Pathway to subnational opposition to globalization.

Table 2.2   Core components of state and community infrastructure
and strategic capital

Asset	Function in promoting local collective action
State infrastructure	
Administrative infrastructure	Citizens may present claims and grievances to local government offices.
Transportation infrastructure	Allows for the strategic application of assertive and disruptive collective action, as well as publicity to bystander publics.
Higher education infrastructure (public universities)	Public university students and staff sympathize with anti-privatization efforts and have time and flexibility to mobilize other sectors.
Community infrastructure	
Nongovernmental organizations	As some of the few organizational units operating in rural and impoverished regions, nongovernmental organizations maintain social networks of trust with communities outside urban centers and have experience with organizing and mobilization.
Opposition political parties	With expanded democratization in the developing world, opposition political parties operate as one of the only nationally organized bodies that can synchronize actions with local memberships to participate in national protest campaigns and also strengthen their electoral power.
Labor-based associations	Unions, professional associations, and labor coalitions maintain organizational structures in larger cities and towns.
Strategic capital	
Strategic experience	Critical information and know-how in coordinating local collective action grows out of experience with prior campaigns.

mounting collective action campaigns in response to free market reforms. Protest campaigns against economic liberalization erupt on the national political landscape from dozens of local actions at the community level combined with mass demonstrations in the capital. Localities vary in terms of their structural and strategic assets. In their review of the mobilizing structures literature, Bob Edwards and John D. McCarthy (2004: 118) state that "the resources crucial to the initiation or continuation of collective action are unevenly distributed within societies." Such unequal distributions of state and community infrastructures generate spatial inequalities (Lobao, Hooks, and Tickmayer 2007). A subnational perspective highlights key state, community, and strategic assets that are unevenly dispersed across political subdivisions. The elements of state and community infrastructures and strategic capital provide a foundation for community members and activists to launch collective action in their localities as part of broader campaigns addressing economic integration and globalization. These campaigns are more likely to be especially potent and sustained when broad multisectoral alliances emerge across civil society and the national territory.

Conclusion

In this study I examine the most extensive campaigns against globalization in Central America. Protest campaigns involve "a set of discrete actions that can be subsumed under a common but specific goal or slogan" (Rucht and Neidhardt 1999: 68). Protest campaigns are shorter-term collective actions, in contrast to more enduring social movements, which often maintain multiple goals and objectives. Campaigns center on specific policy measures (in this case, policies directly tied to economic globalization such as privatization, labor flexibility, price control deregulation, or free trade agreements). Protest activities in the global South more often take the shape of campaigns than of longer-term social movements. With significant portions of the population living near the poverty line and lacking material resources, sustained and enduring mobilization is difficult to attain (Boudreau 1996). However, people can commit to shorter-term mobilizations that directly affect their livelihoods, such as access to health care, utilities, affordable food, clothing, transportation, and social services. Ordinary people strive for social resilience, well-being, and health in the face of neoliberal threats (Hall and Lamont 2013). Campaigns also have well-defined boundaries of beginning and ending dates, policy outcomes (e.g., was the privatization implemented or not?), and territorial reach.

For these same reasons, protest campaigns are easier for scholars to analyze empirically. Moreover, campaigns can offer more reliable data than less direct forms of opposition to economic liberalization such as public opinion surveys or voting behavior. When people publicly and purposively mobilize against specific neoliberal measures, it is a more direct and transparent sign that the economic policy is driving opposition to globalization. The systematic reconstruction of protest campaigns against neoliberal policies offers the best possible evidence that common people sacrifice their valuable time and meager resources to resist unwanted economic programs associated with globalization and transnational capital and allows for comparisons across other regions of the global South.

Costa Rica, Guatemala, El Salvador, Honduras, Nicaragua, and Panama have all experienced specific campaigns bounded in time and unified under the goal of preventing unwanted economic restructuring. The following chapters are organized by briefly summarizing the state-led development histories of each country in the mid-twentieth century. I then examine the largest campaigns against economic globalization, highlighting the crucial roles of state and community infrastructures and strategic experience in generating subnational resistance. I pay special attention to the multisectoral nature of the opposition. The concluding chapter compares these six Central American states in terms of common features of state and community infrastructures in sustaining campaigns and major differences in the composition of opposition coalitions based on particular state-led development trajectories.

3

Costa Rica

The Prototype for Mobilization against Globalization

Costa Rica entered into its debt crisis and democratized before the other nations of Central America. Because of these early experiences with neoliberalism and democracy, Costa Rican mobilization offers a prototype of the forms and protagonists of collective action observed in subsequent decades throughout the global South. This chapter traces four major campaigns against globalization in Costa Rica. They include the 1983 protests against IMF-imposed electricity price hikes, the structural adjustment loan of 1995 (SAL III), the privatization of telecommunications and electricity ("el Combo"), and resistance to the Central American Free Trade Agreement. These protest campaigns represent the largest outbreaks of mass contention in modern Costa Rica (Mora Solano 2011). To better understand the buildup of state infrastructure, political parties, and civil society organizations undergirding these campaigns and others like them in the global South, however, we need to begin in the 1930s.

Early History of the Left and the Rise of Social Movement Partyism

Early-twentieth-century socialist and social democratic-oriented political parties such as the Partido Reformista formed alliances with urban labor associations in Costa Rica, especially with the trade union movement organized in the Confederación General de Trabajadores (CGT) (García Quesada 2011). However, with the emergence of the Communist Party, the relationship between protest campaigns and the party solidified. The Communist Party of Costa Rica (CPCR) formed in 1931 and organized its first May Day mobilization in 1933. The CPCR immediately began organizing banana workers on Atlantic coast plantations owned by the United Fruit Company and domestic agrarian capitalists (Chomsky 1996). The party also rapidly began setting up local organizational structures with labor unions and communities in Heredia, Grecia, Puntarenas, Cartago, Limón, Turrialba, Tibas, Desamparados, and Alajuela and founded a weekly newspaper, *Trabajo*, in circulation between 1931 and 1948. In the 1930s the communists also surged as an electoral force. The party ran in local municipal elections in 1932 under the name Bloque de Obreros y Campesinos (BOC) and won two out of eight seats on the San José municipal council.[1] In 1934, the BOC ran candidates for national parliament in two out of the country's seven provinces and competed in seven municipal elections in San José, Heredia, Alajuela, and Limón provinces. The party won two seats in the national legislature and seven municipal seats (*regidores*) out of the 34 in which it competed; it also sponsored street marches of unemployed workers and strikes by bakery workers, shoemakers, and sugar cane cutters (Molina Jiménez 2007). However, the most important mass mobilization of the decade occurred on the banana plantations of the Atlantic.

Immediately after winning their national parliament seats, the two Communist Party representatives introduced a petition for banana workers that included provisions for medical supplies on farms (e.g., antimalarial drugs), payment of wages in cash instead of company store tokens, and the legalization of labor unions (Seligson 1980; Contreras 2009). The United Fruit Company pressured parliament to strike down the legislation. After the majority of the assembly obliged the transnational fruit company, a major strike broke out in the banana enclave cantones on the Caribbean coast in August and September 1934.[2] CPCR operatives had organized the banana workers in the months prior to the strike. Militants of the party such as Carlos Luis Falla (popularly known as "Calufa"), Jaime Cerdas, and Arnoldo Ferreto coordinated many of the actions during the strike. Ferreto was also a newly elected regidor for the party in the city of Heredia (Contreras 2009). The party's urban cadre mobilized supplies and financial donations for the strikers and held dozens of protest actions (Sibaja Barrantes 1983: 313). Hence, the strike reached a rudimentary level of multisectoralism with the rural banana workers in the Caribbean region of the country cooperating with local Communist Party cells, urban craft workers (shoemakers, carpenters, tailors, print shop workers), and municipal public-sector employees. These acts of solidarity were a relatively impressive achievement given the limited scale of economic development in the 1930s and the difficulties of communicating between the Atlantic coast and the cities in the central plateau. Communist legislative representatives such as Manuel Mora Verde mobilized inside the parliament to investigate the strike and the economic conditions of the banana workers.

The strike resulted in better working conditions for the laborers, but only after participants endured state repression and mass arrests (Sibaja Barrantes 1983). The strike also consolidated banana worker unions as a base of support for the CPCR through the early 1980s, including in the southern Pacific region where the industry expanded in the late 1930s. Even though this labor battle took place in the early 1930s, it already exhibited core features of protest campaigns in the globalization era: democratic spaces allowed left-oriented political parties to unite with multiple subaltern classes against transnational capital and unfavorable linkages to the world economy (in this case the United Fruit Company).

The CPCR continued organizing efforts throughout the 1930s and 1940s, especially among skilled workers and the unemployed in the cities and towns of the central plateau. Hence, from its very inception the CPCR practiced "social movement partyism," which would be an important legacy when the government re-legalized it in the late 1970s. In 1943 the party changed its name to the Partido Vanguardia Popular (PVP), which it continues to use to the present day. In the early 1940s, the party aligned with President Rafael Ángel Calderón Guardia and the Catholic Church hierarchy to push through a series of social reforms (Díaz Arias 2009). The reforms included the establishment of the University of Costa Rica (1940), a national social security system including health care and pensions (1941), a labor code legalizing unions and the right to strike (1943), among others (Molina and Palmer 2007: 102–3). The social reforms became enshrined as the "Social Guarantees" in the Costa Rican constitution in 1943 with a corresponding mass march of 100,000 people on September 15 (Abarca Vásquez 1992: 12).

The PVP and the labor movement continued to mobilize in the streets to protect the Social Guarantees throughout the 1940s (Díaz Arias 2009). The party used its influence in labor-based groups such as the Unión General de Trabajadores (UGT), Comité Sindical de Enlace, the Confederación de Trabajadores de Costa Rica (CTCR), and the even the Catholic-supported Confederación Costarricense de Trabajadores Rerum Novarum (CCTRN), to back the early welfare state policies of the 1940s. As late as 1947, the PVP organized street marches in the capital by Pacific Coast banana workers to support the Social Guarantees (Rojas Bolaños 1978). When National Republican Party and PVP deputies nullified the presidential elections of 1948, claiming systematic irregularities at the polls and electoral registration, the country fell into a brief civil war.[3] During the five week-long conflict (which resulted in over 2,000 deaths), the PVP aligned with Calderon, but this side was roundly defeated by political dissident José Figueres and his insurgent army.[4] From 1948 to 1975, the PVP was banned by Law 98 in the constitution.[5]

Even though it was officially outlawed and many of its leaders jailed in the years immediately after the civil war, the PVP began to rebuild itself underground. This work was carried out in labor and neighborhood associations (*juntas progresistas*). The party maintained influence in skilled labor such as graphics, carpentry, textiles, leather products and shoemaking, and emerging manufacturing industries. It also continued its organizing efforts on banana plantations and with landless rural workers on the Atlantic and southern Pacific coastal agricultural regions. In the 1970s, it began to infiltrate public-sector unions.[6] By 1953, the party reestablished a leftist labor confederation, the Confederación General de Trabajadores, with 29 unions and four federations (Abarca Vásquez 1992). At this same time, other social democratic confederations, the CCTRN and the Confederación Costarricense de Trabajadores Democráticos (CCTD), were gaining influence given the repression suffered by leftist labor associations.[7] All labor confederations believed in an expanded welfare state, as did the largest political parties, the National Liberation Party (PLN) and Social Christianity (Paige 1997). Indeed, the state and the dominant political parties remained committed to the Social Guarantees passed in the early 1940s and continued to expand the state infrastructure in the decades following World War II. The two hegemonic political parties' withdrawal from welfare state and social citizenship commitments in the late twentieth and early twenty-first centuries would be precisely what led to the largest outbreaks of popular unrest over privatization and free trade in the country's history.

Expanding the Welfare State

From the 1940s to the 1980s, the Costa Rican state engaged in massive public infrastructure development expanding the size of the middle and urban working classes (Cordero 2005). Between 1950 and 1980, Edelman (1999) reports that the government established nearly one hundred new state institutions (ranging from banking and petroleum refining to public housing and port administration), culminating in a "tropical welfare state." The central government built new universities and extension campuses, erected major national highways, and expanded telecommunications to reach remote rural areas. It also nationalized banking and insurance. In 1950, less than 25% of workers in the formal sector were covered by the social security health system, the Caja Costarricense de Seguro Social (CCSS). But by 1973, over 50% of workers were covered by public health insurance (Aguilar Hernández 1992), and by 1980 up to 86% of the population was covered (Edelman 1999). Similar trends could be observed in public education, with enrollment of school-aged children increasing from one-third in 1950 to over half by 1973 (Aguilar Hernández 1992). The Instituto Costarricense de Electricidad (ICE) was established in 1949, adding telecommunications in 1963 (Peña Martínez 1982). The ICE had an enormous influence on the lives of ordinary people. In 1940, 40% of households were connected to electrical power. By 1980, the number had nearly doubled to 79% of homes (Bull 2008: 127).

The University of Costa Rica (UCR) was established in 1940 in a suburb outside of the capital San José in the cantón of Montes de Oca. The UCR served as the first public university in the nation. By the 1970s several regional campuses had commenced operation—Limón (1975), Liberia (1972), Puntarenas (1975), San Ramón (1968), and Turrialba (1971). In 1971, the PLN administration authorized the formation of a new technological university, the Instituto Tecnológico de Costa Rica (ITCR), which opened its doors on the central campus of Cartago in 1973. It inaugurated regional campuses in San Carlos in 1975 and in San José in 1978. The national government opened another major public university system in 1973, the Universidad Nacional de Costa Rica (UNA). The central campus of UNA is located in Heredia, with satellite campuses in Peréz Zeledón (1973) and Liberia (1973).[8] (See figure 3.1 below for the geographical distribution of these campuses.) The magnitude of university growth in the 1970s was astonishing. As late as 1965, enrollment in public universities was 5,800 students (Wickham-Crowley 1989). By 1978 that number reached 42,700.[9] A particularly rapid growth in university enrollments occurred in the years immediately preceding the largest protest campaign in decades, the battle against Alcoa mining operations in 1970. Between 1966 and 1970, the university student population more than doubled, from some 6,000 students to 16,000 (Alvarado 2001: 118).

ALCOA, Pueblo Unido, and the Formation of Modern Multisectoral Campaigns, 1970–1983

By the late 1960s, the communist PVP was finding ways to enter the electoral arena. Along with dissident members of the social democratic PLN party the

PVP formed the socialist political party Partido Acción Socialista (PASO). In 1970, PASO won two seats in the national parliament—one of the representatives elected was Manuel Mora Verde, the historic leader of the PVP. The party also gained regidores in the municipalities of San José, Golfito, Osa, and Limón. At the same time, the 1970s witnessed a flourishing of leftist political parties that broke off from the PVP and the PLN. These "new left" parties included the Partido de Trabajadores, the Partido Socialista, the Movimiento Revolucionario del Pueblo (MRP), and the Partido Popular Costarricense (Salom 1987). In 1975, the government removed the official ban on the PVP. From 1975 to 1977 it worked on earning its legal inscription as an electoral political party.

Another transnational linkage to the global capitalist economy that multiple groups in civil society perceived as a threat (similar to the 1934 United Fruit Strike) provided the drama that inaugurated the 1970s in Costa Rica. A government mining agreement with the Aluminum Company of America (ALCOA) in early 1970 launched the largest protest campaign since the Costa Rican civil war. The campaign baptized a generation of students and activists in protests against a multinational corporation. ALCOA was in the process of receiving a generous government concession to mine bauxite in the Perez Zeledón region. The contract allowed ALCOA to extract the bauxite and directly export it as raw material for processing in the United States without establishing any backward linkages to the Costa Rican economy. The multisectoral protest campaign included two months of street marches, rallies, pickets, teach-ins by newly elected leftist politicians from the PASO party, and other creative actions.

The Federation of University of Costa Rica Students (FEUCR) set up an encampment in the gardens outside of the National Assembly in March 1970 to protest impending approval of the ALCOA mining contract. By mid-March, labor confederations such as the Confederación de Obreros y Campesinos Cristianos (COCC) and the Confederación General de Trabajadores Costarricenses (CGTC) had joined student marches in the capital.[10]

More mass marches took place in late March, including students traveling from Perez Zeledón.[11] Protestors in the capital received solidarity messages spanning the national territory from Guanacaste to the banana plantations in the cantones of Limón. One group of students marched from the city of Alajuela all the way to San José to join the demonstrations.[12] At the massive March 20 street demonstration, participants carried banners reading "aluminum for ALCOA and a big hole in the ground for Costa Rica," "a contract for Alcoa would be selling out the country," and "Congressman defend ALCOA or defend Costa Rica."[13] Similar types of nationalist and anti-imperial sentiments would resonate in campaigns against privatization and free trade in subsequent decades. By mid-April the pace of mobilization accelerated. These actions included a march of 15,000 students on April 22 and a pilgrimage from Heredia to San José on April 23.

On April 24, over 50,000 participants sponsored by a loosely coupled multisectoral coalition of a reported 83 civic, student, labor, communal, leftist party, and professional organizations joined in a demonstration.[14] The mass mobilization resulted in 350 arrests and multiple injuries when police cracked down on the protests while the legislature simultaneously ratified the mining contract.[15] The ALCOA mobilizations represented the largest demonstrations in Costa Rica in a generation. The university and high schools (in San José, Alajuela, and Heredia) went on strike while the CGTC, the National Association of Public Employees (Asociación Nacional de Empleados Publicos, ANEP), and taxi drivers participated in short-term solidarity strikes.[16] One final set of May Day mobilizations in 1970 in eleven different towns—where the ALCOA contract was publicly denounced in each rally—solidified the coalition that would resist globalization pressures for the next four decades: labor unions, public-sector employees, student associations, teachers, community groups, and leftist political parties.[17]

The activists in the 1970s also worked with the Juntas Progresistas and the Dirección Nacional de Desarrollo Comunal (DINADECO). DINADECO was established in 1967 as a state-led effort to organize community self-help associations throughout the national territory. It serves as a prime example of a state-created organization that also would be used for a variety of collective action purposes. The issue that began to organize multiple sectors (including community associations) by the end of the 1970s was the high cost of living. By 1980, there were over 1,000 DINADECO community associations distributed across Costa Rica's 80 cantones as leftist political party militants attempted to unite them in a single confederation.

After marginal election results in 1970 and 1974, three leftist parties decided to unite in a single leftist coalition called Pueblo Unido to compete in the 1978 elections. The three leftist parties included the Partido Socialista, the MRP, and the PVP. Pueblo Unido drew its base of support from popular movements and civil society associations, especially the university community, public-sector workers, skilled workers, and the agricultural proletariat on the

Caribbean and southern Pacific coasts. In late 1977 the Pueblo Unido coalition selected candidates to run for parliament. Nine out of the ten candidates came out of the leadership of popular struggles in the labor, agricultural, and student movements—a clear indicator of social movement partyism or the alliance between opposition parties and protest groups.[18] Each leftist party in the coalition ran candidates for parliament. The electoral race resulted in the coalition winning more than 60,000 votes and three legislative seats in the parliamentary elections held in February 1978. The leftist parties won representation at the local level as well with regidores in 22 of the country's 80 municipalities, up from only four in 1970.[19]

Upon taking seats in parliament and in local governments, the left parties increasingly engaged in issues that supported popular causes, such as price controls and local infrastructure development. The financial crisis was deepening between 1978 and 1981. This led to several mass marches against the high cost of living and transportation prices. The marches addressing the global financial crisis and its local effects were the largest mobilizations in the late 1970s and early 1980s. In addition, the labor movement began holding major strikes in the public sector. Several important strikes occurred between 1970 and 1978 in the public health care system, the ccss (Ramirez Amador and Rojas Corrales 1981), as well as a major strike in the ICE (telecommunications and electrical power) in 1976. The May Day marches, where workers clamored against price hikes and called for a single confederation uniting the country's labor unions, also grew in size throughout the late 1970s. In mid-1980, left-leaning labor unions formed the Confederación Unitaria de Trabajadores (CUT). The CUT affiliates included organized federations of left-leaning public-sector unions (FENTATRAP),[20] along with rural unions, especially in banana cultivation zones. The CUT remained the largest labor confederation in Costa Rica through the early 1980s. In short, between the 1970s and early 1980s a more class-based labor union movement (*sindicatos clasistas*) emerged in the public-sector unions; it fought not only for immediate labor based demands but also over systemwide economic distribution issues.

The CUT held two one-day general strikes in 1981 against the high cost of living, with the highest participation rates in localities with labor associations affiliated with the confederation. Further mobilization against austerity and the debt crisis played out during the elections of 1982. The general strikes against austerity helped support Pueblo Unido in the 1982 elections, in which the coalition won four national legislative seats and 21 regidores. This win set the stage for the first major national mobilization against globalization—the 1983 popular campaign against IMF-imposed electricity price hikes. The 1983 nonviolent uprising represented the largest sustained mass action at the national level in the early 1980s.[21]

The IMF had negotiated a price escalation on consumer electricity rates with the indebted Costa Rican government in November 1982 as part of a letter of intent. As one of the first developing countries to default on its external debt, in July 1981, Costa Rica was forced to cut back on its subsidies for electricity consumption in order to secure future lines of credit from the IMF and to reduce domestic budget deficits. By April and May 1983, community committees sprang up to resist the rate increase, many of these ad hoc committees emerged from preexisting DINADECO organizations that had a leftist leadership from Pueblo Unido–affiliated political parties, especially the PVP (Alvarenga Ventulo 2005).

May Day demonstrations around the country in 1983 included an end to electricity price hikes as a central demand. In May further demonstrations against escalating electricity bills erupted in working-class districts in San José and its surroundings, including Hatillo, Desamparados, Guadalupe, San Pedro, Tíbas, Alajuelita, and other more distant towns such as Turrialba and Alajuela. On May 7 alone, there were 15 reported public gatherings against the price increases in San José. Average citizens organized in community associations comprised the bulk of these demonstrations, but they also included known leftist leaders within the PVP and the CUT. In mid-May, five major women's associations issued a public statement denouncing the electricity price increases.

By early June, local-level protests were surfacing in various districts around the country. Community groups employed the novel tactic of the roadblock, which had proven to be successful just months before with a coalition of small farmer groups, Unión de Pequeños Agricultores Nacional (UPANACIONAL), demanding the renewal of subsidies for agricultural inputs (Edelman 1999). Parliamentary representatives of Pueblo Unido joined the protesters at the barricades—a clear sign of social movement partyism that characterized Costa Rica in the late 1970s and early 1980s. The roadblock would become a favored tactic of groups resisting neoliberal forms of capitalism throughout Central and South America in the 2000s (Silva 2009). At the peak of the movement in the second week of June, citizens erected a reported 36 roadblocks around the country.[22] The government finally conceded to demands to reduce electricity prices back to their December 1982 level after days of barricades and street protests throughout the nation. On June 9, leaders and legislative representatives of Pueblo Unido organized a street march to the National Assembly where they celebrated the victorious outcome.[23] Activists would pass down use of the roadblock as strategic experience almost a generation later in the campaign against the privatization of telecommunications and electricity.

Mass Resistance to Structural Adjustment Loan III

After the 1983 IMF protests, opposition forces splintered in Costa Rica. The origins of the crisis are rooted in a difference in strategy during two major banana strikes, in the Atlantic region in 1982 and on the southern Pacific coast in 1984.[24] The conflict split the PVP into two factions, and divided other organizations affiliated with the left, most importantly, the CUT. The internal divisions dampened the level of popular mobilization (especially multisectoral struggles) for nearly a decade between 1985 and 1995, even as the debt crisis continued and two major structural adjustment loan (SAL) programs were implemented (SAL I in 1985 and SAL II in 1990) (Raventos 1995).

Popular struggles were also weakened by the massive infusion of U.S. financial aid to the Costa Rican government between 1983 and 1989 to prevent a deeper financial crisis and avoid the revolutionary conflicts from neighboring countries spilling into the country (Seligson and Muller 1987). Some of these funds could be used to soften the blows of structural adjustment by investing in social programs. At the same time, this aid assured the United States of a solid geopolitical ally in the region, as the Reagan and Bush administrations sponsored counterinsurgency and counterrevolution in El Salvador, Guatemala, and Nicaragua.[25] Costa Rica became the second largest recipient of U.S. aid in Latin America (Seligson and Muller 1987). Outbreaks of popular mobilization did still occur in the mid- to late 1980s, with a vibrant anti-interventionist Central American peace movement and urban struggles for low income housing.

Activists and labor-based associations reactivated popular mobilization in 1995 during a major strike by teachers and public-sector workers. As discussed in chapter 2, public-sector employees are among the few groups in the developing world organized on a national scale (Cook 1996). Several mass mobilizations reaching up to 100,000 participants took place in July and August 1995 over a new pension plan that would raise the age of retirement and force greater contributions. The pension program, along with mass layoffs and privatizations in the public sector, was part of the third structural adjustment loan (SAL

III) pushed by the World Bank and IMF and agreed upon by the country's two dominant political parties to reduce the government's national budget deficit. The teachers associations had been legalized at the beginning of the state-led development era in the late 1940s. In this protest campaign, educators drew on universities and public-sector unions, sectors also benefiting from state-led development.

Prior to the 1995 conflict, with the exception of the peasant sector and the 1983 IMF electricity price hike protests, large sectors of the population in Costa Rica did not resist austerity measures. In some cases, the government would negotiate with labor leaders before economic reforms were enacted. In other cases, civil society resistance was limited to the particular sector affected by the reforms. This was the case for small farmers in the 1980s contesting agricultural subsidy and tariff reductions (Edelman 1999), cuts in the university budget in 1991 that led to a strike in higher education, austerity measures in public education that resulted in teachers strikes in 1992 and 1993, and a May 1995 campaign by state telecommunication workers against the takeover of cell phone administration by Millicom, a transnational corporation. These smaller economic liberalization conflicts won some concessions (Sandoval Coto 1995); teachers, for instance, prevented a negative change to their pension program in 1993, during the administration of President Rafael Ángel Calderón Fournier (1990–1994). Scholarly observers in Costa Rica classify the 1995 austerity conflict and teachers strike as the first major national campaign against economic globalization in the 1990s (Cedeño Castro 1996, 122; Gutiérrez, Raventós, and Sandoval 1996).

The 1995 mobilizations began in June when the leaders of the two major political parties, the PLN and PUSC, signed a pact (Pacto Figueres-Calderón) agreeing to pass a series of neoliberal forms in the following six months. State policy makers were under enormous international pressure after the World Bank had refused to give the government a $350 million loan earlier in the year when the administration failed to make reductions in the state sector (Sandoval Coto 1995). In addition, the IMF waited with a standby loan, available as soon as the state instituted the economic reforms (a situation referred to as "cross-conditionality"). International lenders expressed concern over Costa Rica's domestic budget deficit, which ran at about 8% in 1995. One strategy to shrink the deficit involved restructuring the retirement system for public school teachers as well as mass layoffs in other public-sector branches. With the austerity measures associated with SAL I and SAL II, the central government already had slashed the budget for public education from 34.5% of social spending in 1982 to 24.4% in 1991 (Trejos and Valverde 1995: 16).

The austerity plan would reduce pension payments from 100% of a teacher's final salary to 80%, along with requiring greater teacher contributions to the system and raising the age of retirement. The legislative assembly introduced and passed the restructuring plan (Law 7531) on July 9, 1995, while teachers were on vacation. Moreover, policy makers scheduled the legislative debate and passage over the weekend with scant parliamentary debate. The pension reform was specifically requested as a condition to receive the standby loan from the International Monetary Fund (Calvo Coin 1995). The measure served as an integral component of Costa Rica's third major structural adjustment program since the early 1980s (known as SAL III) (Rodríguez Molina 2000: 4).

Knowing the legislation was in the pipeline, teachers began demonstrating outside the parliament building while educators from Heredia set up a tent city. The teachers called on fellow public educators to return from vacation immediately and organize to resist this economic threat. The teachers formed a coalition made up of the four major teachers' associations in the country; they called the coalition the Frente de Organizaciones Magisteriales (FOM). The FOM represented between 35,000 to 50,000 teachers. By July 11, 1995, the teachers entered into a coalition with a new ad hoc labor organization, the Comité Cívico Nacional (CCN), composed of 33 labor organizations largely from the state sector. The CCN was mainly concerned about other neoliberal reforms in the Figueres-Calderón Pact and SAL III (cutting 8,000 public-sector jobs, increasing the value-added tax by 50%, increasing the prices of public utility services, and privatizing state institutions). In addition to supporting the teachers, the CCN demanded a 15% pay raise and price subsidies on 500 basic consumption products. The FOM also enjoyed the support of the four national universities, including faculty, staff, and students. Though these coalitions appear wide, they were largely confined to the educational sector and public-sector unions. In addition, the public-sector unions mobilizing efforts did not materialize with the force that organizers anticipated.

The public educators decided to open the school year with a complete strike, which began on July 17, 1995, affecting a reported 700,000 students. The following week, a few public-sector unions from the CCN began to hold solidarity work stoppages. The teachers held daily rallies in San José and intermittent demonstrations in provincial towns (Menjívar Ochoa 1999). On July

26 and again on August 7, the FOM held massive demonstrations in the capital reaching up to 100,000 participants, making them the largest street mobilizations in decades (Dobles Oropeza 1995). The wide geographic reach of the mobilizations is illustrated in Figure 3.1. By August 11, leaders from the FOM and CCN began to hold negotiations with the government, while more public-sector unions joined the strike and threatened to escalate the protests to culminate in a general strike. On August 18, leaders from the FOM agreed to end the strike and set up a special commission with representatives from the government, the FOM, the CCN, and the private sector to further discuss the pension law and other reforms without any guarantees of rescinding the pension law or the structural adjustment agreement (Menjívar Ochoa 1999). The next week teachers returned to work, and the reforms remained in place years after the commission was set up. The teachers had failed to overturn the pension law (an economic austerity measure), which was their explicit goal.[26]

Several other social sectors, such as peasants in Cartago and judicial workers, held group-specific protest campaigns simultaneously that neglected to link to the teachers movement during the first week of the strike.[27] Information about the level of external solidarity achieved in the 1995 teachers strike is shown in figure 3.2. The large majority of the reported protests were held by teachers alone. External allies participated in only 31% of documented protest events during the strike. Nonetheless, because teachers and public schools are located throughout the country, the July-August mobilizations covered much of the territory and resistance was especially intensive in localities with public universities and provincial capitals with administrative offices (figure 3.1). Labor unions and worker associations in Costa Rica tend to be small, with 60% of unions maintaining 100 members or less (Trejos and Valverde 1995). Hence, the three main teachers associations represent some of the largest labor-based organizations in the country. Public opinion appeared divided in its support for the teachers' demands.[28]

Other public-sector labor leaders in key organizations inside the CCN, such as the water workers (AyA), social security and health care employees (UNDECA), and ANEP disclosed to field reporters covering the strike that they were having a difficult time convincing rank-and-file union members outside of the educational sector to support the teachers' demands.[29] In other words, some of the constituencies of key external allies (i.e., other public-sector workers) did not clearly perceive that the teachers' battle was tied to a larger slate of neoliberal

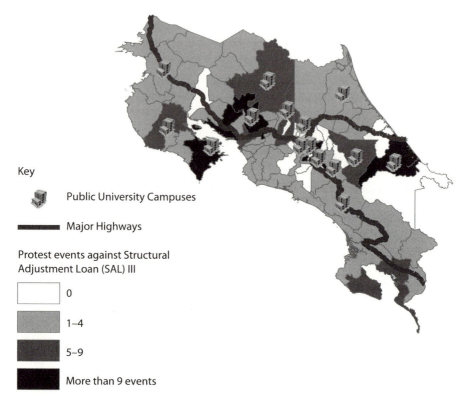

Key

🏛 Public University Campuses

▬▬▬ Major Highways

Protest events against Structural
Adjustment Loan (SAL) III

⬜	0
◻	1–4
◼	5–9
⬛	More than 9 events

Figure 3.1. Subnational resistance to Structural Adjustment Loan III, Costa Rica,
July–August 1995.

reforms under the Figueres-Calderón Pact or that state sector union solidarity
could play a critical role in impeding liberalization measures unfavorable to
the working-class as a whole. Even though the formation of the CCN and the
solidarity strikes by public-sector workers strengthened the teachers' bargain-
ing power, the recent past of sector-specific forms of organizing against neoliberal reforms in the late 1980s and early 1990s constrained the overall degree
of multisectoral mobilization achieved. Nonetheless, the mass actions in the 1995
campaign against structural adjustment demonstrated the geographical reach
of teachers as a mobilized force and the importance of attempting cross-sectoral
ties with the labor movement.[30] Without the formation of the FOM and the CCN
alliances, mass mobilization may not have surfaced. However, in the short

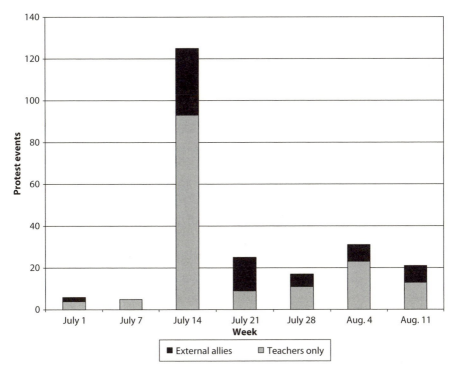

Figure 3.2. Weekly protests against pension system reform, July–August 1995.

term, the sense of defeat following the 1995 campaign worked its way deep into the labor movement's consciousness, to the point that union organizers failed to convoke the traditional May Day rally the following year.[31]

Protests against Telecommunications and Electrical Power Privatization, 2000

On March 20, 2000, the Costa Rican national assembly voted in favor (with 45 out of 57 votes) of a new law allowing for the partial privatization of the state-run institute of telecommunications and power distribution, the ICE.[32] Public opinion stood overwhelmingly against the privatization of the ICE. People viewed the state institution as a relatively efficient and affordable system that should not be left to the whims of international telecommunications and energy corporations (Alvarenga Venutulo 2005). Telecommunications and electricity cover over 95% of the national territory.[33] Civil society groups, realizing that this legislation was in the works, began to meet in the spring of 1999. Earlier attempts to privatize the ICE had stalled for legal and bureaucratic reasons. In March 1995, ICE labor unions held a weeklong strike and successfully stopped the institute's cell phone service from being sold to the multinational telecommunications firm Millicom. In May 1997, the ICE labor associations held another national strike to impede the privatization process. In 1999, after a series of negotiations between the two dominant political parties, the PUSC and PLN, policy makers decided to combine the separate initiatives into one single piece of legislation that would allow for the partial outsourcing of ICE operations.

ICE labor union leaders learned from the failed 1995 teachers' strike and their own 1997 strike and adopted a more inclusive organizing template of multisectoral struggle to battle telecommunications privatization in 1999 and 2000.[34] It was a strategy that proved successful in the short and medium term. Indeed, ICE workers had been active participants in the 1995 strike, marching in unison with the public educators on several occasions. Propaganda from the ICE campaign referred to the failures of the popular mobilizations in 1995 and called for opposition leadership not to negotiate with the government without a prolonged consultation and approval from the grassroots organizers at the base of the campaign.

The ICE labor associations organized anti-privatization events and forums between April and July 1999.[35] The coalition against privatization was composed of some 15,000 ICE state workers organized in eight associations and united in the Frente Interno de Trabajadores (FIT) del ICE, university students, university workers unions, communal associations, environmentalists, the progressive Catholic Church,[36] and left-wing opposition political parties (Fuerza Democrática, Pueblo Unido, and Partido Revolucionario de Trabajadores). The coalition reached such a breadth of civil society participation that even high school students participated in large numbers. The newly formed coalition, led by the ICE unions, held a few anti-privatization actions in the second half of 1999. By the end of 1999 the coalition had begun calling itself the Liga Cívica.[37] By early 2000, several more opposition factions in civil society emerged against the privatization.[38] As the ICE privatization neared a vote in Costa Rica's unicameral legislature, the opposition factions began to unify and coordinate, fearing a repeat of 1995 when the government proved less than transparent in implementing neoliberal reforms and defeated a divided protest campaign.[39] In late January 2000 another overlapping multisectoral coalition formed entitled the

Frente Cívico Nacional composed of the ICE labor associations, students, and opposition political party members from the Fuerza Democrática.

The group met each Wednesday in the capital and distributed an estimated 30,000 anti-privatization flyers in the month of February. The FIT, Liga Cívica, and Frente Cívico Nacional organized a mass street march on February 28 in which participants dressed in yellow (the official color of the ICE) to demonstrate their solidarity with the public institution.

Just days before the vote, on March 17, 2000, the coalition organized another mass street protest, which ended at the legislative assembly while in the interior of the country roadblocks on strategic transportation routes began. The ICE unions (organized in the Frente Interno de Trabajadores) effectively advertised the March 17 demonstration and other activities as fighting inevitable price increases if the ICE were privatized and as a multisectoral struggle of neighborhoods, students, church parishes, and environmentalists.[40] On March 20, 2000, after almost a year of building a diverse opposition coalition, demonstrators surrounded the assembly building, holding placards warning the legislators with slogans such as "nos vemos en las calles" (see you in the streets). The anti-privatization campaign referred to the ICE privatization program in a derogatory fashion as "El Combo" because it combined the dismemberment and privatization of electricity and telecommunications in a single piece of legislation. Opposition propaganda employed the imagery of a fast food outlet's "combo" meal to mock the government's "great bargain" in selling off the national patrimony as students wore cheap paper Burger King crowns during street protests.

The assembly passed the ICE privatization law, even as the protestors surrounded the parliament. The opposition coalition had already organized up to 40 roadblocks and protests in all seven provinces of the country (see figure 3.5 below). University and high school students along with public-sector workers manned barricades throughout San José and at strategic points on highways in the interior. Unlike the 1995 protest campaign, organized peasants in the Cartago region united their demands against cheap agricultural imports with the ICE anti-privatization movement and erected barricades with students in the opening days of the conflict (Alvarenga Venutulo 2005).

For these disruptive protests, several dozen protesters faced arrest while police dispensed tear gas at hundreds more. On March 23, 2000, in a defining moment for Costa Rica in the new century, the opposition coordinated a massive street demonstration with a reported 100,000 participants.[41] Several other cities held simultaneous marches on the same day. In the cities of Heredia, Cartago, Alajuela, and Limón newspapers reported that the high schools were practically empty as students, teachers, and parents joined the demonstrations. Several other cities and towns reported protest activities on March 22.[42]

Between March 20 and March 25 several public-sector unions held one day or partial strikes including the Federación de Trabajadores Limoneses (FETRAL), which encompasses city employees and dock workers in Limón; ICE workers nationwide; the public health care system employees (UNDECA), which held strike actions in 80 clinics and hospitals; the petroleum refinery workers (Recope); and several other state-sector unions, including teachers. Four university students initiated a 12-day hunger strike on March 20 in front of the ICE central administration building. Roadblocks, street marches, labor strikes, and rallies continued across the country through the last week of March. In the face of this massive outpouring of civil society resistance, the main opposition political party, the PLN, came out publicly and stated it would not vote in favor of the privatization in the next round of parliamentary voting.[43] According to the Costa Rican constitution, pending legislation needs to pass two rounds of parliamentary approval before it can be enacted into law.[44]

At the height of the campaign, there were more than 120 protests per week (figure 3.3). A progressive general strike began to take shape in the first week of April, bringing in port and refinery workers from Limón on the Caribbean coast and dock workers on the Pacific coast, and several public-sector unions organized by ANEP. Besides the ICE workers' strike, which began immediately following the passage of the privatization law on March 20, the majority of other protest actions included external groups. In total, external allies were present in over two-thirds of the reported protest events (68%). This multisector representation was in stark contrast to the teachers' unsuccessful 1995 protest campaign, which only counted multiple groups in less than one-third of protest events (31%).

The large multisectoral and combative resistance in civil society and the PLN's reversal of support for the privatization led the PUSC government of President Miguel Ángel Rodríguez to enter a dialogue with the opposition by the first week of April. The disruptive mobilizations marked the largest outpouring of citizen protest participation in decades. Between March 1 and April 6, 2000, there were 473 distinct protest events across Costa Rica's 81 cantones (figure 3.4).[45] Fifty-one percent of protest events involved obstructing traffic, and nearly every municipality transected by one of Costa Rica's major highways experienced a protest event.

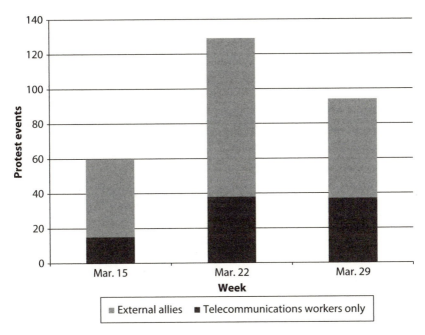

Figure 3.3. Weekly protests against telecommunications and electrical power privatization, March 2000. (Data from *La nación.*)

A CID-Gallup polling team conducted a survey during the historic demonstration on March 23, sampling 660 protest participants. The poll found that 44% of the protesters blamed the legislature for the ICE crisis, and 27% faulted President Miguel Ángel Rodríguez of the PUSC.[46] In a telephone survey conducted by the University of Costa Rica of 460 citizens on March 24 and 25, 2000, 53% of the population stated they were against the privatization legislation and only 20% responded in favor of the newly proposed law. The poll showed that 84% of respondents preferred a direct referendum on the privatization as opposed to delegating the issue to congressional authority; 71% were in favor of the anti-privatization marches; and 42% stated they approved of the highly disruptive tactic of the roadblocks.[47] Clearly, public opinion in early 2000 was against privatization of telecommunications and electricity, especially in the form it was being carried out.

On April 4, 2000, the opposition coalition (in the midst of an escalating general strike) signed an agreement with the government. The government

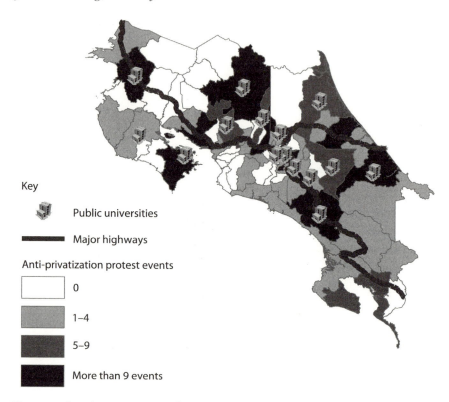

Key

Public universities

Major highways

Anti-privatization protest events

0

1–4

5–9

More than 9 events

Figure 3.4. Local opposition to telecommunications and electricity privatization, March–April 2000. (Municipalities reporting protest events are shaded. Data from *La nación* and *Diario extra*.)

agreed to shelve the privatization of the ICE and assigned a special commission to create an alternative plan for its future. The special commission included key sectors of the opposition coalition, including ICE labor associations, university students, environmentalists, and the progressive Catholic Church. In exchange for the halting of the privatization process, the civil society groups agreed to cease all disruptive protests and agitation.[48] A final crucial outcome of the Combo campaign involved the innovation of a new mobilizing strategy called *sindicalismo-ciudadano* (citizen unionism).[49] Public-sector labor unions coined the term after discovering they needed to involve ordinary citizens in their campaigns, and not rely solely on other labor associations, if they stood any chance of success. This multisectoral approach of unions aligning with multiple groups in civil society was empirically verified with the struggle to rescue the ICE from privatization. Costa Rican unions carried the sindicalismo-ciudadano strategy into the next major globalization battle, the monumental conflict over the Central American Free Trade Agreement.

A comparison of municipalities in Costa Rica that did not participate in collective action and those registering at least one protest event against ICE privatization shows that communities with greater levels of administrative and community infrastructure and strategic experience were more likely to mobilize (table 3.1). All seven provincial capitals experienced protest. None of the 30 nonparticipating communities in Costa Rica house a provincial capital, a strategic administrative location to express collective grievances against government privatization policies. Some provincial capital cities also have preexisting multisectoral coalitions at the local level, such as FETRAL in Limón and the Coordinadora de Organizaciones Sociales de Puentarenas (CORGASOP), which formed in 1998. State road infrastructure is also more developed in the participating municipalities. Over one-third of participating communities have a major highway passing through their municipal boundaries while only 10% of nonparticipating localities are connected to a major transportation route. Over 50% of protests involved blocking roads, and Costa Rica's two major highways (the Pan-American Highway and the San José–Limón/Braulio–Carrillo Highway) provided strategic points for activists to disrupt economic activity during the campaign.

Not one of the localities that failed to mobilize against ICE privatization contains a public university establishment, while nearly 30% of participating communities have such higher education institutes. The expansion of the higher educational infrastructure in Costa Rica between 1940 and 1980 (discussed earlier in this chapter) provided a university campus or extension in nearly 20% of Costa Rica's cantones. Municipalities with a public university (even an extension campus) reported some of the most confrontational protests between youth and security forces in the campaign (i.e., where mass arrests or injuries occurred) such as in San Pedro, Heredia, Pérez Zeledón, Liberia, and Puntarenas. In the town of Turrialba, in the province of Cartago, the extension campus of the University of Costa Rica served as the hub of the local campaign. The university community there coordinated several highway road blockades, street marches, and public forums between March 21 and March 27, 2000 (Comité Cívico de Lucha 2000).

Participating and nonparticipating communities also show differences in community infrastructure. Nonparticipating municipalities have on average

2.8 nongovernmental organizations while participating municipalities have on average 7.5 NGOs operating in their local territory (median of four NGOs). Participating municipalities also tend to display higher levels of influence of left-leaning opposition political parties.[50] Political parties such as Fuerza Democrática and Pueblo Unido were able to use their membership contacts in various locations throughout the national territory to organize protest events. Participating communities also had more ICE offices or power plants, where the ICE labor unions are located and served on the front lines of the resistance. Nonetheless, the 15,000 ICE workers did not have the capacity alone to sustain a nationwide campaign. Such urban-based public unions need the solidarity of other sectors such as public universities and opposition political parties to reach communities beyond the larger cities. One group of ICE workers in Naranjo, Alajuela province, was so aware of this issue that they sent a letter to high school students in their municipality thanking them for participating in the protests and roadblocks immediately after the campaign.[51]

Finally, those municipalities that resisted the privatization efforts had higher indices of participating in past anti-neoliberal protest campaigns (in 1983 against the IMF price hikes and the 1995 mobilization against SAL III). The strategic experience of organizing community members and setting up roadblocks made a difference in the 2000 campaign against the privatization of the ICE. In summary, table 3.1 demonstrates that communities opposing economic liberalization harbor elevated levels of state, community, and strategic infrastructure (across multiple indicators) compared with localities that did not participate in protest actions. Moreover, in a separate multivariate analysis of the *intensity* of protests against the ICE privatization (number of events per locality) state and community infrastructure and strategic experience were associated with heightened levels of popular contention (Almeida 2012).

CAFTA Protests, 2003–2007

The protests against the Central American Free Trade Agreement were more protracted and extensive in Costa Rica than in any other country in the region. Mobilizations reached up to 150,000 participants and forced the government to hold its first ever popular referendum. One scholar-observer finds that CAFTA "generated the largest and most sustained mass mobilization in more than half a century" (Raventos 2013: 81). CAFTA was viewed as a threat to the entire social welfare system and the Social Guarantees the state established in the 1940s, guarantees that were the envy of many developing states. Of special

Table 3.1 Differences between participating and nonparticipating municipalities in collective protest against privatization, Costa Rica, March–April 2000

Category	All municipalities (n=81)	Nonparticipating municipalities (n=30)	Participating municipalities (n=51)
State infrastructure			
Administrative infrastructure			
Percent with a provincial capital	9%	0%	14%
Transportation infrastructure			
Percent with a major highway in municipality	27%	10%	37%
Higher education infrastructure			
Percent with a public university campus	19%	0%	29%
Community infrastructure			
Mean number of nongovernmental organizations	5.79 (median=2)	2.83 (median=2)	7.53 (median=4)
Opposition political party			
Median number of left opposition party votes (1998)	532.0	204.5	701.0
Labor-based associations			
Percent public-sector employees	14%	13%	15%
Mean number of Instituto Costarricense de Electricidad establishments (1999) (focal labor organization)	1.44 (median=1)	0.90 (median=1)	1.77 (median=2)
Strategic capital			
Strategic experience			
Mean number of participation in past anti-neoliberal campaigns in 1983 and 1995 (0–2)	1.06	0.87	1.18
Median population density	67.80	64.45	99.80

concern to the sectors opposing CAFTA was the privatization of telecommunications, insurance, and health care (all developed during the era of state-led development), along with greater access to natural resources by multinational corporations. The anti-CAFTA campaign stretched to an even wider variety of actors than the Combo protests had, with the participation of opposition political parties, public-sector labor unions, environmental NGOs, student organizations, women's collectives, indigenous groups, small farmers, teachers, and artists. These groups, more often than not, coordinated their opposition in large multisectoral coalitions. (Table 3.2 lists the most prominent multisectoral umbrella organizations mobilizing against CAFTA and the specific sectors involved.)

Popular organizations and small leftist parties that had battled against the privatization of the ICE maintained links into the early 2000s, especially through the Comisión Nacional de Enlace (CNE), which was chartered in 2000. Other multisectoral groups that emerged on the political scene in 2003 and 2004 would provide the civil society nexus of organizations that opposed CAFTA. These included Encuentro Popular (2003), Coordinadora Unitaria Sindical y Magisterial (CUSIMA) (2004), Movimiento Cívico Nacional (2004), El Conversatorio, Frente Nacional de Lucha, Movimiento Patriótico contra el TLC,[52] and several others (see table 3.2) (Seguro Ballar and Coronado Marroquín 2008).

The mobilizations began in 2003 with a few rallies and mass marches directed against the first round of trade negotiations. In July and August 2004, organizers launched major strikes and national campaigns with anti-free-trade demands, including 24-hour general strikes by the CUSIMA-affiliated labor confederations and public school teachers. As part of this series of actions, there was a major campaign in the last week of August 2004 in which wage increases, cost of living complaints, the removal of a transnational transport inspection company (RITEVE), and CAFTA were the central issues. The campaign involved a series of roadblocks using cargo trucks (driving purposely at a snail's pace) along with demonstrations in towns and cities that shut the country down for nearly a week. In 2005, even larger multisectoral organizations began to form as it became clear that political elites would not allow popular organizations or labor unions (or civil society in general) a seat at the CAFTA negotiating table. By 2006, there were more major strikes and protest actions taking place against CAFTA, including a national teachers strike in June and a two-day general strike in late October that involved dozens of street actions around the country. The mobilizations peaked in February 2007 when organizers coordinated a street march of 150,000 people in San José, the largest protest march in modern

Table 3.2 Multisectoral organizations mobilizing against the Central American Free Trade Agreement

Organization and year formed	Member organizations	Civil society sectors represented
Comisión Nacional de Enlace (2000)	Coordinadora Unitaria Sindical y Magisterial Comité de Defensa de la Seguridad Social Movimiento de Mujeres 12 Puntos Movimiento Ecologista Movimiento Campesino Movimiento Estudiantil Consejo de Defensa de la Institucionalidad Asambleas del Pueblo Encuentro Popular América Nuestra Foro de Acción Política	Teachers, social security employees, women's rights advocates, environmentalists, small farmers, university students, human rights advocates, religious groups, neighborhood associations
Plataforma contra el Libre Comercio (2002)	Unión Nacional de Empleados de la Caja y la Seguridad Social Asociación de Profesores de Segunda Enseñanza Asociación Nacional de Empleados Publicos Asociación Servicios de Promoción Laboral LOS (AS) NADIES Federación de Estudiantes de la Universidad de Costa Rica Grupo Carmen Lyra	Social security institute labor association, high school teachers, public sector labor unions, labor and environmental nongovernmental organizations, university students, women's groups, peasant organizations, think tanks

(*continued*)

Table 3.2 (continued)

Organization and year formed	Member organizations	Civil society sectors represented
	Grupo Centro de Estudios del Mundo Contemporáneo Movimiento de Trabajadores Costarricenses Federación Costarricense para la Conservación del Ambiente Departamento Ecuménico de Investigaciones	
Comité Patriótico Nacional (2002)	Asociación de Talleres Independientes de Costa Rica Asambleas del Pueblo Confederación Nacional de Asociaciones de Desarrollo Comunal Consejo Nacional de Trabajadores Bananeros Movimiento de Trabajadores Costarricenses	Auto repair shops, community development associations, banana workers, peasant associations
Encuentro Popular (2003)	Escuela de Economía de la Universidad Nacional Consejo de Defensa de la Institucionalidad Departamento Ecuménico de Investigaciones Asociación de Profesores de Segunda Enseñanza Unión del Personal del Instituto Nacional de Seguros Frente Interno de Trabajadores / Instituto Costarricense de Electricidad	Labor unions, students, women, neighborhood associations, political parties, nongovernmental organizations, indigenous peoples, university students, high school teachers, state insurance employees, telecommunications workers, environmental groups from the northern and southern regions of the country including from Guanacaste and Puntarenas

América Nuestra (2003)	Sindicato de Empleados de la Universidad de Costa Rica	University employee unions, port workers, banana workers, high school teachers, social security institute labor association, ICE workers, labor confederations
	Sindicato de Trabajadores de la Universidad Nacional	
	Sindicato de Trabajadores de la Junta de Administración Portuaria	
	Unión de Empleados de la Universidad Estatal a Distancia	
	Sindicato Empleados del Banco Nacional de Costa Rica	
	Asociación de Profesores de Segunda Enseñanza	
	Sindicato Patriótico de la Educación 7 de Agosto	
	ATTAC-Costa Rica	
	Unión Nacional de Empleados de la Caja y la Seguridad Social	
	Asocición de Funcionarios y Funcionarias del Instituto Tecnológico	
	Central de Trabajadores de Costa Rica	
	Amigos de la Tierra Costa Rica	
	Centro de Estudios del Mundo Contemporáneo	

(continued)

RARITAN VALLEY COMMUNITY COLLEGE
EVELYN S. FIELD LIBRARY

Table 3.2 (continued)

Organization and year formed	Member organizations	Civil society sectors represented
Movimiento Cívico Nacional (2004)	Asociación Nacional de Empleados Publicos	Public-sector workers, ICE labor unions, high school teachers, small farmers, taxi drivers, bus drivers, constitutionalists, university students, truck drivers, banana plantation workers, nurses
	Asociación de Empleados del Instituto Costarricense de Electricidad	
	Asociación de Profesores de Segunda Enseñanza	
	Unión Nacional de Pequeños Agricultores Costarricenses	
	Cámara Costarricense de Transportistas Unitarios	
	Asociación Nacional de Empleados	
	Instituto Defensoría Ciudadana	
	Asociación de Talleres Integrales Costarricenses	
	Federación Nacional de Organizaciones de Taxis	
	Sindicato de Estudiantes Universitarios de Costa Rica	
	Asociación de Transportistas de San Carlos	
	Cooperativa de Industrialización y Comercialización del Pacifico Sur	
	Asociación de Taxistas Independientes de Heredia	
	Sindicato Costarricense de Taxistas	
	Sindicato de Traileros	
	Comité Cívico de Talamanca	
	Cooperativa de Transportistas del Valle, R.L.	

Coordinadora Unitaria Sindical y Magisterial (2004)	Asociación de Equipos Especiales a Granel	Private- and public-sector labor union confederations, public school teachers associations, state bank workers, state water and aqueduct workers, social security institute workers, electrical power employees, state insurance employees, port workers, state housing institute employees, municipal workers
	Cámara Sindical de Taxistas	
	Coordinadora de Sindicatos Bananeros	
	Asociación Nacional de Profesionales en Enfermería	
	Federación Nacional Campesina	
	Unión de Taxistas Costarricenses	
	Sindicato de Educadores Costarricenses	
	Coyotes Moto Club	
	Asamblea del Pueblo	
	Confederación General de Trabajadores Costarricenses	
	Central del Movimiento de Trajadores/as Costarricenses	
	Confederación de Trabajadores Rerum Novarum	
	Confederación Costarricense de Trabajadores Democráticos	
	Asociación Nacional de Educadores	
	Sindicato de Trabajadoras y Trabajadores de la Educación Costarricense	
	Sindicato Patriótico de la Educación 7 de Agosto	
	Banco Nacional	
	Acueductos y Alcantarillados	
	Caja Costarricense de Seguro Social	
	Instituto Nacional de Seguros	
	Instituto Costarricense de Electricidad	
	Japdeva	

(continued)

Table 3.2 (continued)

Organization and year formed	Member organizations	Civil society sectors represented
	Fuerza y Luz Instituto Nacional de Vivienda y Urbanismo	
Coordinadora Nacional contra el Tratado de Libre Comercio (2005)	Magisterio en Acción Comisión Nacional de Enlace Movimiento Cívico Nacional Coordinadora Unitaria Sindical y Magisterial Encuentro Popular Coordinadora Estudiantil Asambleas del Pueblo Frente Interno de Trabajadores / Instituto Costarricense de Electricidad Frente de Cultura Frente de Universidad de Costa Rica Inter-Universitaria Frente Amplio Partido de Acción Ciudadana	Teachers, major umbrella organizations, cultural workers and artists, university staff and students, opposition political parties, women's groups
Conversatorio (Grupo de Jueves) (2005)	Asociación Nacional de Educadores Asociación Nacional de Empleados Publicos Asociación de Profesores de Segunda Enseñanza Asociación de Empleados del Instituto Costarricense de Electricidad Consejo Nacional de Cooperativas	Public school teachers, public-sector labor unions, ICE unions, cooperatives, state community development associations, state liquor company employees, health care system employees, small farmers, academic and business sectors

Frente Nacional de Apoyo a la Lucha contra el Tratado de Libre Comercio (2006)

Confederación Nacional de Asociaciones de Desarrollo Comunal Convergencia Patriótica Sindicato Pro- Trabajadores del Consejo Nacional de Producción Unión Nacional de Empleados de la Caja y la Seguridad Social Unión de Pequeños y Medianos Agricultores Nacionales Partido de Acción Ciudadana Coordinadora Nacional contra el Tratado de Libre Comercio Coordinadora Unitaria Sindical y Magisterial Movimiento Cívico Nacional Encuentro Popular Comisión National de Enlace	Multisectoral umbrella organizations opposing Central American Free Trade Agreement

Note: Table constructed from Segura Ballar and Coronado Marroquin (2008) and other sources.

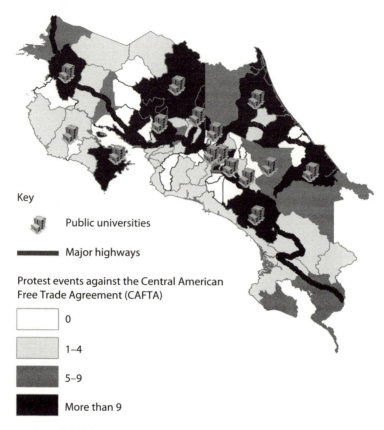

Figure 3.5. Anti-CAFTA protest events, 2003–2007.

Costa Rican history.[53] Altogether, there were 694 recorded anti-CAFTA protest actions distributed across 81 administrative districts between 2003 and 2007, with 596 of the reported protest events (86%) in coordination with one of the multisectoral coalitions (figure 3.5).

The 2006 and 2007 anti-CAFTA mobilizations forced President Oscar Arias and his neoliberal PLN to convoke a referendum on the free trade treaty. It would be the first plebiscite in Costa Rican history. The organizers then switched mobilization strategies to prepare for a special election on CAFTA to be held October 7, 2007.[54] Labor unions and left-leaning political parties used their resources and networks to help form local "Patriotic Committees" to ensure an impressive electoral turnout for the referendum and train locals as election monitors. Between June and early September 2007 the opposition political party, Partido de Acción Ciudadana (PAC), attempted to reach 300,000 households in a door-to-door campaign to rally the vote against CAFTA.[55] Other grassroots "Patriotic Committees" formed within their communities. The opposition, or "No" campaign (Raventos 2013), faced an uphill battle against the dominant PLN party of the two-term president and Nobel Peace Prize recipient, Oscar Arias. The Patriotic Committees held weekly events throughout the country, often using universities, local labor union offices, and high schools to hold public forums and deliberations. A final rally on September 30, 2007, the week before the referendum, once again brought some 150,000 citizens out on the streets of the capital to protest CAFTA. In the end, the No campaign lost by a margin of three percentage points, 756,814 votes (48%) to 805,658 (51%). Since 2007, social mobilization has declined markedly and largely focused on preventing large development projects, such as open-pit gold mining in San Carlos, water aqueducts for tourism in Guanacaste, and the privatization of transportation routes (e.g., the San Ramón–San José Highway) and ports (Cordero 2014).

Sectors benefiting from state-led development between the 1940s and 1980s directed the CAFTA protests (as seen by their representation in table 3.2). In particular, public-sector unions in institutions developed during mid-twentieth century economic modernization, public school teachers associations (legalized in the 1940s) and universities, and other related sectors of the welfare state, such as the community associations of DINADECO, were overrepresented in the opposition to free trade. Other important participants included NGOs (especially environmental and women's groups) and political parties. The multisector style of organizing greatly benefited the capacity to mobilize and reach regions outside of the capital and larger cities. Even though the mobilizations did not defeat CAFTA, the campaign stalled the passage and implementation of the treaty for several years and secured some protections for state-controlled institutions in health care, insurance, and telecommunications. The strength of left-leaning parties in the 2014 presidential and parliamentary elections (PAC and Frente Amplio) is partially attributable to lingering public dissatisfaction with CAFTA's implementation.

Conclusion

The globalization battles in Costa Rica provide important lessons for understanding other struggles in the region. In fact, Costa Rica provides the template for patterns of protest in other Central American countries, and perhaps in the democratizing developing world in general. Thanks to early democratization, an era of state-led development established robust state, community, and strategic infrastructures. Perceived threats to that era's social guarantees from transnational capital (United Fruit, ALCOA, the IMF, and Free Trade) sparked enormous mobilizations at different times. Costa Rican citizens drew on opposition political parties, the labor movement, educational institutions, and the public sector to defend themselves from unfavorable economic changes. The campaigns were more efficacious when citizens combined forces in multisectoral coalitions. These same types of struggles tend to proliferate as other developing countries democratize and face similar conditions of global economic integration and threats from transnational actors. We next analyze neighboring Central American countries to examine these similarities and differences in local resistance to globalization.

4

El Salvador

Opposition Party and Protest Campaigns

El Salvador's path to neoliberal globalization and local opposition is rooted in a repressive military regime that modernized the economy and state infrastructure between the 1950s and 1970s. The military took power in the early 1930s under the dictatorship of General Maximiliano Hernández Martínez (Ching 2014). Following World War II, more reform-minded (but still repressive) military forces took over administration of the government. They created their own political party (PRUD and later the PCN).[1] Military rulers invested heavily in public education, roads, health systems, and telecommunications, and other vital parts of the economic infrastructure. El Salvador's period of state-led development ran from 1950 to 1980, during which the government paved three major highways, the Troncal del Norte, the Pan-American, and the Litoral along the Pacific coast. It also instituted the Social Security Institute (ISSS) in 1950, which provided health coverage to urban workers in the formal sector, and established a modern labor code in 1952. The code was updated in 1963 to allow workers to form labor federations and to strike. The state set up the national telecommunications agency (ANTEL) in 1964. And after 1960, the country saw massive expansion and investment in public education, from the primary to the postsecondary school system (Almeida 2008b; Lindo-Fuentes and Ching 2012).

Even with these social reforms and expansion of state infrastructure, the military governments between 1950 and 1980 could not secure popular legitimacy. The military's alliance with the dominant agro-export class impeded deeper reforms supporting economic modernization and social redistribution (Paige 1997). The state cracked down on growing opposition movements in a manner way out of proportion to their modest demands for more freedoms in the 1960s and early 1970s. Militant organizations began to emerge out of the civil society reform movements after a series of fraudulent elections in the 1970s. Social movements in the labor, educational, church, and peasant sectors that began nonviolent mobilization efforts in the late 1960s radicalized into revolutionary parties in the 1970s after severe military repression against their activities, including killings, disappearances, torture, and mass arrests. These more radical organizations unified into a larger revolutionary organization, the Farabundo Martí National Liberation Front (FMLN) in 1980. Five revolutionary parties composed the FMLN. Growing state and insurgent violence spiraled into a full-blown civil war by early 1981 (Viterna 2013). At the outset of the conflict, the FMLN received international recognition from France and Mexico as a legitimate and representative political force while the Reagan and Bush administrations in the United States funded the Salvadoran army's counterinsurgent operations. The civil war continued throughout the 1980s, with nearly 80,000 deaths, with 85% of them attributed to the Salvadoran government's security and military forces (United Nations 1993).

The Salvadoran democratization process commenced with the Chapultepec Peace Accords signed in January 1992 between the government and the FMLN. The accords put an end to 12 years of civil war and opened up political space for both civil society mobilization and opposition political parties. Before this time, El Salvador had been one of the longest-enduring military-controlled governments in Latin America. With the exception of a few rounds of regime liberalization in the late 1920s, 1960s, and 1980s (see Brockett 2005; Lindo-Fuentes, Ching, and Lara-Martínez 2007; Almeida 2008b; and Gould and Lauria-Santiago 2008), some form of military rule was in effect from late 1931 until 1982, and the Salvadoran armed forces continued to exercise enormous influence inside the state until the United Nations–brokered peace accords (Stanley 1996; Williams and Walter 1997).

Even with the implementation of competitive elections during the civil war in the 1980s, only center-right and far-right political parties participated in the electoral process while a state of emergency was in effect from 1980 to 1987 (Artiga-González 2004). These conditions hampered the ability of groups in civil society to sustain nonviolent campaigns for more than a few weeks at a time. Meanwhile, the government constantly claimed that the most powerful civic organizations and labor unions maintained clandestine links to the FMLN, then still an armed insurgency, which exposed the civic leadership and rank-and-file members of popular organizations to selective forms of state repression until the early 1990s. Soon after the peace accords, the government recognized the FMLN as a legitimate political party; that recognition was a major accomplishment in terms of constructing social peace, as a former insurgent army turned over its weapons and entered local and national elections (Wood 2005). In addition, activists attempting to organize protest campaigns now had a potential ally inside the parliament with the FMLN legalized as a political party. Also, with the peace accords dismantling the notoriously repressive security bodies like the Treasury Police, National Police, and the National Guard, it would be easier to mobilize on the streets in the new democratic context.

With democratization under way, the neoliberal economic model was also coming to dominate policy makers' plans in the region (W. Robinson 2008). Even before the civil war ended, Salvadoran governments were enacting economic-stabilization programs based on guidelines from the International Monetary Fund. Christian Democrat president José Napoleón Duarte's "economic package" of January 1986, for example, included a devaluation of the national currency (Brockett 2005). However, a more consistent neoliberal policy-making trajectory came with the electoral triumph of Alfredo Cristiani and the ARENA party in 1989 (W. Robinson 2003). The Cristiani administration (1989–1994) implemented several neoliberal reforms, including reprivatizing the banking system, closing the Food and Basic Grains Regulatory Supply Institute (IRA), implementing massive layoffs in the public sector, and privatizing coffee export institutes and sugar refineries (Aguilar Guillén 1993). The intensity of neoliberal restructuring would assist the FMLN in becoming a major opposition political party in the post-civil-war era by partnering with protest campaigns. The strategic alliance between the FMLN and anti-globalization resistance efforts consolidated in the early 2000s. In particular, the party's involvement with popular campaigns against privatization and free trade solidified the partnership. The alliance eventually led to the triumph of the leftist party in the 2009 presidential elections and sustains the FMLN as a political party with substantial public opinion support into the 2010s.

In the early 1990s, the FMLN began reconstructing itself as a major electoral party. Historically an uneasy coalition of five left-wing factions, the party suffered from internal ideological disputes over political platforms, programs, and policies in the post–Cold War context. These conflicts blew up at the end of 1994, when seven legislative deputies left the FMLN along with two of the founding factions, the National Resistance and the People's Revolutionary Army (the bases of these two renegade parties largely remained with the FMLN or later returned as sympathizers). As the FMLN struggled to overcome these internal tensions, it focused on elections rather than protest. Many of its top leaders with connections to popular movements, like Humberto Centeno from the telecommunications workers association,[2] enmeshed themselves in electoral mobilization and left behind their earlier organizing work.

Early Anti-Globalization Skirmishes

During the early 1990s as the civil war ended and the country transitioned to peacetime, the civil society organizations also adjusted their strategies and alliances in accordance with the new political climate. The traditional types of labor organizations attempted to confront some of President Cristiani's austerity measures and held short protest campaigns and one-day strikes. These battles of the early 1990s included popular movement coalitions like the Inter-Gremial and UNASTEMA, which fought the closing of the IRA and the mass layoffs in the public sector under the first ARENA government. However, some of the largest conflicts in the period centered on grievances left over from the civil war, like peasant associations and rural cooperatives' struggles for access to land and ex-paramilitary bodies (*patrulleros*) combating the state through violent street actions for ongoing indemnification and benefits for their services during the civil war.

In the 1994 local, parliamentary, and presidential elections, the FMLN had established itself as a substantial, if still minority, political party by forcing ARENA into a second-round runoff election for president and winning 21 seats in the country's 84-member unicameral legislature. With its momentum building, the FMLN went on to take over 51 municipal governments and 27 legislative seats in 1997, nearly equaling ARENA in parliamentary power (Spence, Lanchin, and Thale 2001). The party also triumphed with the election of Dr. Héctor Silva as mayor of San Salvador, the nation's capital. Yet despite these unprecedented electoral gains, the party failed to attract the necessary support to win a presidential election, which it lost in 1999 and 2004 in the first round of balloting. Nonetheless, a new wave of protest activity emerged by the late 1990s, which helped the FMLN sustain its electoral base in local and parliamentary elections in 2000, 2003, 2006, and 2009 (Artiga-González 2004).

El Salvador was transforming into a largely neoliberal political economy, especially with the implementation of a second generation of major economic policy reforms (Segovia 2002). These new reforms centered on privatization, dollarization, and free trade and generated the largest sustained protest campaigns in decades. Under the presidency of Armando Calderón Sol (1994–1999), privatization measures were implemented via the executive office's State Modernization Program. The reforms began in earnest in 1994 with the announcement of massive layoffs in the public sector (Anner 1996). In early 1995, Calderón Sol announced plans to increase the value-added tax and privatize ANTEL, electrical power distribution, and the state-run pension system. Popular movement groups and the FMLN responded to these reforms with a few mass street marches, but these mobilizations lacked the capacity to sustain a unified opposition campaign, given the period of adjustment to the emerging neoliberal environment. Activists also only reached the largest cities in these campaigns and failed to engage supporters in smaller towns and more remote regions.

The majority of resistance waged between 1995 and 1998 was fought out in individual sectors, as telecommunications workers battled privatization, the

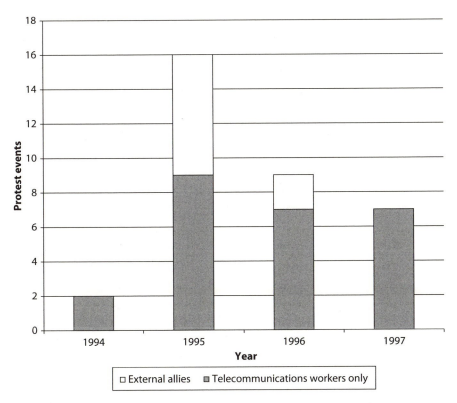

Figure 4.1. Protests against telecommunications privatization, El Salvador, 1994–1997.

public works labor association (ATMOP) fought mass layoffs, state pension workers (SITINPEP) tackled pension privatization, and consumer-defense NGOs mobilized against the regressive value-added tax and electricity price hikes. In one of the larger campaigns of the mid-1990s, the telecommunication workers failed to bring enough external allies into their battle against privatization and to extend the struggle into towns and villages beyond San Salvador, botching efforts to produce a multisectoral coalition across the national territory (figure 4.1). In the end, the telecommunications system, one of the most profitable state institutions, was sold off to multinational firms in France, Spain, and Mexico; thousands of workers were dismissed and the labor unions decertified. Throughout the 1990s, the popular sectors made futile attempts to unify their skirmishes against privatization into a larger campaign and broaden conflicts to multiple geographical regions. At the same time, the key political ally of anti-neoliberal mobilizations inside the parliament, the FMLN, lacked the political capital and representation to prevent privatization measures from being passed in the legislature. Nonetheless, the balance of power began to shift in favor of both the popular movement and the FMLN in late 1999, when the government moved to outsource a key component of the public health care system.

The Battles over Health Care Privatization

Soon after taking office, Francisco "Paco" Flores, the third consecutive ARENA president (1999–2004), pursued an initiative, begun in the mid-1990s with the assistance of the World Bank and Inter-American Development Bank, to outsource the services of the country's premier medical institution, the ISSS.[3] The doctors of the ISSS—who had just formed a labor union (SIMETRISSS) in 1997 and launched a successful strike in 1998 for better wages and more voice in the restructuring initiatives—immediately joined forces with the health care workers union (STISSS). Their combined protest campaign proved to be different from the episodes of resistance to economic policies in the 1990s. Most notably, the health care unions formed an effective coalition with other groups in civil society (Kowalchuk 2011) and with the FMLN (Almeida 2006, 2008a; Almeida and Delgado 2008). This successful new coalition came into existence largely as a result of a change in the structure of Salvadoran civil society in the late 1990s. After the isolated, sector-specific campaigns in the mid-1990s, several new multi-group and multisectoral alliances were established. In the health sector, the Tripartite Commission came together in 1998 to defend public health and included the newly formed SIMETRISSS, the physicians in the general hospital system, and the Medical College, the doctors' professional association.

In the labor sector, the Movement of Integrated Labor Organizations (MOLI) brought together more than a dozen public-sector unions, while the Union Coordinating Committee of Salvadoran Workers (CSTS) united workers in the government, construction industry, and maquiladoras, as well as informal workers. These two labor coalitions then joined municipal employees, teachers, and several important organizations beyond urban labor (including the two most prominent university student organizations, peasant associations, and community-based confederations) under the loose umbrella structure of the Labor and Social Alliance (CLS). The CLS formed in June 1999 to fight state sector privatization, state repression, increase the minimum wage, and prevent flexible labor laws.[4] In the NGO sector, an important coordinating organization, the Foro de la Sociedad Civil (Civil Society Forum), was already established. Formed in early 1999 in the aftermath of Hurricane Mitch, it counted at least 50 NGOs among its ranks, including the largest agricultural worker associations and rural cooperative federations, as well as important rural community associations (e.g., CORDES and CRIPDES) and women's collectives (Almeida and Delgado 2008). The coordination of a diversity of NGOs under a single organizational umbrella opened up the possibility to mobilize several remote rural regions in a simultaneous fashion. Activists and community organizers in Nicaragua, Guatemala, and Honduras established similar coalitions of NGOs following Hurricane Mitch in late 1998.

Consequently, on the eve of the first major health strike against privatization, a major restructuring had taken place in Salvadoran civil society in which dozens of the most important labor, peasant, student, professional, and nongovernmental organizations entered into multisectoral alliances. The doctors and health care workers tapped into this vast and newly created web of civic associations to launch two of the most important strikes in Salvadoran history and one of the longest-sustained resistance efforts against privatization in Latin America. Activists also would use this network to launch mobilizations against CAFTA in dozens of localities in the mid-2000s.

The first protest against health care privatization started in November 1999 and lasted until the following March of 2000. The nonviolent campaign involved dozens of mass marches in the country's major towns and cities, including some that mobilized up to 50,000 participants (figure 4.2). This round of mobilizations saw participation from multiple groups beyond the health sector. Peasants

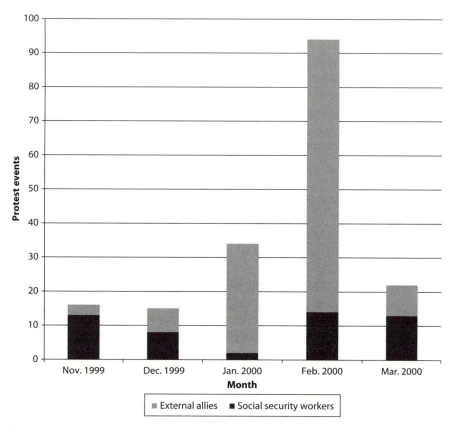

Figure 4.2. Monthly protests against health care privatization, November 1999–March 2000.

from Chalatenango and the lower Río Lempa region boarded buses to participate in marches in the capital. Public-sector labor unions held at least a dozen solidarity strikes. The NGO community formed an ad hoc multisector coalition of 30 groups to support the strike called the Civil Society Movement against Privatization. The Civil Society Movement against Privatization coordinated many campaign actions outside of the capital. In the face of the mounting multisectoral resistance occurring in a variety of localities, the government was forced to back down from privatization and negotiate with STISSS and SIMETRISSS.

The health care protests occurred at the same time as legislative and municipal elections. The FMLN publicly supported the strike, and health care activists campaigned for the party, which partly explains the FMLN's electoral success in 2000, when the party surpassed ARENA for the first time in the number of legislative seats. But the struggle was not over. In mid-2002, the ARENA government, working closely with the private business association ANEP, decided once again to try outsourcing medical services in the ISSS. This triggered an even larger and more enduring protest campaign, from September 2002 to June 2003, led by STISSS and SIMETRISSS. The doctors and health care workers called on their allies in NGOs, schools, political parties, women's rights collectives, and public-sector labor associations, who again played decisive roles in mobilizing civil society. This time, they erected dozens of roadblocks on the country's major highways and organized massive streets marches, known as the *marchas blancas* (white marches), that involved up to 200,000 participants (Smith-Nonini 2010).

The FMLN joined the mobilizations, dispatching not only rank-and-file party members but also legislative deputies and mayors to the marches and highway barricades—in fact, the entire FMLN parliamentary faction joined anti-privatization marches as its own protest contingent. The FMLN also used its weekly public rally, the Tribuna Abierta, to call on supporters to join the protests. The party introduced legislation that would prohibit health care privatization, but it was overturned when small right-wing parties changed alliances in parliament. As before, the second anti-privatization campaign occurred during municipal and parliamentary elections. The FMLN once again benefited from its open support of the anti-privatization mobilizations, winning enough votes to maintain its representation in the legislative assembly and in local governments, including the capital. The campaign once again forced the government to halt its outsourcing efforts.

The health care privatization campaigns had much more activity and external support from civil society than the mobilizations against telecommunications privatization (figures 4.1–4.3). In a single week the health care campaigns generated more protests than the entire four-year effort against telecommunications privatization. Nearly two-thirds of health care protest events included participation of groups outside the social security sector and its constituent labor unions, while less than one-third of events during the telecommunications protests between 1994 and 1997 involved groups outside of the unions in the communications sector. Similar to the Instituto Costarricense de Electricidad

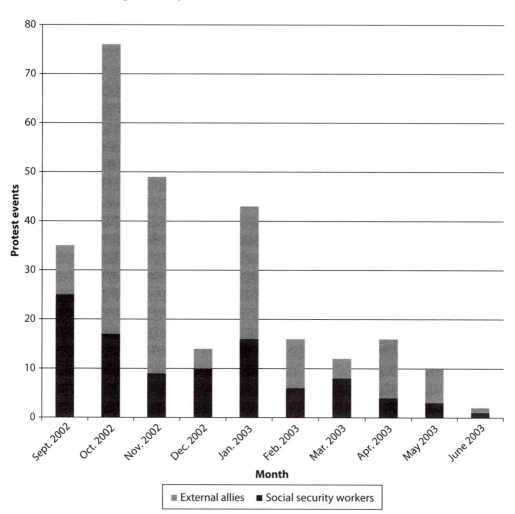

Figure 4.3. Monthly protests against health care privatization, September 2002–June 2003. (Data from *Diario co latino*.)

(ICE) privatization campaign in Costa Rica (see chapter 3), the health care unions learned from the failed anti-neoliberal campaigns of the past and used the new post-civil-war democratic space to mobilize multiple groups for relatively successful outcomes.

Another key dimension of the health care battles involves the vast geographical space in which the protesters were able to organize on a national scale. The defense of health care campaign drew on both state infrastructure (highways, administrative offices, and public hospitals) and community infrastructure (NGOs, labor associations, and opposition political parties) along with strategic experience to coordinate the campaign in dozens of communities. In the 2002–2003 campaign, 550 anti-privatization protest events were distributed throughout the national territory (figure 4.4).[5]

In table 4.1, communities in El Salvador with no collective action (nonparticipating municipalities) are compared to municipalities registering at least one protest event against privatization, based on the data in figure 4.4. Key state and community infrastructure dimensions are compared between the participating and nonparticipating communities.

In terms of state infrastructure, nearly 20% of participating localities serve as a provincial capital, while only 1% of nonparticipating communities are a

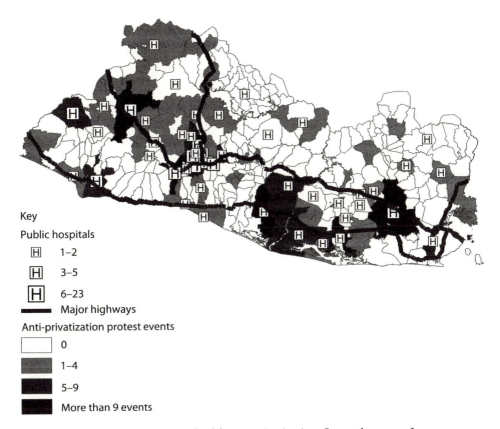

Key

Public hospitals

H   1–2

H   3–5

H   6–23

▬▬ Major highways

Anti-privatization protest events

□   0

▨   1–4

▤   5–9

■   More than 9 events

Figure 4.4. Local opposition to health care privatization, September 2002–June 2003. (Municipalities reporting protest events are shaded.)

Table 4.1 Differences between participating and nonparticipating municipalities in collective protests against health care privatization, El Salvador, September 2003–June 2003

Category	All municipalities (*n* = 262)	Nonparticipating municipalities (*n* = 194)	Participating municipalities (*n* = 68)
State infrastructure			
Administrative infrastructure			
Percent with a provincial capital	5.0%	1.0%	19.0%
Transportation infrastructure			
Percent with a major highway in municipality	24.0%	13.0%	54.0%
Higher education infrastructure			
Percent with a public university campus	2.0%	0.0%	6.0%
Community infrastructure			
Mean number of nongovernmental organizations	6.81 (median = 5)	4.82 (median = 4)	12.50 (median = 10)
Opposition political party			
Median number of left opposition party (Farabundo Martí National Liberation Front) votes for legislature (2000)	550.5	461.5	1919.5
Percent left opposition party (Farabundo Martí National Liberation Front) votes for legislature (2000)	29.3%	27.5%	34.6%
Labor-based associations			
Percent public-sector employees	3.0%	2.0%	4.0%
Mean number of public hospitals (focal labor organization)	0.40 (median = 0)	0.07 (median = 0)	1.34 (median = 1)
Strategic capital			
Strategic experience			
Percent participating in 1999–2000 health care privatization campaign	11.0%	3.0%	34.0%
Median population density	171.10	155.58	263.47

regional capital, thus offering fewer opportunities to express grievances to government officials and offices. Over half of the participating communities have a highway intersecting their territory, while only 13% percent of nonparticipating localities maintain a major transportation route. Indeed, nearly one-third of protest events (32%) in the campaign involved roadblocks. Protesters targeted El Salvador's three major highways and shut traffic down for hours at a time, even blocking border crossings into Honduras and Guatemala. Participating municipalities also had more university establishments.[6] It is important to note, however, that the Salvadoran public university system is much more centralized than in other Central American countries, with just one large campus in the capital and three regional campuses in other cities.

As regards community infrastructure, participating communities have significantly more nongovernmental development-type organizations. Civil society organizers formed ad hoc coalitions of dozens of NGOs to support the campaign (such as the Alianza Ciudadana contra la Privatización and the Foro de la Sociedad Civil) and coordinated several of the highway blockades. Many of these participating NGOs (CORDES, CRIPDES, Asociación para el Desarrollo Integral de la Mujer) are most active in distant and poor rural communities out of the reach of urban activists. Progressive NGOs filled the space of the declining organized peasant movement by sustaining ongoing relationships with rural communities on a wide variety of local development projects. NGOs also provide a crucial source of information flow between communities about privatization policies by encountering the extreme distortions of El Salvador's major media outlets (Kowalchuk 2011).

Participating communities also maintain a larger number of FMLN sympathizers. As mentioned above, the FMLN repeatedly called on supporters to actively participate in the health care protest campaign during its weekly public rally, the Tribuna Abierta.[7] Moreover, high-ranking FMLN party officials, such as mayors and members of parliament, participated in street marches and even roadblocks during the campaign. Another measure related to the influence of opposition political parties is the percentage vote for the opposition out of the total vote count. In El Salvador, communities participating in the anti-privatization campaign had a higher percentage vote for the FMLN (34.6% of the vote) compared to nonparticipating municipalities (which had a mean percentage vote of 27.5% for the FMLN). Also, participating communities maintain a larger percentage of the labor force in the public sector and host more public hospital units, where the health care labor and professional associations reside (figure 4.4).

Looking at strategic experience, one-third of participating communities had mobilized in the 1999 protest campaign against health care privatization, while only 3% of nonparticipating localities could count on this kind of communal knowledge of coordinating previous mobilization. While a community's participation in past protest actions of any type would serve as an experiential resource, involvement in earlier campaigns against neoliberalism should especially reduce mobilizing costs given that people in the locality already would be aware of the potential consequences of privatization. In short, Salvadoran communities participating in the campaign to defend the public health care system tended to maintain higher concentrations of strategic experience than nonparticipating communities. Finally, participating municipalities are more densely populated. Overall, communities participating in the campaign against the outsourcing of public health care retain higher levels of state and community infrastructures across multiple dimensions, according to the data in table 4.1. In a separate multivariate quantitative study on the *intensity* of local protest against health care privatization (number of events per community), administrative infrastructure, transportation infrastructure, NGOs, and FMLN penetration were the strongest predictors of heightened anti-privatization contention at the local level (Almeida 2012).

Campaign against the Central American Free Trade Agreement, 2003–2008

After the health care battle in June 2003, the FMLN effectively absorbed much of the popular movements' mobilization capital into its electoral campaigns. The party created a social movement section within its organizational structure that focused on supporting popular sector causes and bringing grievances into the legislative assembly. In October 2003, a new multisectoral organization also came into existence, the Bloque Popular Social (BPS), which maintained close links to the FMLN. Another multisectoral coordinating body, the October 12 Popular Resistance Movement (MPR-12), emerged in 2003 from the Foro de la Sociedad Civil and the Coordinadora Laboral y Social (CLS) and signed accords with the FMLN during election campaigns to offer strategic support while the FMLN incorporated popular organization demands into its election platform.[8] Both the BPS and MPR-12 acted as key multisectoral coalitions in the campaigns against the government's plans to sign on to the Central American Free Trade Agreement between 2003 and 2008. The anti-CAFTA coalitions generated 351 reported protest events between 2003 and 2008 (figure 4.5).[9] Of

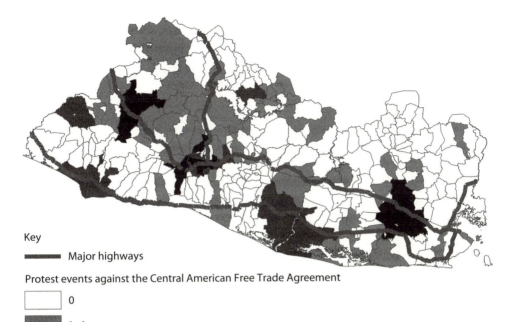

Key

▬▬▬▬ Major highways

Protest events against the Central American Free Trade Agreement

⬜	0
🔲	1–4
⬛	5–9
⬛	More than 9 events

Figure 4.5. Popular resistance to free trade, 2003–2008.

these, 251 (71.5%) were reportedly carried out by multiple groups and/or a multisectoral organization.

The Salvadoran congress passed CAFTA on December 9, 2004, with 49 out of 84 votes. A coalition of right-wing parties led by ARENA voted in unison for the treaty's passage. The 35 votes against CAFTA came from the FMLN and the smaller, center-left CDU party. The congress ratified the agreement at 3:30 in the morning on December 17, while reporters, civil society opponents, and the general public were likely fast asleep. The BPS had held a protest march to the legislative assembly during the previous day. The march was brutally repressed by the elite police force (UMO), and several leaders were injured (including Protestant ministers). The MPR-12 attempted to occupy the legislative assembly for several hours the day after ratification. From this point forward, the anti-CAFTA mobilizations were on the defensive, as the pro-neoliberal political parties had successfully rushed the legislation through the parliament at a dizzying pace.

Anti-CAFTA mobilizations had begun in mid-2003, at the end of the health care privatization campaign. For example, the MPR-12 came to public light in April 2003 while simultaneously protesting health care privatization and the third round of negotiations on CAFTA (Chacón Calderón, Iraheta Fuentes, and Villeda 2008). The first national days of protest explicitly against CAFTA occurred in December 2003.[10] The MPR-12, the women's rights group DIGNAS, university students, and many NGOs participated in the December mobilizations within or near northern and eastern San Salvador Department, such as in the municipalities of Paisnal, Aguilares, San Pablo Tacachico, Chalatenango, Suchitoto, San Martin, Soyapango, and Ilopango. The FMLN was involved in many of these mobilizations.

By June 2004, the BPS organized another round of anti-CAFTA mobilizations with marches in many provincial capital towns and cities. As organizers of the anti-free-trade campaign sensed that CAFTA was moving closer to final approval in the National Assembly they redoubled efforts with a series of actions in the second week of October 2004. This wave of actions reached dozens of municipalities around the country. The Red Sinti Techan ("Maiz del Pueblo" in Nahuatl), another multisectoral organization (Spalding 2007), along with the MPR-12 and the BPS, coordinated the protests. In this wave of activities, organizations set up highway roadblocks and reached out to new communities with educational workshops about the potential consequences of CAFTA's implementation. This type of educational activity is crucial when the general public registers a low level of awareness about issues (Snow and Benford 1988). The workshops took place in rural communities such as Santa Elena and Estanzuela in Usulután, Cinquera in Cabañas, and Atiquizaya in Ahuachapán, as well as large municipalities and provincial capitals, including Mejicanos, Soyapango, San Salvador, Santa Ana, San Miguel, Sensuntepeque, and Chalatenango.

The roadblocks in October 2004 targeted strategic points throughout the national territory. The Colima bridge that connects San Salvador department to Chalatenango was blocked by members of rural communities from the northern part of the country. FMLN mayors from small towns in Chalatenango participated alongside residents of their surrounding villages. The BPS and MPR-12 also blocked multiple routes along the nation's main highways and major roads providing entry into the capital. The BPS launched a new wave of protests and highway blockades on December 22, 2004, just days after CAFTA's ratification. It used its multiple affiliates in the labor, student, NGO, and rural sectors to hold nearly two dozen highway blockades in eleven out of fourteen of El Salvador's provinces.

The campaign strived to keep up momentum in March 2005 with days of action in municipalities in the Department of Santa Ana. In early June, organizations affiliated with the FMLN, BPS, and MPR-12 sponsored a day of anti-CAFTA actions to mark the one-year anniversary of President Antonio Saca in office and to protest the principal achievement of his tenure, the passage of the free trade treaty. The multisectoral alliance held street marches in all fourteen provincial capitals where protesters could easily assemble in recognized public squares. The FMLN and BPS would hold national days of action against CAFTA (and the ARENA Party) on the second and third anniversaries of Saca's presidency in 2006 and 2007. To finish out 2005, the FMLN and BPS sponsored a day of protests in late November, with the participation of over two dozen municipalities around the country. FMLN mayors, city council participants, and rank-and-file members played a large part in these mobilizations.

The final showdown over CAFTA came in early 2006. The treaty was to go into force on March 1. Anti-CAFTA organizations sponsored days of action in late January and late February and set up road barricades and blockades at international border crossings. Nonetheless, the street demonstrations rarely reached over 40,000 people compared to the massive marchas blancas in 2002 and 2003. The government successfully implemented the treaty, but CAFTA would continue to mobilize opposition groups through 2008, including an anti-TLC pilgrimage from San Miguel to San Salvador organized by the BPS, MPR-12, and CRIPDES in October 2006 and another national day of protests in 2007 to mark the one-year anniversary of CAFTA's implementation. The treaty immediately created new conflicts between informal sector market vendors and local authorities. Police units began to clamp down on pirated merchandise (which violated the trade agreement's copyright laws) in the larger cities. DVD and CD street vendors began to form national organizations to defend themselves against the new wave of repression. The ARENA government appeared to have outmaneuvered the opposition by fast-tracking CAFTA (it was the first government to ratify the treaty in Central America). Nationally representative public opinion data reported by Rose Spalding (2007: 104) show that between 2003 and 2006, the percentage of Salvadoran citizens believing that free trade agreements increase poverty steadily rose from 28% to 50%. She partially attributes the growing public misgivings with CAFTA to the mass mobilizations and informational campaigns that occurred in the same period. By the mid- to late 2000s, the FMLN also seemed to be placing more attention and resources into its increasingly successful electoral gains than into grass-roots organizing in the streets.

Electoral Mobilization against Globalization

In 2004, the FMLN chose a major leader from the health care campaign, Dr. Guillermo Mata Bennett (former president of the Medical College), as the running mate of presidential candidate and historic FMLN leader Jorge Schafik Hándal. The party campaigned for the election almost like a protest campaign, going door to door to drum up support,[11] while popular organizations used their affiliates to help bring out the vote. In the end, the ARENA candidate, former TV sports journalist Antonio Saca, garnered a record 1.3 million votes. But the FMLN more than doubled its usual electoral turnout, earning about 800,000 votes. In the 2006 municipal and legislative elections, the FMLN maintained its numbers in parliament and received more than 780,000 votes (in a non-presidential-election year). The FMLN also maintained control of multiple departmental capitals and densely populated working class municipalities near San Salvador such as Soyapango, Ciudad Delgado, Mejicanos, Apopa, San Marcos, Santa Tecla, and Ilopango. This electoral success is all the more remarkable given the schisms in the FMLN with the defection of important factions in 2005. What may have made up for these internal conflicts was the continuing unpopularity of the ARENA government's policies, including privatization, as well as its inability to control consumer inflation, ongoing official corruption, excessive homicide and crime rates, and the decision to continue sending troops to Iraq. This litany of state-attributed social problems often found its way into the protest songs in favor of the FMLN during the 2009 election season (see below).

Following the government's second defeat in the health care privatization wars, it had begun a crackdown on popular mobilizations against CAFTA, environmental degradation, water privatization, and mining. In April 2004, police forces arrested top leaders of the STISSS while they were attempting to occupy the metropolitan cathedral in San Salvador. In December 2004, the interior minister had the faces of anti-CAFTA campaign leaders published in the opening pages of a leading national newspaper. A year later, the government expelled from the country a key SIMETRISSS consultant who was very active in the anti-privatization campaigns. Police continued to harass informal market vendors who violated CAFTA rules by selling pirated CDs and DVDs to scrape out a living. After a rare shootout between police and ultra-left groups in July 2006 killed two police officers, the government enacted the Special Law against Acts of Terrorism. Before this bizarre shootout, most anti-neoliberal protest activity was nonviolent in the post-civil-war era (but often assertive, disruptive, with occasional outbreaks of vandalism). The central government soon used the new antiterrorism legislation to criminalize peaceful demonstrators from the country's leading NGOs who were blocking roads near the town of Suchitoto to protest water privatization in July 2007.

Under pressure from these more stringent government laws, popular movements were unable to generate the level of mobilization they had effectively pieced together for the two health care campaigns and the first actions against CAFTA. Meanwhile, however, the FMLN's ability to hold on to its municipal and parliamentary seats in the mid-2000s set the stage for the extraordinary 2009 presidential elections. In August 2007, on the eve of launching the 2009 presidential campaign, the FMLN invited several civic organizations, social movements, and NGOs into the halls of the National Assembly for a special forum to push for the passage of a national bill that would prohibit water privatization. The head of the FMLN parliamentary faction and its soon-to-be vice presidential candidate, Salvador Sánchez Cerén, implored the attendees active in the anti-water-privatization campaign, "The coming struggle to defend water is going to demand struggle and many mobilizations from the communities."[12]

In late 2007, the party nominated Mauricio Funes and Sánchez Cerén as the party's presidential and vice presidential candidates. Funes, a well-known former journalist with decades of exposure on national television, was an outsider to the party (and remained so after winning the elections). Sánchez Cerén had begun participating in the popular movement in the late 1960s as a local leader of the teachers' labor association ANDES–21 de Junio in La Libertad department. He was also one of the highest-ranking leaders in the Popular Forces of Liberation (FPL) revolutionary organization until it dissolved into the FMLN in 1995.

The FMLN candidates began their campaign in the Cuscatlán soccer stadium on November 11, 2007, with some 50,000 supporters in attendance, almost a year and a half before the elections in March (ARENA did not choose its slate until March 2008). The Funes campaign judiciously used the 17 months at its disposal. Immediately, the FMLN launched the Caravan of Hope (echoing Barack Obama's campaign mantra of "hope"). The caravan traveled through multiple municipalities every weekend, getting out the message that progressive social change stood on the horizon. The campaign rallies resembled the protest gatherings against privatization and free trade of the previous years, with the same slogans and protest songs chanted and sung in unison along with a whole host of new songs crafted just for the election.

The Funes campaign also enlisted the support of radio stations, including Radio Mi Gente, founded by a recently repatriated Salvadoran evangelical minister. Radio Mi Gente broadcasted daily in favor of social change and consistently highlighted the social and economic ills plaguing the nation's popular classes, including neoliberal economic policies, gang violence, official corruption, and the high cost of living. Radio Mi Gente, Radio Maya Visión, the Caravan of Hope, and an army of campaign volunteers also distributed and sold protest songs in support of the campaign. Musicians composed dozens of new songs in multiple popular rhythms, from cumbia and meringue to mariachi, ranchero, and even reggaetón. Protest musicians often took popular songs by artists such as Juan Luis Guerra and Juanes, which were familiar to much of the electorate, and changed the lyrics to electoral propaganda. All of these popular communication and social movement strategies could be seen as overcoming the shortfalls of past electoral campaigns, in which right-wing political parties controlled the three major national TV stations and the most important radio stations in the nation.

The presidential campaign maintained its confidence in the first test of its mobilizing drive, the municipal and legislative elections of January 18, 2009. Although the FMLN lost San Salvador to ARENA for the first time in twelve years—the vote was by a narrow margin but the FMLN had defeated ARENA by an even smaller margin in 2006—the party triumphed in more than 90 municipal governments and took 35 legislative seats (its highest proportion of local governments and legislative deputies to date). In the final two months before the presidential elections, candidates from the smaller parties dropped out of the race, ensuring a final showdown between the FMLN and ARENA to be decided in the first electoral round. The Amigos de Mauricio group played a fundamental role in these final months by attracting the support of disaffected members from other political parties, the military, some business groups, and part of the evangelical Christian population.

The final pre-election test for the FMLN occurred March 7, a week before the elections. Funes and the FMLN convoked a rally in San Salvador along Alameda Juan Pablo II. It turned out to be one of the largest collective political events in Salvadoran history. Crowds stretched from close to Soyapango all the way to the Centro de Gobierno, where multiple stages were set up for political speeches and live music into the evening hours. Three hundred thousand people are estimated to have participated.[13] The historically large crowd may not have heeded Funes's plea to persuade ten more people to come out on election day, but the FMLN sympathizers appear to have been able to bring out at least four more. The final election tally was 1.3 million votes for the FMLN and 1.2 million for ARENA. Since taking power in 2009, the Funes government has managed the unenviable task of moderating FMLN sympathizers' high expectations in the midst of the world financial crisis. Popular organizations continue to mobilize on the streets, especially related to transnational capital such as mining, hydroelectric dams, and other megadevelopment projects in the northern departments. Other groups independent of the FMLN, such as new teachers' unions, have led actions since 2011, and even ARENA has organized protests over the selection of Supreme Court judges.

The FMLN had its own disputes with Funes over integrating into Venezuela's Bolivarian Alliance of the Americas (ALBA) trade program and trying to reduce the cost of telecommunication services for consumers. The FMLN and the Funes government instituted popular social programs and legislation, including price controls on medicine and pharmaceuticals; a reduction in public hospital fees; small monthly pensions for the elderly; free elementary school lunches, uniforms, and supplies; and progressive rural programs of technical assistance and legalizing land titles for small farmers (Perla and Cruz-Feliciano 2013). The First Lady's Office of Social Inclusion established the Ciudad Mujer program in four cities. The initiative provides urgently needed health care and job training to tens of thousands of working-class women. The Funes-FMLN government has experimented with other new social initiatives such as the Foro Nacional de la Salud. The Foro holds popular assemblies in five geographical regions in order to design a new public health care plan that will allow a greater portion of the population more extensive medical coverage in contrast to the privatization schemes of past pro-neoliberal governments. Popular organizations and NGOs from the health care privatization campaigns are coordinating the Foros with the Ministry of Public Health and Social Assistance (MSPAS). The large scale-type anti-neoliberal protest campaigns against privatization and CAFTA have not returned since the FMLN and Funes took power in 2009.

The party selected Vice President Salvador Sánchez Cerén as the presidential candidate for the 2014 elections along with the popular FMLN mayor of Santa Tecla, Oscar Ortiz. The 2014 FMLN ticket ran on a platform of continuing the popular social programs implemented between 2009 and 2014. The presidential campaign reached historic levels of success with the FMLN reaching nearly 1.5 million votes in the final runoff election.

Conclusion

In El Salvador, democratization and neoliberalism converged in the 1990s. These conditions produced a strategic alliance between the leftist opposition political party and protest campaigns confronting particular economic liberalization policies. The coalition had become multisectoral by the late 1990s, with a range of civil society groups participating. Once NGOs, rural cooperatives, public-sector unions, women's collectives, student groups, and the FMLN coalesced in the early 2000s, they launched major campaigns to prevent health care privatization and the implementation of CAFTA. The weakening of traditional peasant movements and labor unions and the loss of their organizational capacity made the new multisectoral coalitions even more vital to civil society. The FMLN's 80,000 member party is organized with affiliates in each of the country's 262 municipalities. Women's groups and rural NGOs have the ability to reach marginal and remote regions. The result is that these multisectoral coalitions can engage communities in many different parts of the country to resist new rounds of neoliberal reforms (as can be seen in the maps in figures 4.4 and 4.5).

The election of Mauricio Funes as president dampened the level of mass participation in protests between 2009 and 2014. The reformist FMLN government made attempts to avoid further privatizations in the public sector (such as water administration) and implemented price controls in vital social services (medicine, hospital fees, education, and telecommunications) in a country where nearly 50% of the population hovers near the poverty line. The FMLN administration credits these social and economic policies with a reported 11% reduction in poverty between 2008 and 2013 (Ministerio de Economía 2014).[14]

5

Panama

The Legacy of Military Populism

The political economy of modern Panama is stamped by the October 1968 military coup that eventually led to the dominance of General Omar Torrijos from 1969 to 1981. Before this time, state modernization had been under way for several decades. Beginning in the 1940s, President Arnulfo Arias established a national health insurance and retirement system, the Caja de Seguro Social (CSS), legalized a public school teachers association and enacted the first labor code. Arias was a conservative populist whose political party (Panameñista) alternated in power with other oligarchic groups and elitist parties to the exclusion of the urban and rural working classes (Gandásegui 1998). After the ascendancy of General Torrijos in the late 1960s, the expansion of state infrastructure continued at a rapid pace.

General Torrijos pieced together a corporatist military regime by building a mass base within the urban labor sector. The Torrijos government created a worker-friendly labor code in 1972 and gave official recognition to a national labor council (CONATO) that comprised the country's main labor federations. The new labor code guaranteed the right to strike, the ability to form worker committees at the factory level, and several seniority protections, including employer obligations to negotiate collective labor contracts (Phillips Collazos 1991). Shortly after the passage of the Torrijos labor code, the number of legal unions and union members tripled, from 67 unions with 21,614 union members in 1970 to 217 unions with 80,500 members in 1975 (Phillips Collazos 1991: 62). The militant construction workers union Sindicato Único Nacional de Trabajadores de la Industria de la Construcción y Similares (SUNTRACS) also was legalized in this period.

General Torrijos also greatly expanded coverage of the social security system to family members of core beneficiaries, providing health care and retirement benefits to nearly two-thirds of the population at the height of the state-led development period. In Latin America, only Costa Rica provides wider state coverage to the general population (Mesa-Lago 2007). Moreover, the populist military regime extended health care and pension coverage to banana plantation and packing house workers. The rapid expansion of the health care system reached its zenith in 1976 with the establishment of a massive centralized hospital complex in Panama City. In addition to these state-building efforts, Torrijos nationalized the electrical power generation and distribution system in 1969.

Torrijos also greatly extended the highway and educational infrastructure by building roads and schools. The regime enacted land reform, distributing parcels to thousands of landless peasants in the interior of the isthmus (Priestley 1986). University enrollments tripled between 1965 and 1975, and several regional campuses were erected in the provinces. The total public university population grew from 7,000 students in 1965 to 26,000 in 1975. By 2002, the University of Panama would count over 74,000 students across its campuses, and the country continues to maintain one of the highest rates of university enrollment in Latin America for young adults between the ages of 17 and 24. The decentralized nature of Panama's university system (established in the state-modernization era) plays a major role in supporting local-level mobilizations in the twenty-first century. The government had also established a national and centralized water and sewage distribution system in 1961, the Instituto de Acueductos y Alcantarillados Nacional (IDAAN), which Torrijos greatly expanded in the 1970s, with drinking water and sewage service reaching 70 percent of households.[1]

The rapid growth of organized labor, health care, education, and water and sewage infrastructure under Torrijos in the 1970s would set the stage for the core of opposition to neoliberalism decades later. General Torrijos died in an airline accident in 1981. In the years just before his death, Torrijos, facing pressure to democratize from the United States, established a political party, the Partido Revolucionario Democrático (PRD). The PRD ruled with smaller political groups and converted military populism into a one-party authoritarian state during the 1980s. After internal power struggles in the early 1980s, Torrijos's chief of military intelligence, General Manuel Noriega, emerged as the leader of the National Guard (later renamed the Panamanian Defense

Forces [FDP]) and the ultimate authority of the one party-dominated state (even with titular civilian presidents) until the U.S. military invasion in December 1989.

1980-1990

As early as 1980, the Panamanian government was implementing reforms suggested by the International Monetary Fund. The country experienced first-generation austerity protests between 1983 and 1986 after signing its first formal structural adjustment package with the IMF and World Bank in 1983. The nation's foreign debt was approaching $3 billion dollars by the early 1980s, and a large proportion of its budget was siphoned to make loan repayments (see figure 1.1). The IMF and World Bank demanded that the government freeze wages in the public sector, cut subsidies to basic industries, and loosen restrictive measures of the progressive 1972 labor code to attract greater foreign investment.

In reaction to the introduction of structural adjustment, CONATO labor federations held a two-day strike in June 1983 (Quintero 2003) and worker protests broke out in Panama City and Colón in October of the same year over price hikes (Walton 1987). A massive campaign against an austerity package was launched in late 1984 by a wide coalition of professional associations (teachers, lawyers, and doctors), small shop owners, and university and high school students called the Coordinadora Cívica Nacional (COCINA). *Cocina* means "kitchen" or to "cook" in Spanish, and many protesters donned cook's hats.[2] Nicolas Barletta, the new president of Noriega's party, implemented the austerity measures. Barletta had served as vice president for the World Bank's Latin American division. A general strike and mass mobilizations by tens of thousands of demonstrators took place in November and December 1984, causing Barletta government to cancel the austerity measures (Beluche 1994). The central actors in this first mass campaign against neoliberalism were teachers, lawyers, small business owners, students, and employees of the social security system, all of whom would play pivotal roles against economic liberalization in the 2000s.[3] Mass demonstrations and strikes also erupted in 1985 as the government disclosed its letter of intent agreement with the World Bank, which called for the weakening of the labor code, wage freezes, and mass layoffs in the public sector. The public-sector unions converged in a new labor federation, the Federación Nacional de Servidores Públicos (FENASEP) as the vanguard in the 1985 mobilizations (Beluche 1990).

In 1986 the IMF and World Bank once again pushed for labor code reforms to attract foreign investment, leading to a national strike by CONATO (and the participation of COCINA) in March that also included several mass marches and actions on the banana plantations in the provinces of Bocas del Toro and Chiriquí. Legislators packaged the impending labor reforms together in Law 46. Immediately after a successful street march against structural adjustment on March 4, CONATO activists went door to door days before the strike pleading with fellow citizens for support and solidarity.[4] The actions included a ten-day general strike involving nearly all the major industries and three mass marches that drew up to 100,000 participants.

Public university students also mobilized for demonstrations during the strike. General Noriega unleashed the Panamanian Defense Forces (FDP) and the notoriously brutal anti-riot police, known as the "Dobermans," to put down the strike. The unions and CONATO lost the battle as the fraudulently elected parliament passed Law 46 in the third and final legislative debate on March 19, 1986. At the height of the strike, dozens of unions were participating, including SUNTRACS and workers from key oil refineries, Coca-Cola and Pepsi bottling plants, breweries, hotels, ports, telecommunications, energy and electricity, banana plantations, water administration, clothing and furniture factories, food-processing plants, and supermarkets (figure 5.1).[5] A communist leader of the Partido del Pueblo and secretary-general of the CNTP (a union confederation affiliate of CONATO), José Manuel Meneses, led the strike for CONATO.

Protesters clearly attributed the labor flexibility laws to the IMF and World Bank. In a demonstration on March 14, labor unionists carried a coffin draped with a banner inscribed, "IMF R.I.P.," while COCINA appealed to nationalist and anti-imperial sentiments by publicly calling the measures "anti-national." Female labor union members and supporters created their own front, the Frente Feminino, and marched at the head of a mass march in the capital on March 18.

In the end, the FDP quashed the strike in several regions and made organizing in the interior of the country difficult under General Noriega's authoritarian rule. Within two days of the general strike, the defense forces dislodged striking workers in strategic industries such as the ports and oil distribution centers in Colón, milk-processing plants in the interior of the country, and impeded workers from holding marches. Noriega's "Dobermans" assassinated a SUNTRACS construction worker, Yito Barrantes Méndez, at point-blank range during a demonstration in the second week of the strike.[6] COCINA tried to con-

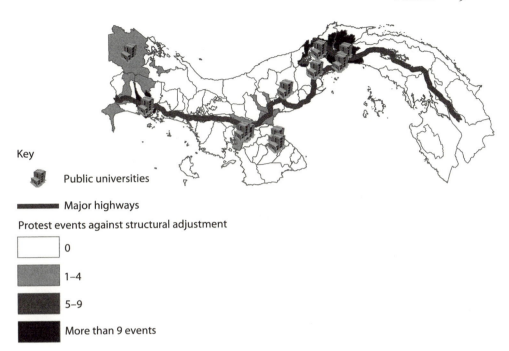

Key

 Public universities

▬▬▬▬ Major highways

Protest events against structural adjustment

▢ 0

▨ 1–4

▧ 5–9

■ More than 9 events

Figure 5.1. CONATO strike, Panama, 1986.

vince CONATO to prolong the strike, but the costs became unbearable. Of the 112 reported protest events, 39 (34.8%) involved groups outside of the private-sector labor unions, such as university students, small merchants, and civil servants.

Participants in the first-generation campaigns against economic liberalization in Panama failed to sustain mobilization and hold together broad coalitions. The lack of democratization greatly hampered the formation of organizations and coalitions that could freely exercise rights of association and public assembly. Democratization in Panama would not begin in earnest until the early 1990s. Threats of economic adjustment were still relatively new, and each affected social sector struggled against them in largely independent ways. A long-term collective consciousness based on experiences of several rounds of economic reforms had yet to congeal with the subaltern classes. These conditions had begun to change by the late 1990s.[7] However, in the late 1980s middle- and upper-class groups placed their collective energies in overthrowing the Noriega regime. These groups formed the coalition Cruzada Cívica

(Nepstad 2011). Labor leaders in the late 1980s such as in CONATO and FENASEP had largely silenced the more radical class-based elements in the union movement (*corrientes clasistas*) and struck individual patronage deals with the Noriega regime.

Democratization and the 1989 U.S. Invasion

Guillermo Endara assumed the presidency during the U.S. military invasion of Panama in late 1989. Between 1990 and 1994 he attempted to implement neoliberal reforms, including restructuring the highly popular social security system. The administration passed a privatization law (Ley Marco de Privatización) in 1992 to begin selling off state assets.

A large march against privatization occurred in mid-October 1990, and labor unions followed up with a one-day national strike in December to prevent massive layoffs (Tyroler 1990; Cambra 1994). At the same time, a new left leadership assumed influence in the Asociación de Profesores de Panama, the oldest organization of Panamian teachers, and took over SUNTRACS (the construction workers' union).[8] The corporatist labor structure General Torrijos had established, and that CONATO exemplified, was weakening after the fall of General Noriega. In 1991, more strikes broke out in the public sector to prevent further IMF- and World Bank–recommended cuts in public health and privatization in telecommunications and electrical power. Labor coalitions led many of the struggles in this period such as the Coordinadora de Sindicatos Estatales, the Coordinadora Nacional por el Derecho a la Vida, and the Coordinadora Unitaria Sindical y Popular (Quintero 2003). Most of these mobilizations were short lived and did not attract other social sectors into the campaigns, and two of the strongest unions in these coordinating organizations witnessed the privatization of their institutions, energy (IRHE) and telecommunications (INTEL), by the mid-1990s.

In 1994, Ernesto Pérez Ballardes from the PRD was elected president in the first competitive elections in several decades. Pérez Ballardes kept General Torrijos's party intact during the years following the U.S. invasion and occupation. Immediately upon assuming executive power, the new president implemented a state modernization law, a version of the economic reforms with eerily similar names in Honduras, El Salvador, and Costa Rica in this same time period. Pérez Ballardes enacted labor flexibility reforms and plans for water, electricity and telecommunications privatization as part of the modernization efforts. While the telecommunications and electricity privatizations went through with moderate resistance, civil society groups vehemently protested against labor flexibility in 1995 and water privatization in late 1998. By 1995, 30% of the national budget went to paying off foreign debt, as the IMF and World Bank pressured the government to sell off state assets, outsource public services, and slacken protections on the domestic economy (especially pro-union labor laws) in exchange for debt reduction and new lines of credit.

On May 11, 1995, when a new law to weaken the 1972 labor code was in the legislative pipeline, SUNTRACS organized a street march of over 30,000 workers (K. Robinson 1995). On May 23, labor unions called a one-day national strike against the reforms with the participation of 70,000 workers, including unions in Coclé, Chiriquí, Colón, and Bocas del Toro.[9] At the end of June, SUNTRACS occupied the Labor Commission offices inside the National Assembly, demanding a halt to the labor flexibility reforms. The reforms

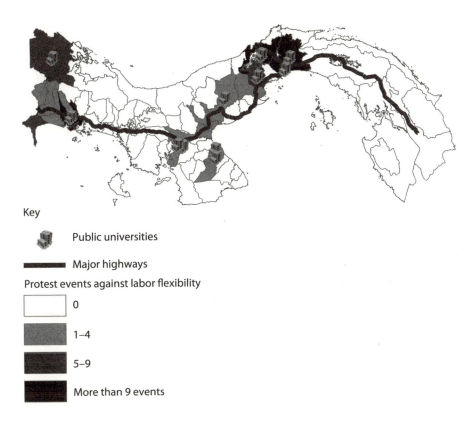

Key

Public universities

Major highways

Protest events against labor flexibility

0

1–4

5–9

More than 9 events

Figure 5.2. Labor flexibility law protests, 1995.

called for wage cuts and employee relocation during economic downturns, along with several other pro-business measures.

The campaign picked up pace in August 1995. This was the first major joint worker action under the democratic government of Pérez Ballardes. Led by the militant SUNTRACS and its leftist leadership, along with the banana industry unions, 49 labor associations held a two-week national strike in August 1995 striving to turn back the new labor measures (figure 5.2). University of Panama students also joined in the protest coalition, and as their participation increased the government temporarily shut down the Panama City, San Miguelito, and Colón campuses. Three hundred participants were arrested during the strike, and government forces killed four civilians, including a SUNTRACS unionist, Rufino Frías.[10] One reporter remarked that the events represented the most intensive conflict since the U.S. invasion.[11]

Forty out of 146 documented protest events (27.4%) involved the participation of allies outside of the private-sector labor unions, including high school and university students, health care employees, public-sector civil servants, peasant organizations, and the Movement of Unemployed People of Colón (MODESCO). As in the CONATO labor reform battle of 1986, the union movement lost and the government implemented the reforms. Nonetheless, from the defeat emerged a new coalition of labor forces called the Confederacion Nacional de Unidad Sindical Independiente (CONUSI), which held its first convention in 1998.[12] CONUSI provided an organizational mechanism to hold together in a loose labor coalition the 49 militant labor associations from the 1995 strike (including SUNTRACS) and characterizes itself as a *clasista* confederation fighting for the working-class as a whole and not just the immediate wage demands of individual unions (Quintero 2003).

MONADESO and the Campaign against Water Privatization, 1998

The first major campaign against public-sector privatization took place at the end of 1998, a year before the most famous battle against water privatization in Latin America in Bolivia. Pérez Ballardes had successfully passed labor flexibility (1995), telecommunications privatization (1996), and electricity privatization (1997) as part of his neoliberal modernization program. In late 1998, he moved to sell the nation's water and publicly administered aqueduct systems. This led to the first successful campaign against privatization, led by a new civil society coalition, the National Movement to Defend Sovereignty (Movimiento Nacional por la Defensa de la Soberanía, MONADESO), which originally had formed to contest the continued presence of the U.S. military (with the potential installation of a drug-enforcement military base), after the Panama Canal officially came under the jurisdiction of the national government in 2000 (Gandásegui 2002). Activists unveiled MONADESO on January 10, 1998, with a special assembly at the University of Panama to commemorate the anniversary of the January 9, 1964, student massacre in the Canal Zone.

Throughout 1998 MONADESO had been organizing for a "no vote" during a plebiscite to allow Pérez Ballardes to run for a second consecutive term as president. The experience served well in the campaign against water privatization, which occurred just a few months after the referendum. The referendum campaign offered an opportunity for MONADESO to reach wider populations. In addition, the activists coordinating MONADESO created an innovative organizational structure by linking *several* social sectors under one loosely aligned coalitional umbrella counting 40 organizations. The coalition included high school teachers and students, university student associations, SUNTRACS, CONUSI (the newly established leftist labor confederation), and community-based groups. This multisectoral structure allowed the mobilizations to reach across the national territory in multiple districts and for protests to be synchronized and held simultaneously. Activists would emulate MONADESO's successful organizing structure in campaigns to come.

After the telecommunication and energy privatizations, Panamanians were already wary of further free market reforms. Public opinion polls show increasing popular hostility to privatization-type measures. In fact, just days before the campaign against water privatization started to gain momentum, the Latin Barometer conducted a representative national survey that found that nearly 80% of the respondents reported a negative experience with the privatization of the state sector in Panama (table 5.1).[13] These public sentiments offered a fertile political atmosphere for labor unions, teachers, students, and other civil society groups to launch their campaign against the privatization of the national water and sewage system, the Instituto de Acueductos y Alcantarillados Nacional (IDAAN).

The protests began in late November 1998 with attempts at roadblocks on the country's two major highways. The mobilizations gathered steam following a massive street march in the capital on Friday, December 3, led by the recently formed MONADESO coalition. The "units to control the multitudes" (an elite and highly trained riot police force that had replaced the "Dobermans" in

Table 5.1   Public opinion on privatization in Panama, 1998–2003

	"Privatization of state companies has been beneficial to the country"	
Survey date	Respondents who agree or strongly agree	Respondents who disagree or strongly disagree
1998 (November)	201 (20.76%)	767 (79.24%)
2000 (February)	217 (22.35%)	754 (77.65%)
2001 (April–May)	368 (37.78%)	606 (62.21%)
2002 (April–May)	305 (33.96%)	593 (66.03%)
2003 (July–August)	102 (11.03%)	823 (88.97%)

the democratic transition) invaded the national university (for the first time since the 1968 military coup) to suppress the student associations' anti-privatization mobilizations. The protests drew more support from civil society groups than previous protest campaigns against economic liberalization measures. In particular, school teachers participated in large numbers by both striking and engaging in street actions and roadblocks, including in the interior of the country (figure 5.3). The protests intensified to such a point that the Pérez Ballardes's government eventually pulled back the water privatization legislation.

The civil society opposition groups learned an important lesson from the their success in the campaign against water privatization. Specifically, the organizing strategy of mobilizing multiple sectors simultaneously in a cross-class coalition or front appeared to have been especially potent, as had been efforts to generate collective action in a range of localities. The earlier campaigns against economic liberalization (such as the mass strikes of 1986 and 1995) largely had been composed of a narrow coalition of labor unions and university students. The December 1998 mobilizations reached beyond the labor movement to a wider base of supporters, including teachers, high school students, and community groups. Nearly every protest action included groups outside of the IDAAN water administration labor union. The multisectoral nature of the struggle also evolved into a nested structure. Mirroring the national struggle, local cross-sectoral coalitions formed to protest privatization efforts. For instance, in mid-December, activists formed the Coordinadora Popular Veraguense (COPOVE) in the province of Veraguas in the center of the country. COPOVE consisted of NGOs, indigenous rural organizations, university students and professors from the regional branch of the University of Panama (CRUV),

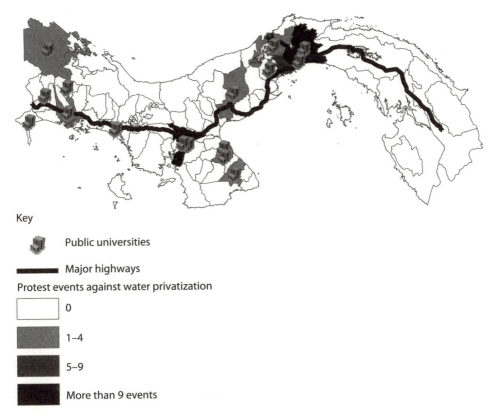

Key

Public universities

Major highways

Protest events against water privatization

	0
	1–4
	5–9
	More than 9 events

Figure 5.3. Anti-water-privatization campaign, 1998.

construction worker unions, anti-mining environmental groups, and the local high school teachers association.[14] Similar coalitions formed in David and Changuinola (e.g., Frente Amplio por la Defensa del Bocas del Toro), in the provinces of Chiriquí and Bocas del Toro, and helped sustain mobilization in the anti-privatization battles of the 2000s at the local and provincial levels. At the same time, MONADESO continued its mobilization drives against privatization and transportation price hikes between 1999 and 2002.

Protecting Social Security and Health Care, 2003 and 2005

Two decisive campaigns against economic restructuring focused on the Caja de Seguro Social (CSS), Panama's national health care and pension system, which covers the health and pensions needs of nearly two-thirds of the population. In

2003, the CSS came under the threat of privatization. The government had signed a letter of intent with the IMF in 2000, in which it agreed to begin restructuring CSS services and benefits. In June 2003, CSS workers and allies in the student, labor, and educational sectors launched street actions to prevent the migration of CSS assets to private banks. In September and October, CSS employees, other public-sector unions (including teachers), students, and construction workers launched two general strikes to protest the attempted privatization, which slowed down the process of outsourcing government pension services and public health care to the corporate sector. CONATO, with its nine labor confederations and 100,000 unionists, also backed the protests, with thousands of workers participating in short strikes and street actions. These massive mobilizations enjoyed wide public support (see table 5.1 above).

Several social sectors vehemently opposed the restructuring and partial privatization of CSS. Many saw the reforms as a direct threat to social citizenship rights. Of the 297 reported protest events associated with the campaign, 178 (60%) involved sectors outside of the labor, professional, and employee associations of the CSS. Using MONADESO as a template, organizers assembled a new coalition, the National Front in Defense of Social Security (FRENADESSO), composed of SUNTRACS, CONUSI, CSS doctors, administrators, and support staff, and several public school teachers associations, university and high school student groups, and community-based associations. In stark contrast to the Cold War era, when civil society fronts gave themselves revolutionary names (e.g., FMLN and FSLN in El Salvador and Nicaragua) with the objective of overthrowing repressive regimes, in the neoliberal era activists name their multisectoral fronts after institutes of the welfare state under threat of privatization and outsourcing to transnational corporations and financial interests.

Organizers officially announced the existence of FRENADESSO at a special mass gathering in the University of Panama in September. The final push to the campaign came on September 10, 2003, when the government expelled the progressive CSS director, Juan Jované, a university-trained economist. Jované had made Herculean efforts to expand CSS coverage within a neoliberal state. He attempted to strengthen financing for the public health system and prevent its reserves from being used to make payments on the foreign debt and transferred to private banks.[15] The IMF had placed heavy pressure on the government to avoid running up deficits in its health and pension system. Jované's leadership attracted support from the popular classes as he placed new hospitals and clinics online and enforced health care coverage and payments for

workers from previously uncooperative business owners.[16] Jovane's firing sig-
naled to opposition groups that the government was heading down the path
toward privatization.

FRENADESSO unleashed a wave of strikes, street marches, and roadblocks over
a one-month period, often shutting down the country's two major highways,
the Pan-American and the Transístmica thoroughfares (figure 5.4). High
school teachers, students from the regional public universities, SUNTRACS
unionists, and public hospital staff manned the roadblocks on the Pan-American
Highway between Panama City and the Costa Rican border in Chiriquí province. At least two mass protests in the capital, on September 12 and October 9,
reached over 50,000 participants and were reportedly the largest street marches

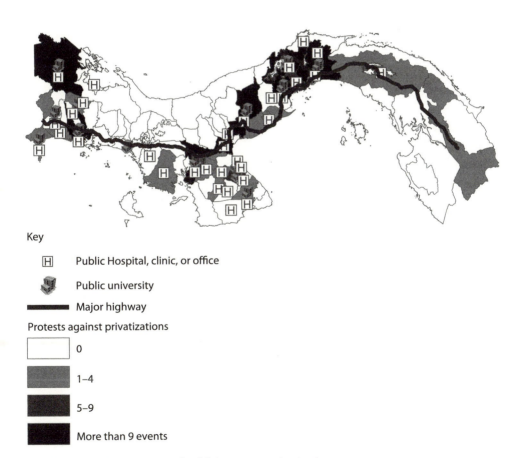

Key

Ⓗ   Public Hospital, clinic, or office

       Public university

━━━   Major highway

Protests against privatizations

☐   0

▨   1–4

▦   5–9

■   More than 9 events

Figure 5.4. Protest against health insurance privatization, 2003.

in the past four years.[17] On September 16, the minister of education temporarily shut down the largest public high school in Panama City, the Instituto Nacional, after massive street protests by its students. Scholarly observers noted that these protests had stretched deeper into the interior of the country and attracted more middle-class support than other mobilizations in recent years (Gandásegui 2003).

The multisectoral mobilizations succeeded as they had against water privatization, and the government of Mireya Moscoso publicly declared it would not privatize the CSS health and pension system. Perhaps President Moscoso also succumbed to the influence of a popular rhyming chant during street demonstrations, "Arnulfo la construyó y Mireya la destruyó," meaning that Moscoso's late husband, three-time president Arnulfo Arias, founded the CSS (back in 1941) and President Moscoso "destroyed it."[18] The mobilizations also reproduced the nested structure of cross-sectoral organizing of the 1998 anti-water-privatization campaign. More groups began to form multisectoral structures at the local level as they emulated FRENADESSO's structure at the national level. For example, in Coclé province in the interior of the country, activists established the Front in Defense of the CSS, which included labor unions, high schools, small farmer associations, and the regional campus of the University of Panama.[19]

Another conflict erupted in 2005 when the government approved a new pension law that increased the age of retirement and, once again, included plans to transfer CSS funds to private transnational banks. This time the government of Martín Torrijos and the PRD was under pressure from the World Bank to restructure the CSS (Gandásegui 2005). Dozens of mass marches took place between April and July 2005, some reaching up to 100,000 participants. Activists and the press described one march in the campaign held on June 1, 2005, as the "mother of all marches." Students, public school teachers, and labor unions also repeatedly set up roadblocks throughout the national territory (figure 5.5). Public opinion was overwhelmingly against the neoliberal CSS reforms (between 70 and 82 percent of the population).[20] Moreover, a majority of the public (55%) also reportedly supported the disruptive street protests early in the strike, providing a particularly receptive environment for FRENADESSO to engage in mass actions.[21]

On May 21, FRENADESSO began coordinating a general strike. The strike included the public schools, the CSS hospital network, the construction industry, and the universities (which involved twenty different student associations). Lasting until late June, it became the longest-enduring general strike in Pana-

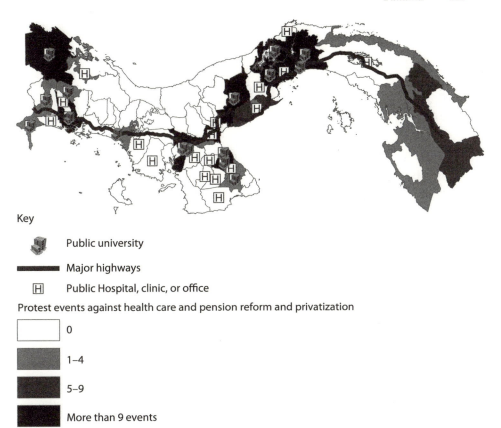

Key

Public university

Major highways

H Public Hospital, clinic, or office

Protest events against health care and pension reform and privatization

0

1–4

5–9

More than 9 events

Figure 5.5. Health care and pension system reform protests, 2005.

manian history. The police apprehended close to 1,300 citizens during the campaign. Because the wide coalition included the public school teachers' associations, the protest movement reached more remote zones, such as in the indigenous Kuna Yala Comarca of San Blas and the tropical districts of Darien province, regions where the css system is nonexistent. Hospital workers, staff, nurses, and physicians also played vital roles in the 2003 and 2005 campaigns to defend the extensive public health care and pension system. (Figures 5.4 and 5.5 and table 5.2 show the close association between css health units and the distribution of the mobilizations.)

Activists coordinating the protest campaign framed the new css legislation (Law 17) as the "law of death" because with the raising of the retirement age,

Table 5.2 Differences between participating and nonparticipating districts in collective protest against health care and pension system reform, April–July 2005

Category	All districts (*n* = 76)	Nonparticipating districts (*n* = 49)	Participating districts (*n* = 27)
State infrastructure			
Administrative infrastructure			
Percent with a provincial capital	12%	0%	33%
Transportation infrastructure			
Percent with a major highway in municipality	36%	18%	67%
Higher education infrastructure			
Percent with a public university campus	21%	4%	52%
Community infrastructure			
Mean number of nongovernmental organizations	2.18 (median = 2.2)	0.29 (median = 0)	5.63 (median = 2)
Labor-based associations			
Percent with a Caja de Seguro Social public hospital, office, or clinic	46%	31%	74%
Strategic capital			
Strategic experience			
Percent participating in 1998 campaign against water privatization	14%	0%	41%
Percent participating in 2003 campaign against social security privatization	35%	14%	74%
Median population density	23.01	18.85	52.10

Panamanian citizens would have to work until they died. In accordance with this macabre theme, demonstrators organized *marchas negras* in which they robed themselves in black dress with at least one activist leading the protest in a grim reaper costume wielding a sickle. In the end, the government of President Martin Torrijos (son of General Omar Torrijos) partially conceded to the movement's demands and watered down the aggressive pension reforms.[22] The opposition coalition in both phases of the conflict (2003 and 2005) maintained a delicate unity under the FRENADESSO coordinating committee. In 2011 and 2012, further government attempts to privatize the Caja de Seguro Social were impeded via strikes and demonstrations by the labor associations within the CSS. Despite a name change and shifts in some of the key coordinating organizations, FRENADESSO continued in existence into 2014, providing continuity for multisectoral coordination in anti-neoliberal protests campaigns.[23]

Table 5.2 compares the differences between localities in Panama that collectively mobilized against the neoliberal reforms to the CSS in 2005 with those regions that failed to organize.[24] This campaign was the largest sustained outpouring against economic liberalization in modern Panama, with a five-week long general strike, the closure of public schools and mass mobilization in communities throughout the nation (see figure 5.5). In terms of placing direct pressure on state actors in administrative offices, all provincial capitals experienced at least one protest event. None of the districts that lacked mobilization houses a provincial capital. Similar to almost every major campaign against neoliberal reforms in Central America, Panamanian citizens also blocked roads with human chains, construction materials, or tree branches. One of the two major national highways (Pan-American or Panama City–Colón / Transístmica) crosses through two-thirds of districts exhibiting organized resistance, while these transportation corridors only penetrate 18% of quiescent communities. Teachers, university students, urban labor unions, and health care associations from the CSS maintained roadblocks on nearly a daily basis at the height of the campaign in late May and June.

Panama's public university system, like Costa Rica's, is decentralized and has high enrollment rates, a product of state-led development between 1960 and 1980. There is a university campus or regional center in 21% of districts, and half of the protesting localities host such a campus. Only 4% of the 49 nonparticipating districts maintain a public university. As mentioned above, the FRENADESSO coalition was founded at a special political rally in the University of Panama in September 2003, and the higher education community contrib-

uted to the protest campaign in 2005 in multiple arenas. Some of the participating student associations (e.g., FER-29, PAT, BPU, MERS, FUAR, MERP) are active
on the regional campuses and maintain the capacity to carry out activities in
the capital and in the provinces. Protest actions on the regional public university campuses (such as in David, Santiago, Colón, Changuinola, Baru, Penon-
ome, Las Tablas, and Chitre) are often in concert with other groups such as
teachers, labor unions, neighborhood residents, and high school students, re-
producing multisectoral coalitions at the local level.[25]

NGOs also were more prevalent in the participating districts (these districts
had a median of two NGOs while nonparticipant districts had less than one). Even
though the campaign was dominated by the health care, teacher, and student
associations along with the SUNTRACS construction union, a few key urban-
based NGOs participated, such as the Catholic-based Cáritas and legal and
human rights associations helping to protect protest leaders from persecu-
tion. The protests followed a pattern close to the distribution of the CSS hospital and healthcare network (see figure 5.5). Of participating districts, 74% have
at least one CSS hospital, clinic, or administrative office. Doctors, nurses, and
health care employee associations (e.g., COMENENAL, AMOACSS, ANFACCS, AMN,
AECSS) under direct threat from the restructuring led many protests near their
workplaces across the country. Their repertoire of actions ranged from vigils
in front of regional hospitals to work stoppages and shutting down the Pan-
American highway for several hours. Only one-third of nonparticipating communities are served by a CSS unit.

Part of the explanation for the unprecedented size of the 2005 campaign re-
sides in the nation's experience with previous economic reforms. As witnessed
in chapters 3 and 4, the mass protest campaigns against neoliberal reforms in
Costa Rica and El Salvador in the early 2000s erupted immediately following
multiple unpopular economic measures in the form of telecommunications and
energy privatization and pension reforms. The strategic experience in Panama
of mobilizing against water privatization in late 1998 and CSS privatization in
2003 provided a new generation of activists with expertise in coordinating
such campaigns. The 1998 water privatization actions also innovated over previous campaigns with the broadening of cross-class and multigroup alliances
with the formation of MONADESO, which eventually evolved into FRENADESSO.
Table 5.2 shows the importance of strategic experience on a geographical scale.
Not one of the communities lacking participation in the 2005 protests organized action in the 1998 campaign against water privatization. Of the districts

Table 5.3 Character of protest events in anti-neoliberal campaigns, 1986–2005

Campaign	Reported protests	Multisectoral	Strike/work stoppage
1986 labor flexibility law	112	6 (5%)	100 (89%)
1995 labor flexibility law	146	24 (16%)	52 (36%)
1998 water privatization	78	36 (46%)	22 (28%)
2003 social security privatization	297	63 (21%)	128 (43%)
2005 social security restructuring	609	179 (29%)	109 (18%)

resisting social security restructuring in 2005, 41% had participated in the 1998 campaign. Organizers also maintained continuity between the 2003 and 2005 protests, with the same districts participating in many of the actions. Since FRENADESSO served as the vanguard of both campaigns, the disparate groups in the coalition called upon the same communities to support the struggle. Protest actions were also more common in more densely populated regions of the country.

Table 5.3 summarizes the largest anti-neoliberal campaigns in terms of magnitude (total number of protest events), how many individual protest events were organized by more than one social sector, and the relative use of the strike as a tactic. Labor unions served as the vanguard coordinating committees of the first two protest campaigns in 1986 and 1995. The 1998 campaign coordinated by MONADESO included several social sectors—high school and university students, private and public-sector labor unions, teachers associations, and community-based groups. The labor confederation CONUSI also formed in late 1998 and looked to join community-based struggles. CONUSI was made up of the 49 labor associations (including the militant construction workers' union SUNTRACS) that led the disruptive 1995 strike that failed to overturn Pérez Ballardes's labor flexibility law. The MONADESO coalition learned from the 1995 strike, as well as from the failed attempts to prevent electricity and telecommunications privatization in 1996 and 1997. MONADESO held together the cross-class and multi-group coalition to present a much more powerful front to power holders, even beyond the 1998 battles against water privatization.

The 2003 and 2005 CSS campaigns were multisectoral in character. Because the cases in table 5.3 require that the particular protest event has at least two different social sectors present to be classified as multisectoral, it may actually underestimate the extent of collaboration. Many of the 2003 and 2005 protests called for simultaneous actions in different communities by a variety of social groups but not necessarily for different groups to be present in the same protest event. Interestingly, many of the multisectoral mobilizations occurred outside of the capital as smaller towns needed to galvanize multiple groups in order to pull off a march or a roadblock with hundreds of participants. Because the largest labor unions, universities, and hospitals are concentrated in greater Panama City, groups there can pull off a moderate to sizable protest event within their own sector.

The protest campaigns diversified their repertoire of actions following CONATO's 1986 campaign against the labor flexibility law, which focused almost exclusively on factory strikes. The 1995 campaign reached out to students, while workers also moved away from their striking factories and banana plantations and engaged in more street-level protests. In 1998, although strikes remained an integral component of the campaign, participants also organized vigils, rallies, marches, roadblocks, and teach-ins. This tactical diversity in multiple sectors contributed to keeping authorities off-balance in their social control efforts and impeded attempts to implement unpopular economic policies at the pace preferred by neoliberal policy makers.

The Chorizo Law, Mining, and Privatization, 2010–2014

Another prominent national protest took place in late June and July 2010 over a new labor flexibility law. The campaign mobilized laborers on banana plantations in the Bocas del Toro region as well as urban workers and resulted in several injuries and deaths of rural indigenous unionists. In June 2010 newly elected president Ricardo Martinelli introduced a combination of unconnected laws (detractors called it the "chorizo" (sausage) package because it stuffed so many disparate issues in a single piece of legislation) into a special rushed session of the Panamanian legislature that passed on June 16. The Chorizo Law (officially called Law 30) limited the right to strike and union recognition, enforced drastic legal penalties on roadblocks, created provisions to protect police involved in repressive actions, and removed legal requirements for environmental impact statements on future mining and construction projects.

The banana worker unions in the province of Bocas del Toro (SITRAIBANA) immediately began organizing their 4,000-strong membership along with citizens in mass marches in the regional city of Changuinola. By July 4, after Bocas Fruit Company (a subsidiary of the transnational Chiquita Brands) refused to take union dues out of paychecks (in effect not recognizing the union), the banana workers in the entire region declared a general strike.[26] Citizens and workers of Changuinola built dozens of roadblocks, cutting off transportation and obstructing the main bridge into the province. The government airlifted security forces into the region on July 7. Between July 8 and July 11, within the province of Bocas del Toro alone, security agents killed a reported five demonstrators, injured up to 716 more, and arrested at least 115 (Gandásegui 2011; Mattson 2010).

Labor unions in Panama City began to prepare for a general strike against the Chorizo Law and to escalate the conflict to a national level. On July 10, police arrested dozens of union leaders during a street march after a press conference by FRENADESSO in the capital; they apprehended other known popular movement leaders the following day. An attempt at a national-level general strike surfaced on July 13 even in the face of the governmental repression with the participation of a militant faction of CONATO-affiliated unions (ULIP), SUNTRACS, CONUSI, high school teachers, Coca-Cola bottling-plant workers, dairy and cement processing plants, the national brewery, Cuadernos Escolares, Plastiglas, Harinas Panamá, and several other industrial plants and commercial services (Beluche 2014). Teachers in the province of Veraguas blocked the main streets of the provincial capital, Santiago, in outrage and solidarity with the repression suffered by the indigenous banana workers of Bocas del Toro. Workers, students, and teachers engaged in actions in the districts of Chitré, Pese, David, Colón, Aguadulce, and Changuinola, while 4,000 indigenous people (Ngobe Buglé) marched in San Felix. The conflict calmed when unions and the government agreed to a 90 day "cooling-off period." By October 2010, the government had overturned Law 30.

In 2011 and 2012, other struggles involving indigenous Panamanian groups have taken place over transnational mining operations and hydroelectric dam construction. In particular, the semi-autonomous Ngöbe-Buglé Comarca in the provinces of Chiriquí, Veraguas, and Bocas del Toro counts a wealth of mineral resources, including one of the largest known copper deposits in the world. The Ngöbe-Buglé and other sympathizers, such as labor unions and environmental NGOs, have resisted changes to the country's mining laws that would allow transnational mining firms to operate in indigenous territory. Protestors erected a series of roadblocks on the Pan-American highway in early 2011 and 2012. The February 2012 roadblocks against mining and hydroelectric dams were sustained by indigenous groups and environmentalists for three consecutive days (along with a string of solidarity actions in other towns and cities) until the Martinelli government agreed to negotiate (Reynolds 2012). Both campaigns appear to have emulated the multisectoral struggles of the mid-2000s in that the Ngöbe-Buglé set up a multisectoral coalition, the Coordinating Body in Defense of Natural Resources and the Rights of the Ngäbe and Buglé Peoples, which brought together a variety of groups, including environmental organizations, beyond the *comarca* (Human Rights Everywhere 2011). This coalition used the roadblock on the Pan-American Highway (in multiple locations) as a core tactic to resist transnational mining and other mega-projects.

As the CSS protest campaigns demonstrate, Panamanian citizens had largely turned against privatization policies in the mid-2000s. On October 21, 2012, the entrepreneurial president Ricardo Martinelli and his political party, Cambio Democrático, approved by parliamentary vote the privatization of lands in the Colón Free Trade Zone (Law 72). An immediate uprising took place in the *corregimientos* comprising the district of Colón. Within days, solidarity strikes and roadblocks were taking place throughout the country, led by labor unions, schoolteachers, university students, and indigenous peoples (opposing transnational mining operations), and an incipient left-wing opposition party rooted in the organizational structure of FRENADESSO called Frente Amplio por Democracia. Ngobe and Buglé ethnic groups erected barricades on the Pan-American highway in San Lorenzo and San Felix districts while holding placards that read, "Panama is our homeland and it is not for sale." The popular uprising reached such intense levels that the president backed down within five days and rescinded the legislation. However, the conflict left at least five people dead, including a nine-year-old child. Once again, the multisectoral form of organizing appeared to be especially potent in fending off the threat of another major neoliberal reform.

Conclusion

In the 1980s, under authoritarian rule, Panamanian citizens had a difficult time sustaining protest for more than a week. By the late 1990s, after several failed campaigns and privatizations implemented, opposition groups in civil society had learned to form alliances across social sectors. Several of the most important battles since the 1998 campaign against water privatization involved a wide multisectoral coalition and achieved a moderate level of success. The 1986 and 1995 campaigns against labor flexibility, though quite disruptive, largely only involved labor unions and university students. The formation of MONADESO and FRENADESSO, in the late 1990s and early 2000s, allowed opposition groups to coordinate actions in many locations and nationalize the opposition to globalization-induced policies beyond the capital and the largest cities.

It is also notable, given Panama's particular form of military-populist state-led development, that key sectors and institutions that expanded in the 1970s would play pivotal roles in the opposition to neoliberal forms of capitalism in the twenty-first century. These were the labor unions in the public and private sector, such as those in the CSS and IDAAN, as well as the university communities and schoolteachers, who acted as the vanguard in the multisectoral struggles against economic liberalization policies. Even private-sector labor associations, such as the militant construction workers' union SUNTRACS, engaged in decisive coordinating strategies in every major campaign since the mid-1980s. The expansion of labor unions in the 1970s, part of the Torrijos populist legacy, helps explain why Panama maintains some of the only private-sector labor groups in Central America capable of generating mass actions on a national scale.

6

Nicaragua

Third World Revolution Confronts Globalization

What makes Nicaragua different from other Central American states in the mid-twentieth century is the rule of a single-family dictatorship, the Somozas. From roughly 1936 to 1979 the family controlled the country and slowly took over strategic components of the national economy for personal and familial gain. The hold on power began with General Anastasio Somoza García, who ruled until his assassination in 1956. He was followed by his two sons, Luis Somoza Debayle (ruling from 1956 to 1967) and Anastasio "Tachito" Somoza Debayle (ruling from 1967 to 1979). The reign of the Somozas also involved brutal repression and little tolerance for political dissent, much less for organized opposition. At the same time, as elsewhere in the global South, the dictatorship engaged in state building by expanding highways, public schools, water and hydroelectricity systems, urban infrastructure, and establishing a weak social security system in the 1950s. However, because of the personalistic nature of the authoritarian regime, many state institutions and production units were headed by allies of the dictatorship. Economic modernization and social welfare projects were limited until the Nicaraguan Revolution of 1979.

The Nicaraguan Revolution marked a major political moment in twentieth-century Latin America (Martí Puig 2012). It was the fourth major social revolution in the region (after Mexico, Bolivia, and Cuba). The revolution was led by the Frente Sandinista de la Liberación Nacional (FSLN), or the "Sandinistas." The FSLN takes its name from Augusto César Sandino, an opposition leader who fought a guerrilla war against U.S. occupation of the country in the late 1920s and early 1930s. General Anastasio "Tacho" Somoza García ordered the assassination of Sandino in 1934 to prevent political competition. Sandino's opposition force was resurrected in the 1960s and 1970s as the FSLN launched a guerrilla insurgency against the Somoza dictatorship. By 1978 and early 1979, mass strikes along with rural and urban insurrections reached such a high level of intensity that the dictatorship was overthrown and the repressive national guard fled the country (Booth 1985).

Immediately upon taking power the FSLN built a large infrastructure of civil society organizations with between 500,000 and 1 million active members by the late 1980s (Serra 1991; Grigsby 2005) with a reported majority of the adult population participating in at least one mass organization (Stahler-Sholk 1990). These calculations are based on the size of the following organizations: Asociación de Mujeres Nicaragüenes Luisa Amanda Espinoza (AMN-LAE), Unión Nacional de Empleados (UNE), Juventud Sandinista 19 de julio (JS), Central Sandinista de Trabajadores (CST), Unión Nacional de Agricultores y Ganaderos de Nicaragua (UNAG), Asociación de Trabajadores del Campo (ATC), Sindicatos de Obreros de la Construcción (SCAAS), Federación de Trabajadores de Salud (FETSALUD), Asociación Nacional de Educadores de Nicaragua (ANDEN), and the Movimiento Comunal Nicaragüense (MCN). All of the mass organizations were created late into the Somoza dictatorship or in the immediate aftermath of the revolution. The organizations maintained representation on the Council of State, the government's most important policy making body during the early 1980s (Vilas 1986). Most importantly, in terms of collective action, the popular organizations developed deep levels of solidarity with one another at the local level as they administered municipal governments in the 1980s (*las juntas municipales de reconstrucción*) until the mayor-city-council system was established in the 1990s.

The Sandinista government erected a large welfare state during its rule in the 1980s. The Área de Propiedad del Pueblo (APP) served as the core of the state infrastructure. The APP was composed of nationalized mines, factories, and agricultural lands that had belonged to relatives and allies of the Somoza dictatorship or transnational capital. Nearly 100,000 rural families benefited from the redistribution of land and agrarian reform. Poor and middle-level peasants received government support through credit for agricultural inputs by the Banco Nacional de Desarrollo (BND), especially for domestic production (Enríquez and Spalding 1987). The Sandinista government also created a food regulation and distribution institute, Empresa Nicaragüense de Alimentos Básicos (ENABAS), and a centralized state-run water and sewage infrastructure, the Instituto Nicaragüense de Acueductos y Alcantarillado (INAA). The socialist government nationalized the banking system within months of seizing power and modernized the nearly bankrupt social security system the Instituto Nicaragüense de Seguridad Social y Bienestar (INSSBI), expanding coverage to the general population and incorporating health care into the program in addition to pensions, disability insurance, and veterans' benefits. Indeed, Kampwirth (1997:116) reports that between 1979 and 1989 the INSSBI went from covering 202,518 to 1,813,415 citizens (nearly 50% of the population).

In addition, the FSLN strengthened the public education system in the early 1980s, nearly doubling junior high and high school enrollments, as well as shrinking adult illiteracy from over half of the population to around 13%. The literacy campaign served as one of the early accomplishments of the revolution. Thousands of urban college and high school students and public school teachers worked in voluntary literacy brigades in rural regions, building stronger ties of solidarity ties between town and countryside. The government quadrupled the number of school teachers in the public education system. It also invested in higher education, establishing regional branches of public universities in the provincial capital towns of Esteli, Matagalpa, Juigalpa, and eventually Jinotepe.

Throughout the 1980s the Sandinista government faced an intense counterrevolutionary insurgency of former National Guard officers, Somoza loyalists, and better-off farmers sponsored by the United States (Horton 1998). The counterrevolutionaries were known as the Contras. The Contras inflicted millions of dollars of damage to the country's economic infrastructure and caused the loss of thousands of lives in a low-intensity war. The conflict greatly hampered the FSLN's development plans as precious and scarce resources had to be redirected to national security and defense. As the conflict dragged on into the late 1980s, the hostilities forced the Sandinista government to impose unpopular policies such as mandatory military conscription and economic austerity measures.

After a decade of governance, the FSLN party stepped down from power in early 1990 after losing presidential elections.[1] The center-right government of Violeta Barrios de Chamorro assumed power and a $10 billion foreign debt and immediately initiated multiple austerity programs encouraged by the United States Agency for International Development (USAID), World Bank, and IMF. These measures sparked mass mobilizations of labor unions and other sectors (agricultural cooperatives, civil servants, students, teachers, bus drivers) throughout the early 1990s (Stahler-Sholk 1994).

The austerity measures and privatizations implemented by the Chamorro administration proved extremely aggressive (Vargas 1999). This was not a mere transition of executive power but a hostile (and largely successful) attempt at dismantling the cornerstones of the Sandinista Revolution, namely, agrarian reform and the mixed economy. Hundreds of state-run firms, farms, and production units were privatized in just a few years. One observer of the process of revolutionary reversal referred to it as a "slow motion counter-revolution" (W. Robinson 2003: 76).

When the FSLN lost the election in early 1990, most of the popular mass organizations remained intact, but they were weakened by a lack of state support. The opposition to Chamorro's economic policies came from the sectors that benefited from the socialist modernization experiment of the first Sandinista government.[2] The popular organizations realigned with the formation of the Frente Nacional de Trabajadores (FNT) in May 1990. The FNT acted as a novel multisectoral coordinating unit for the major labor and rural associations affiliated with the Sandinista Party. Before the revolution in 1979, a reported 11% percent of workers had been affiliated with labor unions. By the mid-1980s, unionization reportedly reached up to 56% of the labor force (Stahler-Sholk 1995), one of the highest rates in the developing world. The Sandinista government legalized hundreds of labor unions in the first years of the revolution and created a central labor confederation in the Central Sandinista de Trabajadores (CST). In 1979, a reported 133 labor unions existed; by the end of 1983 that number had swelled to 1,100 (Serra 1985), including dozens based in the countryside. The FNT maintained this organizational legacy and redirected these pro-Sandinista sectors into the battles against neoliberalism and globalization in the 1990s and 2000s. At its founding in mid-1990, the FNT claimed to represent some 200,000 agrarian and urban workers.[3]

Austerity and Structural Adjustment Campaigns in the 1990s

The FSLN, similar to the FMLN in El Salvador, originated as a clandestine revolutionary party in the 1960s that led an armed struggle against the dynastic dictatorship of the Somoza family. Following its electoral defeat in 1990, the FSLN remained the largest opposition political party. Between 1990 and 2006, three successive governments ruling Nicaragua subscribed to neoliberal economic programs as the country suffered from a massive external debt (W. Robinson 2003). Popular movement organizations and civic associations created during the revolutionary period and after attempted on several occasions to coalesce with the FSLN to fight the economic policies of the postrevolutionary neoliberal governments. The party maintained close relations with civic organizations in the cities and countryside that were once part of the party's formal structure.

The FSLN reorganized its leadership in the early 1990s to compete in the liberal democratic electoral process. The party created a new governing body of nearly 100 representatives called the Sandinista National Assembly. Many representatives on the national assembly were affiliated with one of the FNT organizations. Indeed, the election results for the inaugural national assembly of the FSLN held at the first national party congress in 1991 reveal a tight relationship between civil society organizations and the opposition political party. Of the 98 national assembly members, 30 (31%) also served as activists in mass organizations, an unambiguous sign of popular-movement links.[4] This *doble militancia* (Luciak 2001) creates ties between opposition parties and popular organizations at the individual level. These ties assist protest campaigns when individual activists convince an opposition party to provide organizational resources to sustain a particular mobilization (Almeida 2010b).

Austerity Protest Campaign, May–October 1990

Beginning in 1990, the new government of President Violeta Barrios de Chamorro (1990–1996) began to enact austerity and privatization policies, and pro-Sandinista labor unions of the FNT led resistance against the measures. The FNT drew its largest support from state-sector unions in government ministries, education, and health care, as well as from organized farmers and agricultural laborers. The FNT sponsored a series of massive general strikes and demonstrations between May and October 1990, which forced the government to slow the pace of austerity (Stahler-Sholk 1994). Within a month of taking office, President Chamorro began to make a string of decrees that threatened major gains of the revolution, such as undermining collective labor contracts (abolition of the Ley de Servicio Civil) and privatizing land confiscated during the agrarian reform of the 1980s (Decrees 10-90 and 11-90). From May 12 to May 17, the FNT launched its first major strike wave against the economic austerity policies. The mobilizations were preceded by May Day rallies against austerity in the towns of Chinandega, León, Esteli, Ocotal, Managua, Jinotepe, Juigalpa, Granada, and Somoto, often led by Sandinista officeholders.[5] Several mass marches took place in Managua and the major cities of the country. The Asociación de Trabajadores del Campo (ATC) occupied farms in the Departments of León and Chinandega. The teachers union, ANDEN, convened a 48-hour national strike, while nearly all government institutions went on strike and civil servants occupied buildings. The May 1990 events served as the largest acts of nonviolent civil disobedience since the late 1970s and baptized Nicaraguan civil society into the globalization era.

Many of the protest actions literally occupied the institutions of the welfare state of the previous socialist administration, such as the social security institute (INSSBI), public sector banks, telecommunications and postal services (TEL-COR), and state-run factories, farms, and processing plants administered by the APP. Urban and agricultural workers attempted to defend the social service and production agencies established by the revolution by seizing them. The new government was forced to negotiate with the FNT and provide concessions in order to end the strike, while the FNT agreed to terminate the disruptive protests and end the building and farm occupations.[6]

The FNT unleashed an even larger national campaign and strike from late June to mid-July 1990, when the Chamorro government reneged on earlier agreements from the May strike and continued plans to privatize agrarian reform lands and lay off thousands of public sector employees. This protest campaign included up to 120,000 participants and was geographically widespread with over one hundred cotton farms occupied in the western region of the country and daily marches and strikes by workers, students, and professionals in the major towns and cities of the country, as well as factory and workplace occupations (figure 6.1). Multisectoral coalitions occurred at the local level with Sandinista mayors, legislative representatives, and members of popular organizations from a variety of sectors appearing in the same protest event, including artists performing revolutionary songs from the late 1970s and early 1980s. The government finally agreed to negotiate a truce with the FNT on July 11 after movement sympathizers began to erect dozens of brick barricades throughout the capital Managua and other towns.[7] The population drew on its strategic experience of the barricade as a tactic against Somoza's repressive security forces in the years immediately preceding the revolutionary triumph in 1979.

A final wave of mobilizations by the FNT took place in late September and early October 1990 to force the government to agree to earlier concessions and temporarily halt a plan to dismiss an additional 15,000 public sector workers (O'Kane 1990b). The strikes and mass protests between May and October 1990 were the largest actions in a decade. They resulted in wage increases, greater worker participation in the privatization process, and a more gradual process of economic liberalization, along with the executive's dismissal of

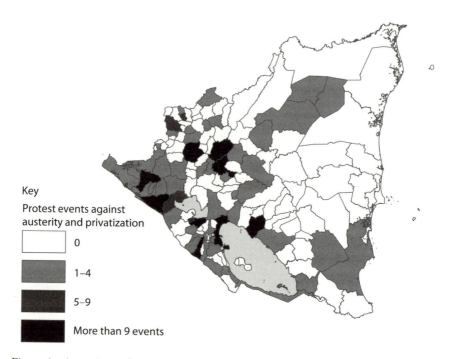

Key

Protest events against
austerity and privatization

☐   0

▨   1–4

▧   5–9

▮   More than 9 events

Figure 6.1. Austerity and anti-privatization protests, Nicaragua, May–October 1990.
(Data from *Barricada*, May 1–October 31, 1990.)

Francisco "Pancho" Mayorga, the chairman of the Central Bank and architect
of the aggressive austerity measures and currency devaluation.[8] Nonetheless,
neoliberalization continued to deepen, albeit at a slower pace given the multisectoral resistance in dozens of localities throughout the national territory.
Other major outbreaks of popular unrest would occur in 1995 and 1997 and
were tied to agricultural privatization and structural adjustment. Additional
mass actions in the decade of the 1990s largely focused on a specific social sector such as bus drivers, university students, teachers, and health workers. The
political transition of the early 1990s allowed for more confrontational labor
union mobilization, while the threat of mass layoffs, salary freezes, and privatizations motivated the protests. In the late 1980s labor mobilization was difficult
under a state of emergency and the prohibition of strikes in the context of ongoing foreign aggression with the Contra war (O'Kane 1990a).

The extent of the massive outbreak of protest against austerity and privatization of the neo-liberal Chamorro government in 1990 is shown in figure 6.1.[9]

Table 6.1 Differences between participating and nonparticipating municipalities in anti-austerity and anti-privatization protests, Nicaragua, May–October 1990

Category	All municipalities (*n* = 144)	Nonparticipating municipalities (*n* = 80)	Participating municipalities (*n* = 64)
State infrastructure			
Administrative infrastructure			
Percent with a provincial capital	12.0%	1.0%	25.0%
Transportation infrastructure			
Percent with a major highway	33.0%	18.0%	53.0%
Higher education infrastructure			
Percent with a public university campus	4.0%	0.0%	4.0%
Community infrastructure			
Opposition political party			
Percent of left party (Sandinista) votes in municipal elections (Feb. 1990)	40.0%	35.6%	45.6%
Percent with a Sandinista mayor (Feb. 1990)	21.5%	16.0%	28.0%
Percent of left (Sandinista) party votes for president (Feb. 1990)	38.8%	34.8%	43.9%
Median total votes for Sandinista presidential candidate (Feb. 1990)	1,847	1,212	3,467

Collective resistance to neoliberal globalization took place in 64 out of 144 municipalities (44.4%). Table 6.1 compares protesting municipalities with those that remained quiescent during the largely nonviolent, though extremely militant and disruptive, anti-neoliberal revolt. Participating localities were more likely to house a provincial capital. These provincial capital towns have a higher number of state institutions such as social welfare agencies, state banks, telecommunication offices, and health care and social security services, places where public-sector employees occupied their work sites. Over half of rebelling communities are transected by a major highway, while only 18% of nonparticipating municipalities maintain a connection to a transportation route (remarkably similar to the distribution of highways and popular resistance to neoliberalism in El Salvador).

Community participation against privatization also occurred where public universities are located (though only a few municipalities are home to university campuses). The role of the left party is evident as well, with protesting municipalities registering higher voting rates for the FSLN and a higher proportion of local governments run by the FSLN. The number of FSLN votes also was much higher in communities exhibiting collective resistance, indicating the absolute number of sympathizers of the opposition party was higher in communities resisting economic liberalization. In sum, the local resistance to the aggressive austerity and privatization measures took place in communities with state infrastructures and relatively greater levels of Sandinista political party structures and support.

Campaigns against Agricultural Structural Adjustment, 1995–1997

The Nicaraguan government signed its first full-fledged structural adjustment program with the IMF in 1994. A key component of the accord prohibited the recapitalization of state-sector banks, including the National Development Bank. The IMF structural adjustment agreement forced the BND to close dozens of rural branches and raised interest rates on loans to poorer farmers (Enríquez 2000). By 1998 the BND, the most important source for credit to small farmers and one of the oldest banks in Nicaragua, had permanently closed its doors after 85 years of existence (Rocha 1998). The situation created a severe rural credit crunch, and 50,000 peasants were denied loans in 1994 (W. Robinson 2003). Even before the 1994 structural adjustment accord, the Chamorro government had begun to cut off funding and end price controls for state-sector rural cooperatives and small farmers, the core beneficiaries of agrarian reform

(Everingham 2001). Instead, the governments of Chamorro (1990–1996) and Arnoldo Alemán (1997–2001) redirected new international loans into private commercial banks that largely provided financing and credit to large-scale agro-export operations. This strategy reintegrated Nicaragua into global commodity networks, with a heavy emphasis on nontraditional export crops (W. Robinson 2003). These conditions drastically reduced the production capacity of a large sector of rural producers and set the stage for two massive nonviolent insurrections against agricultural structural adjustment, in 1995 and 1997. A field survey of 60 farmers by Laura Enríquez (2010) conducted in four municipalities (with varying crops and activities) in the departments of León and Matagalpa shows a drastic reduction in bank credit to small farmers between 1990 and 1997. Her survey data is consistent with national-level measures that confirm a similar trend through the late 1990s (Everingham 2001).

The May 1995 Campaign

An ad hoc coalition called the Movimiento Nacional en Defensa del Crédito, la Propiedad y la Vida (MNDCPV) led the 1995 campaign against agricultural structural adjustment. The MNDCPV formed in early May 1995.[10] Its demands included a reduction of interest rates on loans, more agricultural credit, and an end to rising costs of basic services and utilities. These three principal issues united urban and rural groups in a single protest campaign. The mobilizations began in similar fashion as the 1990 protest campaign with May Day rallies and marches in several cities under the banner of the main demands of the MNDCPV. Campaign organizers set up roadblocks on the country's main highways and strategic intersections.

The campaign occurred at the same time the country was celebrating the 100th anniversary of Sandino's birth, which added to the opposition culture of resistance (Foran 2005). The protests also took place in the context of the debate on the privatization of TELCOR, the state telecommunications and postal agency. The FSLN took out full-page ads and newspaper articles encouraging the population to join the protests—an even stronger version of social movement partyism than witnessed in the 1990 protest campaigns. Other groups strengthened the MNDCPV, such as 20,000 striking public-sector health workers in the FETSALUD federation of doctors, nurses, and staff, as well as the nationally organized neighborhood groups in the MCN. Even ex-members of the Contra insurgency joined the MNDCPV in protests, a clear demonstration that one of the last conflicts of the Cold War had ended and the battle against neoliberal globalization acted as the new dividing line between privileged classes connected to emergent international markets and those excluded from them.

The April–May 1997 Campaign

The 1997 campaign lasted nearly 30 days and involved hundreds of protest events demanding a renegotiation of the agricultural debt, an end to farm foreclosures, and legalization of land and property titles negotiated under the two former regimes (all of these grievances shaped by agricultural structural adjustment). This round of protests involved even more roadblocks on the country's major transportation routes, which cut off commerce (including international trade) for weeks at a time. As in 1995, the FSLN called on its estimated 100,000 party members to support and participate in the collective actions against IMF pressure to defund credit sources for medium and small-scale farmers. Even though the protest campaigns in 1995 and 1997 led to short-term compromises, they did not resolve the fundamental problem of agricultural debt and lack of credit. By the early 2000s, rural producers in the departments of Jinotega, Matagalpa, Chinandega, Madriz, Esteli, and Nueva Segovia were engaging in mass encampments and hunger marches to the capital, walking past overgrown weeds in the parking lots of the shuttered state banks en route to make their desperate pleas to the National Assembly. With the advance of rural free markets and the breakdown of solidarity ties, rural mobilization over land has declined since the late 1990s (Horton 2013).

Elite Pacts, Privatization, and the Labor Movement

The individual affiliates of the FNT became more autonomous in their organizational decision making even as they retained close ties to the FSLN. At times the FSLN negotiated with the ruling government over workers' issues such as privatization, wage freezes, and layoffs in the public sector without the FNT's input. At other times it acted in concert with the FNT, including the participation of thousands of party members in street protests. Throughout the 1990s and early 2000s, the FNT maintained its organizational structures and political influence. However, labor protest was largely defensive in these economically austere times. Tens of thousands of public-sector workers lost their jobs between 1988 and the mid 1990s (O'Kane 1995). Hundreds of firms were privatized in the 1990s, especially in manufacturing, mining, and commercial services. By the end of 1993, the Chamorro government had already privatized 289 public enterprises (in a period of less than four years). By 1998, the Nicaraguan Central Bank registered 343 privatized firms and production units (Freije Rodríguez and Rivas 2005). Around this same time the international financial institutions moved into a new wave of privatizations targeting the basic economic infrastructure, public utilities, and services such as water, electricity, and social security (Baker 2014: 197–99), setting the stage for popular mobilization in Nicaragua in the twenty-first century as in other parts of Latin America and the global South.

The labor-based struggles of the early 1990s forged a strong relationship between the opposition party and protest campaigns, which would endure throughout the globalization era. During the 1990s, the FSLN could be inconsistent—sometimes aligning with protest campaigns on the streets and supporting mass mobilization, sometimes cooling protests through negotiations with the government, as in a series of pacts made between the FSLN's top leader Daniel Ortega and President Arnoldo Alemán beginning after the April–May 1997 mobilizations (Perla, Mojica, and Bibler 2013). Also, the FNT's mobilizing capacity suffered from a major split in the CST, the country's largest labor confederation, in 1996. After the 1999 agreement between Alemán and Ortega, there was a decrease in nationwide protest campaigns of the type witnessed in 1990, 1995, and 1997 (Pérez Baltodano 2012: 74). With the reduction of unionized workers (via ongoing privatizations) along with pacts between political elites, new sectors would need to emerge in the early 2000s to compensate for the decrease in traditional union organizations in the labor movement. NGOs partially filled this gap in civil society organizing in the first years of the new millennium. Other social sectors began to coordinate actions by the late 1990s and early 2000s, including university students and a variety of consumer protection-based groups.

An Era of Increased Global Pressures, 2000–2007

Besides cuts in agricultural credit to small producers and the privatization of public services such as telecommunications, structural adjustment agreements between the government and the IMF had called for the decentralization of water management and distribution. By the late 1990s, letters of intent with the IMF included the privatization of water and electricity and the elimination of subsidies to public transportation (Quirós Víquez 2005). Indeed, the first wave of privatizations in the early 1990s largely affected factories, mines, farms, and commercial services, not the social and economic infrastructure, as the privatizations of the late 1990s and early 2000s would do. As these neoliberal restructurings slowly worked their way through the national legislature, the government also agreed to raise consumer prices on water and electricity. Electricity distribution was officially privatized in 2000 and sold to the Spanish transnational corporation Unión FENOSA for $115 million. These agreements to privatize water administration and outsource electrical power generation and distribution to transnational firms allowed the Nicaraguan government to enter the Heavily Indebted Poor Countries Initiative (HIPC) supported by the G-8, IMF, and World Bank. The HIPC erased $6 billion dollars of Nicaragua's external debt (see figure 1.1). At the same time, these controversial policy changes provided the catalyst for a new round of local mobilizations against globalization in the 2000s, especially over water, electricity, and public transportation.

In 1999, the Nicaraguan government also emboldened emerging civil society organizations by finally implementing a new consumer defense law (Law 182), first passed in 1994. The government established the Dirección de Defensa del Consumidor (DDC), an agency housed in the Ministry of Industry and Commerce Promotion (MIFIC), to administer and enforce the new legislation. The law provided guidelines and a template for consumer-protection groups to appeal abuses in the delivery and cost of public utilities and services. Most importantly, Articles 60 to 65 of Law 182 actively encouraged the formation of community-level consumer defense associations to participate in DDC activities; these associations would be provided with a local budget to inform and educate the public about consumer protection issues within their municipalities (Ministerio de Fomento, Industria y Comercio 2002). This new institutional access during the transition from Third World socialism to neoliberal capitalism encouraged a wave of community organizing along consumer defense issues just at the time the state began to engage in the privatization of basic services and public utilities.[11]

The coalitions behind the protest campaigns in the 2000s brought in new sectors of civil society, especially new consumer-based NGOs. NGOs accelerated in growth in the 1990s, with many former Sandinista militants transforming into NGO activists (Borchgrevink 2006). The consumer NGOs rallied around the provisions of the Consumer Protection Law and demanded the government live up to the financial support and citizen participation stipulated in the new legislation. Three major organizations that defined protest campaigns in Nicaragua in the 2000s were the Coordinadora Civil, the Red Nacional de Defensa de Los Consumidores (RNDC), and the Unión Nacional de Asociaciónes de Consumidores y Usuarios de Nicaragua (UNACUN).

The Coordinadora Civil emerged after Hurricane Mitch as a federation of NGOs in late 1998. As the neoliberal state was unable to respond to the thousands of hurricane refugees and destroyed villages, civil society organizations such as UNAG and the MCN worked with dozens of NGOs to meet community needs after the disaster (e.g., rebuilding houses, water systems, and schools and replenishing food and clothing supplies). By 2000, the Coordinadora Civil had turned to other demands such as anti-water privatization and debt relief. In 2001 it mobilized multiple community protests at local Empresa Nicaragüense de Acueductos y Alcantarillados (ENACAL) and INAA agencies over increasing household water and sewage bills. The mobilizations culminated in a petition to the Supreme Court that resulted in an unprecedented favorable verdict for the consumer-based movement. The court ruled that the escalating water and sewage bills were unreasonable and should be reduced (Quirós Vízquez 2005).

The Red Nacional de Defensa de los Consumidores emerged in late 2001 as an advocate against exorbitant consumer prices in food, transportation, and utilities. Two FSLN officeholders during the revolutionary period led the RNDC at the national coordinating level (Grigsby 2005). Individual community activists and association leaders first met in October 2001 to discuss organizational strategies to confront increasing water prices (Red Nacional de los Consumidores 2002). The RNDC officially took its name in January 2002 during a general assembly in the public National Engineering University (UNI). Within months, local "consumer committees" affiliated with the RNDC had formed in Managua, Tipitapa, Ciudad Sandino, Masaya, Rivas, Granada, Boaco, Matagalpa, Larreynaga, La Libertad, Chinandega, León, Jinotega, Juigalpa, and even in the distant Corn Island off the Caribbean Coast. The RNDC local committees often represented several neighborhoods of a town, and multiple social sectors participated, including communal, student, and women's organizations. The organization held educational workshops on the new law of Consumer Defense. In its first year of existence, the RNDC launched campaigns against water privatization, electricity price hikes, and bus fare increases, the major economic liberalization issues mobilizing Nicaraguan civil society in the new millennium. The RNDC also established a long-term relationship with a major national newspaper (*El nuevo diario*). The paper reported on consumer issues and struggles on a nearly weekly basis and often provided them front-page coverage.

The Unión Nacional de Asociaciónes de Consumidores y Usuarios de Nicaragua formed in 2005 over similar issues as the RNDC and was organized nationally. A key affiliate of the UNACUN is the oldest consumer defense organization in the country, the Liga de Defensa del Consumidor de Nicaragua (LIDECONIC), which formed in the mid-1990s. Together, these umbrella organizations aligned with the sectors fighting austerity and privatization in the 1990s, especially university students, the FNT, and the communal movement (MCN).

Water Privatization Wars, 2000-2007

The process of privatizing Nicaragua's water distribution system began in 1998. Under the Somoza dictatorship, private companies administered water in the cities, and few rural zones had access to potable water and sanitation services. When it took power in 1979 the Sandinista government created a centralized water regulatory and administrative agency, the Instituto Nicaragüense de Acueductos y Alcantarillado (INAA). As part of negotiations with the International Monetary Fund and Inter-American Development Bank in the late 1990s, the Nicaraguan government agreed to replace the INAA with a new water-distribution agency, the Empresa Nicaragüense de Acueductos y Alcantarillados (ENACAL). INAA would serve only as a regulatory unit of the government. ENACAL would slowly decentralize water distribution through a series of public-private partnerships or an incremental privatization process (Quirós Vízquez 2005). This was the same moment that conflicts over transnational corporate control of water and sewage systems were emerging as a major issue across the developing world. Water privatization conflicts in South America (especially in Bolivia and Uruguay) began to influence other countries, including Nicaragua. International NGOs began financing campaigns in poorer countries to educate and mobilize the public about the outsourcing of water and sewage services. Progressive Nicaraguan NGOs took advantage of some of these transnational priorities (Bob 2005) and gravitated toward water-related issues (Quirós Vízquez 2005).

The first stage in the water privatization process involved the selling off of the country's largest hydroelectric plant, HIDROGESA in Jinotega. This move sparked mobilizations by communities and NGOs in the region, including indigenous groups that sought to reclaim territory the Somoza regime had confiscated to build the plant. Other pilot projects of public-private partnerships began to emerge in Chinandega and León in the early 2000s, which led to more coordination between grassroots organizations, NGOs, universities, and farmers groups such as UNAG. For example, in the provincial capital León, in August 2002, a local RNDC-affiliated consumer defense committee (ADECONLE) coalesced with the local public university (both administration and students) and mobilized against municipal water privatization.

These grassroots groups successfully slowed down the water privatization process on several fronts. First, they stopped the privatization of the HIDRO-GESA hydropower plant, petitioning the attorney general to halt the sale in 2002 (while under multiple bids from transnational energy corporations, including the Texas-based firm ENRON). Coalitions of NGOs next forced the National Assembly to proclaim Law 470 in July 2003, which forbid *any* private water contracts until a general law on water was passed in the congress.

To halt water privatization, NGOs and other grassroots groups banded under multisectoral umbrella organizations and coalitions. The NGO coalitions coordinated the efforts of the local grassroots associations concerned with water privatization. These included the RNDC, Alianza por la No Privatización y Derecho de Acceso al Agua (ANPDAA), Coordinadora Civil, and GPAE (an agro-environmental coalition of NGOs). The ANPDAA was composed of 30 civil society organizations, including the Coordinadora Civil with its vast network of local NGOs. These multisectoral organizations drafted their own water legislation, gathered signatures, and held popular consultations on water laws in dozens of municipalities (figure 6.2).

Dozens of grassroots groups led the territorial mobilizations against water privatization at the local level. In the municipalities of León, Juigalpa, Chinandega, Corinto, Chichigalpa, Malpaisillo, San Rafael Sur, Diriamba, La Concepción, and Managua, the environmental youth association Club de Jóvenes Ambientalistas played a decisive role. In Jinotega, Culcumeca was the key organization. The farmer organization UNAG organized forces in San Rafael, El Crucero, San Carlos, Mateare, and San Francisco Libre. The MCN, mobilized against water privatization in the departments of Ocotal, Madriz, Granada, Masaya, and León (Barrios Jackman and Wheelock Díaz 2005). These community actions against the transnational corporate administration of water eventually were able to stop the privatization legislation.[12]

ANPDAA activists reached many localities for the popular consultations against water privatization because they were geographically contiguous (figure 6.2). The consultations involved local assemblies in which organizers informed the population and city council of the executive office's General Water Law and popular alternatives. NGOs in the Alianza reached 64 municipalities, and 46 of those communities (72%) passed resolutions or issued public statements against water privatization. Table 6.2 analyzes the differences

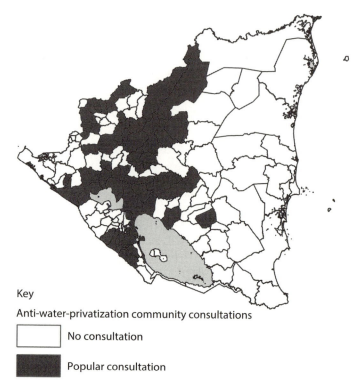

Key

Anti-water-privatization community consultations

☐   No consultation

■   Popular consultation

Figure 6.2. Local popular consultations against water privatization, 2003.

between the communities where popular consultations were held against water privatization and those that were not reached. Participating localities tended to have more of a state infrastructure within their territorial boundaries: 16% of them housed the provincial capital, while only 8% of nonparticipating regions did. Participating communities also maintained a larger public water distribution infrastructure, making privatization a greater threat to access to water and sewage services in these communities.

Participating communities also had slightly more NGOs active in their zone. Consultations took place in municipalities that received a higher percentage of the vote for the opposition FSLN in the 2001 presidential elections and total votes in the 2000 local elections. Pro-FSLN communities and NGO activists likely found a more receptive climate in municipalities with more favorable preferences for state intervention in the economy and basic social welfare services. Finally, participation in the 1990 anti-privatization protests discussed

Table 6.2 Differences between participating and nonparticipating municipalities in anti-water-privatization consultations, 2003

Category	All municipalities (n = 152)	Nonparticipating municipalities (n = 88)	Participating municipalities (n = 64)
State infrastructure			
Administrative infrastructure			
Percent with a provincial capital	11.0%	8.0%	16.0%
Percent of population covered by Public Water Administration	52.5%	48.2%	58.3%
Transportation infrastructure			
Percent with a major highway in municipality	32.0%	30.0%	36.0%
Higher education infrastructure			
Percent with a public university campus	9.0%	8.0%	9.0%
Community infrastructure			
Mean number of nongovernmental organizations (2003)	7.8 (median = 1)	6.2 (median = 1)	9.9 (median = 1.5)
Opposition political party			
Median total votes for left opposition party (Sandinista) in municipal elections (2000)	2,033.5	1,823.0	2,555.0
Percent of left opposition party (Sandinista) votes for president (2001)	39.7%	38.0%	42.0%
Strategic capital			
Strategic experience			
Percent participating in the 1990 anti-neoliberal protest campaign	43.0%	39.0%	50.0%
Median population density	56.8	48.6	68.7

above was more common in the communities participating in the consultations. The strategic experience of local collective action over economic liberalization in the past decade likely helped the anti-water-privatization campaign to penetrate these more receptive communities.

In addition, several protest actions occurred in local towns, at the legislative assembly, and the offices of ENACAL. In October 2004, the ANPDAA sponsored its largest protest to date, a 15,000-person march in Managua. It also gathered an impressive 30,000 signatures in a short time period in order to have its own progressive water law introduced to the Legislative Assembly in 2004. After its 2006 victory in the presidential elections, the new FSLN government appointed Ruth Selma Herrera (one of the principal leaders of the RNDC) as the head of ENACAL, where she strengthened the organization and prevented further privatization (Romano 2012). ENACAL now functioned as a state water distribution agency and moved away from the earlier private-public partnership model of the late 1990s and early 2000s. In 2007, the Sandinista government passed a new general water law that explicitly prohibited the privatization of water and sewer systems and hydropower plants (ENACAL 2009).

Consumer Campaigns against Electricity and Public Transportation Price Hikes, 2000–2006

The 2000s also were marked by an increase in mobilizations against price hikes in electricity and public transportation. These issues were closely related to the water privatization battles. First, many NGOs fought against water privatization and the rising costs of household sewage and water bills simultaneously. Second, the issues of escalating costs for household electrical power and public transportation were consumer defense issues, similar to water privatization. Therefore, coalitions like the RNDC, the Coordinadora Civil, and UNACUN could easily incorporate electricity rates and bus fares into their protest campaigns and mobilize similar groups of consumers. The bus fare issue also brought high school and university students into the campaigns.

Electrical power began to rise in cost immediately after the privatization process was complete in 2000. Unión FENOSA, the transnational firm administering electricity distribution, witnessed the first protests against it in 2000. This trend continued for the next six years. Eventually, more explicit pro-Sandinista groups joined the struggle for electricity price reductions. For example, in June 2005, the FNT workers federation organized the Coordinadora Social, a coalition of some 40 civil society associations to fight electricity price hikes. It held dozens of protests against Unión FENOSA between 2005 and 2006, including defacing recently installed meters, to make them illegible to bill collectors. In 2006, the Coordinadora Social, along with the RNDC, the Movimiento Comunal Nicaraguense, and the Unión Nacional de Asociaciónes de Consumidores y Usuarios de Nicaragua (UNACUN), convoked mass mobilizations in Managua, Ocotal, León, Bluefields, Bilwe, Juigalpa, Granada, Esteli, and Masaya against electricity price hikes and poor water services (Serra 2006).

Transportation battles first broke out in 2000 and 2001 to protest exorbitant bus fares. Students were largely involved in the actions. As the world price of oil skyrocketed in the mid-2000s, and the Nicaraguan government faced continued pressure from international financial institutions not to subsidize public transportation, larger campaigns erupted against public transportation fare hikes. A 30% price hike for bus fares between the capital and major provincial towns in March 2005 set off disruptive protests on a national scale. Protests, rallies, and roadblocks were held in Managua, Ciudad Sandino, Tipitapa, La Conquista, Jinotepe, Chinandega, Matagalpa, Esteli, Juigalpa, Realejo, and León. The protests brought in not only students (though clearly they were the vanguard in the skirmishes) but also the neighborhood organizers in the MCN, workers in the FNT, consumers in the RNDC, and market vendors and maquiladora workers that depended on long-distance bus travel on a daily basis but whose wages were barely enough to support their families. Even distant departments like Nueva Segovia threw their support behind the protesters with public calls of solidarity from FSLN-linked organizations and politicians in Ocotal and Jalapa.

While these grassroots mobilizations for consumer protection were under way, the FSLN was increasing its electoral fortunes at the municipal level. It won 43 municipalities, including the city government in the capital Managua, in 2000 and then over half of the country's 152 municipal governments (including 15 of 17 provincial capital cities) in the elections of 2004. The newly elected FSLN mayors and city councils aligned with consumer groups, students, and pro-FSLN bus driver cooperatives (URECOOTACO) to oppose public transportation price hikes in 2005, the most contentious episodes of collective action of the year.[13] Finally, after major national strikes in the health care and public education sectors (between 2005 and 2006), as well as the nationwide protests against bus fare increases, the FSLN won back the presidency in the elections of November 2006. Similar to the case of El Salvador, a left-wing opposition party not only used its organizational resources to mobilize in the streets but also channeled popular grievances against neoliberalism into electoral triumphs.

Conclusion

The legacy of Third World socialist revolution and the state-sponsored buildup of mass organizations in the 1980s provided Nicaraguan activists a rich set of resources and experiences to use in campaigns to resist neoliberal measures in the 1990s and 2000s. The May–October 1990 protest campaigns against austerity and privatizations demonstrated how the surviving Sandinista labor associations and party structures could be deployed to uphold one of the most intensive mobilizations against free market reforms in Latin America in the early 1990s. In each campaign, opposition forces formed local multisectoral coalitions that emulated the national-level alliances driving the episodes of collective action against economic liberalization. In the 1990s campaigns, local FNT chapters aligned with FSLN office holders, communal groups, agricultural cooperatives, women, and students. In the campaigns against privatization and price hikes in the 2000s, multisectoral alliances materialized in dozens of municipalities and consumer defense NGOs emerged as key actors in community coalitions. The local-level coalitions used highways, universities, government offices, and opposition political parties to make their claims and demand protection from the economic harms associated with global integration. The water privatization campaigns were largely successful because of their sustained cross-sectoral nature and the ability of activists to take the struggle beyond the capital and into the interior of the country. The protests against bus fare price hikes also successfully brought down fares through multisectoral efforts.

Since retaking state power in 2007, the FSLN has moved to reinforce state institutions that were weakened in the 1990s and 2000s, including the food supply and regulation institute, ENABAS, and water system administrator, ENACAL. The Sandinista government has also launched several new initiatives that seem to have reduced the anti-neoliberal protests of the previous decades. Most importantly, the Poder Ciudadano (Citizens' Power) program has set up a structure to channel the population's most pressing grievances and distribute social services down to the community level. Other initiatives include assisting with housing and agricultural supplies in the countryside that have benefited over 30,000 families (Perla, Mojica, and Bibler 2013). The FSLN social policies (such as the "zero hunger" campaign) may have reduced national poverty levels by as much as 5% in its first four years in executive power (Perla and

Cruz-Feliciano 2013). The government has benefited economically from its membership in the Alternative Bolivarian Alliance with Venezuela by receiving a mass infusion of petro-dollars, highly subsidized oil imports and engaging in joint venture projects. Nicaragua also remains an integral member of CAFTA. When substantial protest occurs, it is largely *political* and not based on neoliberal economic grievances. Many of the major protest events between 2007 and 2013 centered on contested local and national elections (especially in terms of transparency and constitutional changes allowing consecutive presidential terms).

7

Guatemala and Honduras

Anti-Neoliberal Resistance

Both Guatemala and Honduras experienced a series of massive protest campaigns against neoliberal policies beginning in the 1990s after their respective governments reversed over a half century of state-led development strategies. Guatemalan civil society emerged from a repressive military regime and three decades of low-intensity civil war and learned to coordinate actions among multiple social sectors. By the 2000s, Guatemalan indigenous, peasant, student, labor, and nongovernmental organizations consolidated one of the strongest campaigns against the Central American Free Trade Agreement. Local communities would go on to resist transnational mining and electricity price hikes into the 2010s. Honduran citizens faced two major rounds of structural adjustment and established large umbrella coalitions to coordinate campaigns against unwanted economic policies. These same coalitions provided the organizational basis of resistance to the military coup in Honduras between 2009 and 2011. The anti-coup campaigns have now been converted to a major left-leaning political party poised to challenge for parliamentary and executive power in elections.

Guatemala: Campaigns against Globalization

After a short ten-year period of political liberalization and democratization between 1944 and 1954, a Central Intelligence Agency–backed mercenary force overthrew the reform-minded Guatemalan government headed by Jacobo Árbenz. President Árbenz's populist regime had expropriated immense tracts of land from the transnational United Fruit Company and distributed the parcels to an estimated 100,000 impoverished farming families. In the aftermath of the coup, Guatemala was largely under military rule until the 1980s, and indirectly until the 1990s (Inclán and Almeida 2013). The repressive government expanded the state infrastructure, public utility system, and basic social services, and it instituted a social security system (the IGSS), unleashing a period of economic modernization. In the 1950s and 1960s the government constructed telecommunications, established the Instituto Nacional de Electrificación (INDE) to build the national power-distribution grid (Véliz 2010), and constructed new highways (Bull 2008). At the same time, domestic and international human rights groups identified the various military governments between the late 1960s and early 1980s as some of the most repressive in Latin America (Grandin 2004). During military rule, some 150,000 people were reportedly killed and another 50,000 persons "disappeared" (Figueroa Ibarra 1991; Garrard-Burnett 2010). Investigators estimate that Mayan ethnic groups made up to 90% of the victims, in a country where indigenous people constitute nearly half of the population. The military and police targeted the repression at insurgent guerrilla forces and their purported sympathizers (labor unions, students groups, rural cooperatives) in the capital and in the indigenous highland communities (Jonas and Chase-Dunn 2001). A final peace agreement between the military and the guerrilla forces (Unidad Nacional Revolucionaria de Guatemala, URNG) was not reached until late 1996.

Early attempts to mobilize against IMF reforms took place in this extremely repressive context. Consecutive competitive elections without civil war did not occur until the late 1990s, and it was not until the early 2000s that civil society would enjoy enough democratic space to launch sustained campaigns against globalization. Indeed, it took two decades for civil society to emerge from the dark days of the genocidal early 1980s. Some of the first organizations to appear in the mid-1980s included victims' families of the state repression, such as the Grupo de Apoyo Mutuo (GAM) and the Coordinadora Nacional de Viudas de Guatemala (CONAVIGUA) (Brockett 2005). In the late 1980s and early 1990s with the return to civilian rule, new indigenous and campesino groups emerged, such as the Co-ordinadora Nacional Indígena y Campesina (CONIC), the Coordinadora Nacional de Organizaciones Campesinas (CNOC), the Consejo de Comunidades Étnicas–Runujel Junam (CERJ), and Defensoría Maya (Brett 2008). In 1995, CONIC and CNOC joined with militant labor groups in the Unidad de Acción Sindical y Popular (UASP) in a three-month campaign called "Recuperación de Madre Tierra." The campaign involved land invasions, street demonstrations, and roadblocks to bring attention to landless and poor rural and indigenous communities (Brett 2008). These same groups would form sustained coalitions with traditional labor movements and a growing NGO sector by the 2000s to work in concert to battle free trade, mining exploitation, and exorbitant consumer electricity rates.

First Protests against Neoliberalism, 1985–1998

Guatemala first experienced economic liberalization reforms in the 1980s. In April and September 1985, a series of riots and looting erupted in the capital while thousands of teachers and public sector employees engaged in strikes and job actions against an IMF austerity program that encouraged budget cuts, new taxes, and price increases in food and public transportation. The protests spread to the second-largest city of Quetzaltenango, where pacific street marches took place. In these events, up to ten people were killed and two thousand arrested (Garst 1985). The collective violence and austerity protests occurred in the final year of military rule, and the army occupied the Universidad de San Carlos (the largest public university) to quell the popular discontent, including deploying tanks, armored vehicles, and 1,500 soldiers to crush student-erected barricades in September 1985. In the end, the government decided to roll back bus fare increases, place price controls on basic foods, and give government sector workers a slight raise (Walton 1987).

Another mass strike broke out in 1987 in which 200,000 public sector workers participated, leading to the formation of the multisectoral Unidad de Acción Sindical y Popular (UASP) (Figueroa Ibarra 1999). More protests against price hikes and austerity cuts occurred in 1988. The UASP, founded in a period of political liberalization with a civilian president, would continue to play a vital role in popular mobilization in the 1990s and 2000s by unifying rural and urban groups in collective defiance of successive neoliberal policies emanating from the central government.

In the 1990s campaigns took place to prevent the privatization of electricity, railroads, and telecommunications. When the UASP organized a general strike against IMF-recommended austerity measures in May 1993, public-sector employees and students participated en masse. During this campaign, organizers used the terms "privatization" and "neoliberalism" as an integral component of their mobilization appeals, a sign that Guatemala stood on the cusp of the era of resistance to globalization. Another mass march of 3,000 public-sector workers sponsored by the UASP in March 1997 called for a reversal of government plans to privatize power distribution, postal services, and telecommunications. In 1998, the government of Álvaro Arzú passed a new national mining law proving extremely generous to foreign capital. The neoliberal government attempted to out compete neighboring Honduras and El Salvador for foreign direct investment in the mining sector by requiring foreign firms to only pay 1% of profits in royalties to the state (Dougherty 2011). The privatizations, economic liberalization policies, and mining laws of the late 1990s set the stage for an unprecedented series of protest campaigns in the 2000s against the new penetration of transnational capital in the territory (Yagenova and Véliz 2011).

Sales Tax Protests, 2001

Increasing the national sales tax has proven a common neoliberal reform in Latin America to increase government revenues, make up for budget deficits, and finance loan repayments (Mahon 2004). Taxing income directly is more of a state-led development strategy, and Guatemalan capitalists already pay one of the lowest tax rates in Latin America. The popular sectors view raising the sales tax on the general population as a regressive economic policy.

Between May and July 2001, under IMF pressure, the Guatemalan government debated and passed such a sales tax increase from 10 to 12%. The UASP and the Guatemalan labor confederation (CGTG) formed an alliance with university students, community-based organizations, the public school teachers' union (SMG), informal sector workers, and even the conservative Coordinating Committee of Agricultural, Trade, Industrial and Financial Associations (CACIF) to resist the unwanted changes. Public opinion was overwhelmingly against the sales tax hike.[1] The oppositional coalition convoked the largest mass protests since the end of the civil war. Beginning in May, each Friday the anti-tax campaign held a rally in the plaza of the Obelisco monument in Guatemala City. Mass marches, civic strikes, and coordinated actions occurred in dozens of cities, including in the departments of Alto Verapaz, Baja Verapaz, Izabal, Quetzaltenango, Sacatepéquez, Sololá, Suchitepéquez, and Totonicapán. By late June, some 50 civic organizations formed an ad hoc alliance to resist the tax hike.

The Alianza Nueva Nación (ANN) served as the primary campaign-sympathetic political party, which held less than 10% of the legislative seats (9 out of 113). In addition, the Unidad Nacional de Esperanza (UNE) party stood against the reforms. Both parties convinced the largest opposition party, the PAN, to abstain from voting in favor of the new tax hike.[2] Nonetheless, the legislative assembly passed the new tax increase on July 26, 2001, by a vote of 65 to 0 (all dissenting oppositional parties abstained in protest).[3] The dominant Frente Republicano Guatemalteco Party (FRG), led in the national assembly by former military dictator Efraín Ríos Montt, passed the legislation with the assistance of the much smaller Christian Democratic Party and the Democratic Union Party (each provided one vote). At the time of the law's passage, the FRG controlled both the presidency, under Alfonso Portillo, and the parliament (with an absolute majority of 63 seats). In response to the tax increase, the protest coalition redoubled its efforts and coordinated mass protests in the days immediately following. On August 1, 2001, the popular opposition held a twenty-four-hour national strike (denominated "Day of National Dignity"), which included a mass march of between 20,000 and 50,000 in the capital, and protest events in all 22 provinces of the country. Many of the protesters dressed in black as a symbol of national mourning. Newspaper correspondents on the scene reported demonstrators chanting the rhyming grievances, such as "El alto costo de vida, el pueblo deja sin comida" (the high cost of living leaves the people without food) and "La canasta básica aumenta, y los sueldos no se incrementan" (the price of consumer goods increases but not our wages).[4] One faction began a hunger strike in front of the Supreme Court in the hope that the law would be declared unconstitutional. The hunger strikers collected 50,000 signatures opposing the tax hike. By early September, however, the protests had petered out, and the new tax law went into effect.

Sales Tax Campaign, 2004

Under pressure from the IMF as part of a stand-by loan agreement signed in 2002, the government moved in 2004 to raise the sales tax once again (to 15%) (Fonseca 2003). This time a coalition of labor unions, students, NGOs, and indigenous peasants successfully resisted the measure by holding a nationwide general strike and roadblocks on June 8 and 9. The 2004 general strike also called for end to negotiations on CAFTA and the cessation of electricity price hikes by the newly privatized (and transnational) energy distribution companies.[5] Organizing began months earlier as indigenous, campesino, and labor groups held demonstrations in the capital and in the interior of the country on March 23 and March 30, respectively, against CAFTA.

The June general strike was multisectoral and one of the largest national mobilizations since the signing of the peace accords in 1996 (M. Sandoval 2004). The police dispatched 30,000 units around the country two days before the strike, while the government's underfunded human rights office sent out 33 observers to document and try to avoid state repression of the protests. Some local communities, such as municipalities in Sololá, protested against contracts to multinational mining companies for mineral exploration, while others demonstrated against

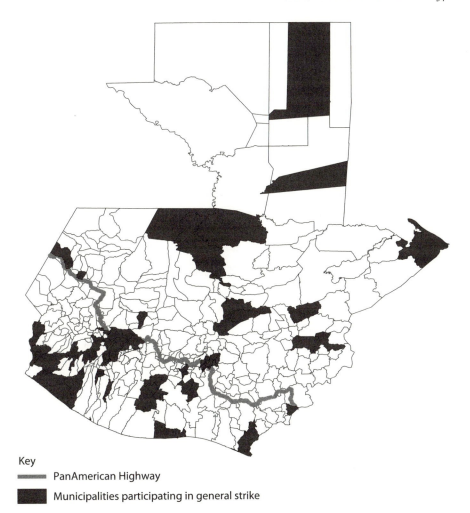

Key

━━━ PanAmerican Highway

▮ Municipalities participating in general strike

Figure 7.1. General strike against CAFTA, tax hikes, and electricity prices, Guatemala, June 8.

electricity price hikes by the privatized energy companies. Hence, opposition to CAFTA, transnational mineral extraction, and elevated electricity prices that would fuel Guatemalan collective action for the next decade, were all combined as grievances in the June 2004 general strike. Many of the protests occurred in the interior of the country along the Pan-American, Pacific, and Atlantic highways (figure 7.1). The government immediately began to negotiate with the opposition before the national strike went into a planned second day of mass actions.

A key outcome of the strike was the formation of a large multisectoral organization, Movimiento Indígena, Campesino, Sindical y Popular (MICSP). The coalition managed to maintain solidarity across a wide range of social sectors much longer than earlier attempts had done. The MICSP counts rural labor unions, urban students, public-sector employees, indigenous groups, and a wide variety of NGOs in its ranks, including federations of NGOs such as the Mesa Global and the Coordinación de ONGS y Cooperativas (CONGCOOP). The formation of the MICSP marks the most important advance in civil society organizing in Guatemala since the peace accords. The MICSP would take the lead in organizing resistance both to the Central American Free Trade Agreement and to government plans to outsource basic services and lease land for mining operations.

The Central American Free Trade Agreement, 2005–2006

The anti-neoliberal coalition resurrected itself in early 2005 to resist CAFTA with the coordinating assistance of the newly formed MICSP. The Guatemalan popular sectors produced the second-largest sustained mobilization against CAFTA in Central America (after Costa Rica) and perhaps the most intensive in terms of disruptive protest. Throughout February, March, and April 2005, students, indigenous organizations, and labor unions held mass marches and blockaded the nation's major highways as the Guatemalan legislature debated, and subsequently approved, CAFTA. The MICSP gathered 25,000 signatures of citizens opposing CAFTA. The government sparked mobilization when it announced at the end of February 2005 that it would push the ratification of the agreement in the next week as a matter of "national urgency." This showed the government was disregarding agreements from the June 2004 general strike in which it had promised to consult with the population about the contents of the trade treaty (including translations into Mayan dialects) before it would proceed to legislative debate. Once news of the government's plans to rush CAFTA through the legislature came out, mobilization picked up pace.

In early March 2005, marches and rallies often targeted the legislative assembly in the capital. The MICSP also began coordinating actions in the interior of the country with its contacts in peasant, indigenous, and NGO organizations. After the congress passed CAFTA, on March 10, the MICSP called for a general strike on March 14 and 15. Participants in the strike included dozens of popular organizations and thousands of workers. Members of the multisectoral coalition blocked the Pacific, Atlantic, and Pan-American highways in multiple locations. During the national strike, there were street marches in Guatemala City and the provincial capitals. Public school teachers and high school and university students refused to attend school. The police soon cracked down on the roadblocks. Local security forces in Huehuetenango killed one protester and injured a demonstrating school teacher so seriously that doctors had to amputate his leg. Unlike the June 2004 general strike, the government refused to negotiate, and President Oscar Berger of the conservative PAN party signed CAFTA on March 15. The MICSP continued to hold national days of protest against CAFTA throughout 2005 and 2006.

A nationally representative poll (of over 1,200 adults) taken in December 2004, just months before the legislature approved CAFTA, reported that 69% of respondents knew "little" or "nothing" of the free trade agreement (CID/Gallup 2004). This may help explain the popular movement's inability to force the Berger administration into protracted negotiations and the government's interest in pushing the law through before opponents could build a more enduring case against the free trade treaty (given the lack of public deliberation or even awareness of the treaty and its social impacts). The government's tactics were similar to those used in El Salvador, as discussed in chapter 4.

Transnational Resource Extraction and Energy Struggles, 2006–2014

Since the early 2000s, dozens of local struggles have broken out in indigenous communities over the expansion of mining operations and other mega-projects, such as dams, private highways, and the large-scale cultivation of biofuels. Indigenous rural residents and their NGO sympathizers view this round of transnational capital accumulation as a new scramble for Guatemalan resources to be exported to global markets. In the mining sector alone, Michael Dougherty (2011) reports a 1,000% increase in mining contracts and licenses issued between 1998 and 2008 to transnational firms operating in Guatemala. Between 2005 and 2009, local grassroots movements (largely rural Mayan communities) convoked dozens of "popular consultations" in municipalities throughout the departments of San Marcos, Quiché, Huehuetenango, and Sololá over open-pit mining operations in these regions.[6] In each community where a consultation took place, an overwhelming majority rejected the mining plans (Véliz 2009).

The mining and mega-development projects are especially conflictive in western Guatemala where indigenous Mayan groups formed an interdepartmental coalition, the Council of Western Peoples, in 2008. Communities from the departments of Quiche, Sololá, Huehuetenango, San Marcos, Totonicapán, and Quetzaltenango make up the council. These regions remain under the greatest threat of mining, hydroelectric projects, and petroleum drilling (Yagenova and Garcia 2009).

The anti-mining movement received national recognition in late 2004 and early 2005 when dozens of indigenous residents from Los Encuentros, Sololá, manned a blockade on the Pan-American Highway for thirty days to prevent a massive cylinder used for gold mining from reaching its destination in San Marcos province (Dougherty 2011). Security forces eventually took down the highway blockade, killing one demonstrator and leaving over a dozen protesters seriously injured (Yagenova and Garcia 2009). Near that same time, a successful case of mobilization occurred in the western town of Sipakapa in San Marcos department. The Sipakapa people are a Mayan ethnic group and retain their local subdialect. In early 2005, the community voted overwhelmingly in a popular consultation to block gold mining by the transnational extraction firm GoldCorp Inc. When the national government failed to recognize the results of the popular consultation and continued to offer mining rights for gold and other precious materials to GoldCorp Inc. in Sipakapa, mining opponents turned to an electoral strategy and won the city council in 2007. Since this time, local residents have prevented mining in their community even as extractive operations continue in the adjacent municipality of San Miguel Ixtahuacán (Yagenova and Garcia 2009). Local conflicts with multinational enterprises over natural resources appear to be growing in the second decade of the twenty-first century throughout the Central American isthmus.

Since 2008 a renewed effort to mobilize against escalating electricity prices and for the renationalization of energy distribution has taken place. These struggles are led at the national level by the Frente Nacional de Lucha por la Defensa de los Servicios Públicos y los Recursos Naturales (FNL) in coordination with dozens of rural indigenous communities. Leftist governments in Venezuela and Bolivia renationalized their electrical power systems in 2007 and 2012, after they were privatized in the 1990s, at the height of neoliberalization. The FNL formed in 2005 during legislative debate on further privatizations via the Law of Concessions, which planned for a new round of government outsourcing of basic services. When the FNL launched its new mobilization initiative in 2005 it organized nine labor unions (largely in the public sector) and three community-based associations. By 2010, the FNL grew to 168 organizations (including 24 labor unions) coordinated by regional committees in 19 of the 22 provinces in the national territory with a reported membership of 170,000 people.[7] Organizations constituting the FNL include community, women's, and indigenous rural associations along with labor unions (i.e., a truly multisectoral coalition).

The FNL began its campaign for the renationalization of electrical power distribution in 2008. The Arzú administration had privatized electrical energy distribution a decade earlier, in 1998. The state electrical company was sold off to transnational energy firms in Spain, Portugal, and the United States that set up subsidiaries in different regions of Guatemala. Throughout the 2000s, electricity prices continued to escalate, along with ongoing problems of power outages. Between 2008 and 2013, the FNL coalesced with their local affiliate groups in days of national action against electricity price hikes. These mass actions included payment boycotts, mass marches, highway blockades, and the collection of a reported 500,000 signatures petitioning the government to renationalize electricity distribution (Véliz 2010). The mobilizations reached a showdown in early October 2012 when government security forces shot to death six indigenous campesinos on the Pan-American Highway in Totonicapán while they were blockading the highway to protest high electricity prices. The electricity and mining struggles continue unabated in the 2010s. In 2012, a former military general, Otto Pérez Molina, took over the presidency while his Patriotic Party won the most seats in the legislature. The dominant parties in Guatemala subscribe to continued free market reforms as the preferred strategy of economic growth, likely leading to more anti-neoliberal conflicts in the near future.

Honduras: From Resisting Globalization to Resisting a Military Coup

The Honduran military elite also engaged in authoritarian state-led development in the mid-twentieth century.[8] Under the civilian presidency of Juan Manuel Gálvez (1948–1954), the government established a series of national banks and organized central government agencies of economic planning and a Ministry of Commerce. A historic seven-week strike by Atlantic coast banana workers against transnational banana companies in 1954 (which escalated into a national strike of some 60,000 workers) brought about a national labor code and the legalization of labor unions by the end of the decade. Between 1957 and 1963, the Honduran government established a national electrical power institute (ENEE), a social security system (IHSS), an agrarian institute (INA), and a national water and aqueduct agency (SANAA). Military governments continued to expand the state in the late 1960s with a steep increase in the number of central government employees (Bull 2008). The Honduran state also carried out a major agrarian reform program in the 1960s and 1970s, benefiting tens of thousands of poor farmers organized in cooperatives (Kincaid 1987).

In the 1970s, the military governments of López Arellano and Melgar Castro pushed a final new round of state expansion before the foreign debt crisis of the 1980s (Ruhl 2000), including nationalizing telecommunications in 1976 with the creation of HONDUTEL. The foreign debt increased sixfold during the 1970s, as a moderately reformist military continued to invest in expanding state infrastructure. In the educational sector the military government built seven new regional university campuses between 1960 and 1981, in San Pedro Sula, La Ceiba, Comayagua, Santa Rosa de Copán, Olanchito, and Choluteca. The San Pedro Sula campus, in the nation's second-largest city, is an especially extensive public university in terms of size.

By 1978, however, reformism had ended. The Honduran military focused on national security and internal repression of opposition as the neighboring countries of El Salvador, Guatemala, and Nicaragua broke out into revolutionary insurrection and civil war. In the 1980s, Honduras served as a strategic ally for the United States, allowing operations and installations within its territory. The counter-revolutionary Contras set up permanent camps in southern Honduras and from there launched raids of sabotage and armed attacks into Nicaragua to try to overthrow the Sandinista government (see chapter 6). With national security dominating domestic politics, civil society organizations found it difficult to sustain collective action campaigns. For example, the various teachers associations formed the Frente de Unidad Magisterial de Honduras (FUMH) in the late 1970s only to have it crushed in the repressive environment of the early 1980s. Additionally in 1982, the government issued Decree 33, which labeled disruption of public order and roadblocks as attacks on national security punishable as terrorist activities. The country gradually transitioned to civilian rule and held more inclusive competitive elections, but it had accrued a massive external debt. Two massive waves of popular opposition to neoliberalism would crest in the 1990s and 2000s. The organizational basis of this opposition to economic liberalization also provided the backbone of the collective resistance to the military coup between 2009 and 2011.

Structural Adjustment, 1990–1999

Anti-neoliberal resistance in Honduras has its roots in structural adjustment accords between the government and the international financial institutions. Honduras signed its first major structural adjustment loan with the World Bank in 1988. The government failed to live up to the austerity conditions stipulated, placing the state in jeopardy of future funding. The situation changed when Rafael Leonardo Callejas was elected president and assumed executive power in 1990 along with his team of neoliberal technocrats (similar to the Chamorro administration in Nicaragua, discussed in chapter 6). President Callejas immediately enacted a structural adjustment program that placed Honduras back in good faith with the IMF and World Bank. In March 1990 the government issued Law 18-90, which enacted neoliberal measures including currency devaluation, a lifting of price controls and subsidies, and the partial privatization of several public institutions including health care, energy, housing, and public works, along with over a dozen privatizations in government-run services (e.g., hotels, printing) and manufacturing (Hernández 1992).

In September, Honduras signed a second structural adjustment accord with the World Bank in which the government agreed to 18 conditions, including 10,000 employee layoffs in the public sector. In 1991 Callejas signed a new Law of State Modernization (Decree 190-91) and instituted a presidential commission to execute the process, which included the rationalization, decentralization, and privatization of public institutions and services (Barahona Mejía 2008). These austerity policies associated with the structural adjustment loans led to the first sustained social protests (Sosa 2012) since land reform measures in the late 1960s and early 1970s (Kincaid 1987). It was also the first episode of mass resistance to public infrastructure privatization in the region. (As chapters have shown, anti-privatization protests became more common at the end of the 1990s in Central America.)[9]

The first major acts of popular protest occurred in 1990 against President Callejas's Law of "Economic Reorganization" (Law 18-90), referred on the streets as the *paquetazo*. The organizational basis of the mobilizations originated in 1989 with the formation of the Platform of Struggle to Democratize Honduras, the widest coalition of oppositional groups to form in the country in decades (Posas 2003). The coalition put together a gigantic May Day march in 1990. Several actions took place against the economic reforms in 1990 and 1991, including strikes by banana plantation workers, health care workers, and other public sector labor unions such as postal workers, energy sector workers, and public works (Sosa 2010). The high point of the campaign came in 1991 with a reported 118 protest events that year (Sosa 2012). It would take another decade for the popular movement to reach such protest intensity with a new round of structural adjustment.

Workers in the public health sector, on banana plantations, and at the government-controlled electricity institute, ENEE, were at the forefront of the 1990–1991 protests (Sosa 2012). Public-sector unions in Honduras have been generally characterized as *clasista*, launching campaigns beyond wage demands and working conditions to economic distribution issues in society as a whole. The public health care workers launched a 25-day strike in June 1990, denouncing privatization of laundry, food, security, and other services in the public health system tied to the economic reorganization law. The workers organized in dozens of locations (the public health system has a national reach). Sosa (2012) reports the participation of at least 45 subunits (*seccionales*) of the health care union. Workers also demanded a pay raise to keep up with the inflation caused by the economic liberalization package. The strike ended with relative success, blocking the privatization process.[10] On the heels of the health strike, in July, 10,000 banana workers on Chiquita Brands (previously United Fruit Co.) plantations went on strike and barricaded worksites, demanding a 60% raise because of the huge decline in purchasing power caused by the paquetazo (Posas 2003). The workers enjoyed the support of solidarity strikes from other strategic unions such as oil refinery workers. The government sent in the army to quell the strike while Chiquita threatened to abandon the country. In the end, the workers gained a 25% wage increase and remained relatively quiescent for the following two decades (Sosa 2012). In the midst of the health care and banana worker strikes, in June, just as the multisectoral strike campaign was gathering momentum, two union leaders in the social security institute and the Central Bank were mysteriously killed. The repression tactics from the country's Cold War days had not vanished entirely.

The electrical power workers' union (SITRAENEE), led by Gladys Lanza, held strike actions and street protests throughout 1991 to prevent privatization and bring down electricity prices for consumers (Centro de Documentación de Honduras 1992a). SITRAENEE workers attracted solidarity from other labor unions in the left-leaning Unitary Federation of Honduran Workers (FUTH) and public university students from the National Autonomous University of Honduras (UNAH), who also participated in work stoppages and street actions. In May 1991 alone, there were a dozen solidarity strikes in support of SITRAENEE and its anti-privatization efforts (Centro de Documentación de Honduras 1991). Nevertheless, by the end of the year the Callejas government had broken SITRAENEE with the dismissal of 500 workers, including over 100 of the most charismatic and effective labor union organizers (CEDOH 1992a). On top of these losses for the popular movement, the state also began outsourcing some of the services and operations of the ENEE.

In 1992, Callejas passed a wide-ranging neoliberal agricultural structural adjustment law, the Ley de Modernización Agricola. The measure permitted the selling of state and agrarian reform lands to agrarian elites operating in nontraditional export crops and large-scale farming and timber operations. The largest confederation of farming cooperatives and small rural producers, the Consejo Coordinadora de Organizaciones Campesinas de Honduras (CO-COCH), held a series of protest actions and highway blockades in 1992 in an effort to impede the Ley de Modernización Agricola (CEDOH 1992a). The actions failed, and the government created its own parallel peasant confederation to compete with the once hegemonic COCOCH .

By 1993, Eugenio Sosa (2010) contends, President Callejas had successfully demobilized the popular movement via a mix of state modernization, cooptation, and repression. A particularly successful government tactic involved negotiating separately with each of the coalition members in the Platform of Struggle to Democratize Honduras in a divide-and-conquer strategy (Posas 2011). Another tactic was to create parallel unions for each sector with labor militancy and give the pro-government union official legal recognition. The state carried out these actions between 1990 and 1994 in the electricity sector, the rural cooperative movement, and in the women's movement (Centro de Documentación de Honduras 1992a). Other scholarly observers find that the Platform coalition would have generated even more forceful pressure if activists in the labor and cooperative movement were able to reach neighborhood-level groups, especially communal groups organized in the cities as *patronatos* (Centro de Documentación de Honduras 1992a). Even with Callejas's successes in implementing major neoliberal reforms and pacifying the popular movement, the powerful public teachers associations coalesced, for the first time since the late 1970s, in the Federación de Organizaciones Magistrales de Honduras (FOMH) in 1992 (Barahona Mejía 2008). In that same year the most militant leftist unions (*corriente clasista*) established a labor confederation, the Confederación Unificada de Trabajadores de Honduras (CUTH), which includes affiliates from teacher, communal, peasants, and women's organizations (Centro de Documentación de Honduras 1992b). The FOMH formed in response to Callejas's neoliberal "modernization" of the educational sector policies. With the currency devaluation of 1990, teachers experienced a decline in their real wages for the next two decades (Barahona Mejía 2008). The teachers used their newly formed organizational unity to push a through a major law protecting the profession and salary scale of public educators in 1997 (Ley del Estatuto del Docente). The FOMH would remain intact for the next two decades, and its 55,000 teachers distributed in all 298 municipalities would serve as key actors in the campaigns against structural adjustment. The labor unions and popular organizations affiliated with CUTH would also provide a mass base for anti-neoliberal protest campaigns in the 2000s.

Structural Adjustment and Military Coup, 2000-2013

A second wave of popular discontent against neoliberalism emerged in the early 2000s. The basis for the opposition originated in a new round of structural adjustment agreements signed with the IMF in 1999, 2002, and 2004. The renewed engagement with structural adjustment loans from the IMF came on the heels of Hurricane Mitch, which devastated the country in late 1998, causing more than 10,000 deaths and billions of dollars in economic and infrastructural damage. Honduras entered the twenty-first century with over $4 billion in external debt, with 30% of the national budget servicing the loans (see figure 1.1). The adjustment measures in the 2000s were similar to the paquetazo of 1990 but focused more aggressively on the privatization and outsourcing of the core public infrastructure, especially energy distribution, ports, telecommunications, public works, and water and sanitation services.

In addition, the government had already raised the sales tax from 7 to 12% in the late 1990s and passed a foreign mining law in 1999 with extremely favorable terms for transnational mineral-extraction companies (similar to Guatemala's mining law issued around the same time period). In the letters of intent with the IMF, the government promised to make progress in privatizing, implementing the Central American Free Trade Agreement, lifting price controls on basic consumer goods, rationalizing the civil service sector and the social security system, and freezing public-sector wages. The IMF, World Bank, and Inter-American Development Bank rewarded the governments of Flores (1998–2002) and Maduro (2002–2006) with entry into the Heavily Indebted

Poor Countries Initiative (HIPC) and substantial debt reduction. At the same time, policy makers faced stiff opposition from civil society in the implementation of this second wave of structural adjustment reforms.

In 1999, a new multisectoral oppositional organization formed, entitled the Bloque Popular. The Bloque Popular was composed of university students, public sector labor unions, large and militant school teacher associations, and peasant leagues, linking urban and rural struggles under a single organizational umbrella. It engaged in several campaigns against privatization in the early 2000s, resulting in much more anti-globalization mobilization activity than in the 1980s and 1990s (Sosa 2012). Dozens of mass mobilizations took place between 2000 and 2002 related to the 1999 IMF structural adjustment agreement, including anti-privatization marches and road blockades by public sector unions and salary demands by health workers and public school teachers (related to wage freezes in the IMF plan). Many of the actions were multisectoral, even in the provinces outside of the capital.

Water privatization appeared to be the neoliberal grievance with the greatest potential to mobilize the disparate demands of the groups contesting neoliberalism in the early 2000s as a water privatization law worked its way through the national legislature. Local skirmishes against water privatization began to bubble up from the grassroots in 2002, such as the mass mobilization and highway blockade in El Progreso, Yoro province, on December 2, 2002. The multisectoral coalition Asamblea Popular de Progreso contra las Privatizaciones, organized the local mass action with some 37 civil society organizations in the labor, educational, and community-based (patronatos) sectors. Similar protests and roadblocks took place in La Lima, Tegucigalpa, the Aguán Valley, and San Pedro Sula between October and November 2002. The protests succeeded in the short term by temporarily halting the final passage of the water privatization law for seven months (Moreno 2002). Indeed, one Jesuit priest working with the progressive ERIC organization (Equipo de Reflexión, Investigación y Comunicación) in El Progreso prophesized at the end of 2002 the importance of water privatization at the municipal level as a grievance that had the potential to mobilize a sustained cross-sectoral coalition that could unify communities across the country.

> The October and November mobilizations [of 2002] began with water as a concrete problem, first set off in a distant municipality, but in very little time water transformed into the central issue of the traditional popular organizations in all

geographic regions of the country. The water issue united the Sula Valley with Tegucigalpa, to Danlí in the eastern part of the country and to the Aguán Valley in the Atlantic region. The struggle continues. Water has provided a common project and summoned the popular sectors. And this spark could turn into a fire. (Moreno 2002, author's translation)

Just a few months after Padre "Melo" Moreno's predictions, a broader coalition formed to resist privatization of water administration and services, the Coordinadora Nacional de Resistencia Popular (CNRP). With links to the Bloque Popular, it would become the most powerful multisectoral coalition in decades.

As the government entered the HIPC initiative, policy makers came under heavier pressure to decentralize and outsource water and sanitation services. As a condition for another IMF loan agreement, to be signed in February 2004, the National Congress passed a law on August 14, 2003, allowing for the outsourcing of water and sanitation services at the municipal level (Ley Marco de Agua Potable y Saneamiento). Passage of the law came as a surprise to local groups (such as the Asamblea Popular de Progreso) that had negotiated with congress to withdraw the legislation. Opposition groups had even drafted their own alternative general water administration law explicitly prohibiting the licensing of water to private firms for profit (similar to the consumer defense NGOs in Nicaragua discussed in chapter 6). Obviously, policy makers had ignored this proposal, which grassroots organizations presented to the legislature in July 2003 (Ardón Mejía 2005). This impending threat of water privatization welded the CNRP coalition together throughout the 2000s.

The CNRP organized in multiple geographical zones by setting up regional branches with an impressive array of organizations, including Asamblea Popular Permanente (APP) in El Progreso, Patronato Regional de Occidente (PRO) in rural areas of Santa Barbara, and the Committee of Popular Organizations of Aguán (COPA) in the Aguán Valley. The CNRP also incorporated already existing militant organizations such as rural cooperatives like COCOCH; indigenous organizations such as the Consejo Cívico de Organizaciones Populares e Indígenas de Honduras (COPINH); tens of thousands of public school teachers in the FOMH, women's advocates in the Colectivo de Mujeres Hondureñas (CODEMUH); the country's core labor confederations, including the leftist Confederación Unitaria de Trabajadores de Honduras (CUTH), the social Christian Confederación General de Trabajadores (CGT), and the social democratic Confederación de Trabajadores de Honduras (CTH); high school and university student associations; the Unificación Democrática (UD) political party; and even environmental associations such as the Movimiento Ambientalista de Olancho (MAO). Between late 2003 and 2008, the CNRP organizations convened on the first Sunday of every month to plan mobilizing priorities and strategies.[11] The coordination of these preexisting organizations into a unified action structure greatly raised the scale of mobilization potential in localities scattered across the national territory.

The mass days of action organized by the CNRP began with a colossal demonstration through the streets of Tegucigalpa in August 2003 to protest the IMF-backed water privatization measure, wage freezes, and the weakening of collective labor contracts (Posas 2003). People from throughout the country traveled to the capital to take part in the inaugural mobilization. The CNRP quickly followed up and, on October 28, 2003, demonstrated its organizational capacity at the national level with simultaneous marches and roadblocks in La Ceiba, Choluteca, Puerto Cortés, San Pedro Sula, Tela, El Progreso, Tegucigalpa, La Lima, Santa Bárbara, and other towns and strategic locations.

Between 2004 and 2009, the CNRP also organized several national days of protests and civic strikes against particular neoliberal policies (e.g., privatization, wage arrears, free trade, etc.). The Bloque Popular and CNRP also tried to prevent the National Congress from ratifying CAFTA. The two militant multisectoral organizations delivered a petition against CAFTA with over 18,000 signatures in late September 2004. Nevertheless, the legislature ratified the treaty in March 2005. The CNRP and Bloque Popular immediately organized mobilizations, but the campaign failed to change the government's plans, and the treaty went into law in 2006.

The CNRP and Bloque Popular also benefited from the legalization of the Unificación Democrática party in 1997—a direct outcome of Honduran democratization—which gave the coalitions a political ally. The UD was a left-wing coalition of opposition political parties that mobilized on the streets and in the electoral process. There was substantial overlap between party politics and protest campaigns (and *doble militancia*) (Almeida 2010b) among the UD and popular organizations. UD leaders and congressional representatives also served in leadership positions in the FUTH, Bloque Popular, CNRP, COCOCH, and other labor unions (Posas 2011). A similar relationship would develop between the LIBRE party and protest campaigns between 2012 and 2014 eventuating in even more electoral success.

Between 2007 and 2009, the CNRP organized three general strikes and several other days of action against neoliberal policies (Posas 2012). Overturning the water privatization law usually served as item number one on its list of public demands during these mass actions. President Manuel Zelaya, elected as a traditional Liberal Party politician in 2006, appeared to be drawing closer to the popular organizations by the middle of 2008 with the country's entry into the Alternativa Bolivariana para los Pueblos de Nuestra América (ALBA), which the National Congress ratified with a majority vote that October. A mass rally of tens of thousands of citizens occurred on August 25, 2008, in Tegucigalpa to support Honduras's admission into ALBA.[12] In December 2008, President Zelaya declared a 60% increase in the minimum wage, which also garnered the president heightened legitimacy from the popular organizations even as it earned him the ire of upper-class groups. His reformist administration also increased social spending and reduced poverty and income-inequality rates (Johnston and Lefebvre 2013). In June 2009, President Zelaya was overthrown in a military coup as he and his supporters attempted to organize a popular referendum on a constituent assembly. Since 2010, poverty rates and income inequality have increased markedly (Johnston and Lefebvre 2013).

The UD, CNRP, and Bloque Popular would coalesce into a new front, the Frente Nacional de Resistencia Popular (FNRP), to oppose the June 2009 military coup d'état in Honduras (Briceño Jimenez 2010). In this way, the antineoliberal battles of the 2000s established the multisectoral resistance to the coup. The FNRP mobilized several mass campaigns against the coup between June 2009 and July 2011. For example, within weeks of the military coup, the CNRP/FNRP had organized dozens of roadblocks, including a massive 5,000-person blockade of the Choloma bridge (*Puente blanco*), obstructing transportation of goods from the strategic Caribbean port city of Cortés for several days.[13] Eugenio Sosa (2012) has documented the growing use of the road blockade by multisectoral groups such as the CNRP and Bloque Popular in the years prior to the coup and found that by the mid-2000s, roadblocks counted as the fourth most common tactic employed by popular movements (after rallies, street marches, and strikes). Hence strategic experience was well established by popular movement battling neoliberal policies in the years before the military overthrow of Zelaya.

With organizational roots in the CNRP, the FNRP represented a wide coalition of civil society, including organized labor, NGOs, environmentalists, women's groups, students, teachers, peasant and indigenous associations, lesbian-gay-bisexual-and-transgender (LGBT) groups, and even the left wing of Zelaya's Liberal Party (Ruhl 2010). The FNRP faced severe repression; the Honduran Truth Commission documented 76 demonstrations that were repressed by the security forces between 2009 and 2011. In addition, the state and police were responsible for dozens of killings and hundreds of arrests and injuries suffered by suspected sympathizers of the FNRP. Between June 2009 and August 2011, the commission documented 5,418 reported human rights abuses (Comisión de Verdad 2012: 229).

Battles against two decades of punishing austerity and neoliberal policies had given the organizations that made up the FNRP the strategic experience to campaign against the authoritarian coup via sustained nonviolent civil disobedience. Loose coalitions such as the CNRP and Bloque Popular were multisectoral to their core; they began with the labor movement and reached out to students, teachers, indigenous communities, rural cooperatives, peasants, women's groups and political parties to develop a wide base of opposition (Frank 2010). Mario Posas (2011) reports that the FNRP mobilizations represented some of the largest demonstrations in the modern history of Honduras in terms of size and breadth of participation.

Ousted president Manuel Zelaya's return to the country in 2011 sparked one of the largest rallies in Honduran history with a reported 200,000 citizens in attendance at the welcoming ceremony at the Toncontín International Airport in the capital. In June 2011, after the return of Zelaya, the FNRP converted into a political party, Libertad y Refundación (LIBRE), which has begun to emerge as one of the most powerful electoral forces in the country. Indeed, in LIBRE's first electoral test in November 2013, the new party garnered nearly 900,000 votes for president and 30% of legislative seats with a platform of democratic socialism, anti-neoliberalism, and a constitutional assembly. These results transformed LIBRE into the second-largest political force in the country and displaced a century-long system of political rule by two alternating elite political parties.

8

Conclusion

State-Led Development Legacies in the Era of Global Capital

Popular organizations resurrected Central American civil society in the early twenty-first century. Economic threats emanating from a new round of global capitalist integration provided the incentives for a series of protest campaigns throughout the isthmus. Along with the Central American Free Trade Agreement, privatization of water, health care and social security, electricity, telecommunications, and land galvanized the demonstrations with the highest numbers of protest participants. The resistance stretched well beyond the national capitals of the individual countries. In these pages, I have detailed how and why subaltern groups broaden struggles against neoliberal capitalism into the interior of their respective countries. On many occasions, citizens broke national records for the size of the street marches and the territorial reach of the campaigns, especially over social security and health system reforms in El Salvador and Panama, over CAFTA in Costa Rica and Guatemala, and over water privatization in Honduras and Nicaragua. Clearly, more than any other grievance or social conflict, global economic integration-related issues mobilize the greatest number of citizens in this world region.[1] Moreover, the largest cross-class opposition coalitions often name themselves after these neoliberal policy threats: the Citizen's Alliance against Privatization, in El Salvador; the National Coordinator against Free Trade, in Costa Rica; the Progreso Popular Assembly against Privatizations, in Honduras; the National Front in Defense of Social Security, in Panama; and the Alliance against Privatization and the Right to Water Access, in Nicaragua. The scale of these mobilizations, along with the collective identities and banners under which citizens march, provides compelling testimony that we live in the era of accelerated globalization.

The struggles against the economic threats of privatization and social exclusion also occurred during a period of democratic transition, though it was a political transition controlled by domestic economic elites and the transnational factions of their respective political parties (W. Robinson 2003). While acknowledging the strict limits placed on the popular sectors by the electoral contests in terms of campaign funding and access to the mass media overwhelmingly dominated by elite groups and classes (Centro de Competencia en Comunicación 2007), the democratic transitions permitted more groups to enter the arena of political struggle without having to face the severe forms of state repression carried out in the past. Even elite-dominated democratization processes allow more groups to form organizations and mobilize with legal recognition and rights to public assembly (Tilly and Wood 2012). In addition, competitive elections permit the formation of opposition political parties that may also use their newly formed organizational structures to coordinate collective action campaigns with civil society groups outside of parliamentary politics.

As shown in chapter 3, Costa Rica offered a template for how the contours of these anti-globalization battles would likely express themselves, given the country's early historic and nonviolent struggles against transnational capital in relatively democratic contexts, such as the 1934 United Fruit Company banana strike, the 1970 Alcoa anti-mining campaign, and the first skirmishes against the International Monetary Fund in response to the foreign debt crisis in the early 1980s. All of these campaigns confronting global capital mobilized some combination of opposition political parties, urban labor unions, students, communal groups, and rural workers participating in a multisectoral alliance. Decades later, we observe similar types of coalitions emerging throughout Central America and the global South, as the recipe for generating mass multi-group resistance—the mixture of democratization with economic threats emanating from the global capitalist economy—is reproduced in dozens of national and subnational contexts. In Central America the wave of mass discontent against neoliberal democratization in the twenty-first century was first observed in rudimentary forms in twentieth-century Costa Rica.

Commonalities of Anti-Globalization Struggle

Struggles against globalization across Central America share many commonalties. All of the protest campaigns covered in these pages focused on some kind of unwanted economic policy such as privatization, free trade, labor flexibility, or price hikes. More successful episodes of collective resistance in terms of the

size, scale, and intensity, as well as final outcomes, relied on multisectoral coalitions steering the campaigns. In Costa Rica, El Salvador, Panama, and partially in Honduras, anti-neoliberal campaigns in the early to mid-1990s relied
on relatively narrow groups within the opposition. The battle against structural adjustment program III (SAP III) in Costa Rica, even with impressive mass
marches, was largely composed of the educational sector and state workers. In
El Salvador, the opposition coalition against telecommunications privatization, made up of the telephone workers and a few allies in other public sector
unions, proved too weak to impede the policy. The Panamanian protests
against labor flexibility laws drew support largely from urban unions, banana
workers, and university students.

Although the Platform of Struggle to Democratize Honduras organized
multiple sectors against President Callejas's IMF-backed reforms in the early
1990s, in actual protest campaigns each sector largely focused on particular
threats of wage freezes, mass layoffs, and privatization. The failure of sustained
multisector coalitions to materialize resulted in the passage of most neoliberal
measures by 1993 and the ascendancy of the transnational faction of the domestic capitalist class (W. Robinson 2003).[2] After major defeats in each of these
campaigns across Central America, activists and organizers adapted their organizational strategies and were able to create broader alliances in the next major battles against globalization, battles that often stretched across expansive
tracts of the national territory and forced power holders to make substantive
economic concessions favorable to the opposition.

Strategic experience with economic liberalization measures converted past
failures into relatively more efficacious campaigns in subsequent rounds of
collective action. Activists learned that the shrinking public sector labor movement alone could not defend civil society from austerity and privatization. By
the late 1990s and early 2000s, organizers pieced together more inclusive coalitions and took advantage of emerging social sectors such as opposition political parties, women's collectives, NGOs, high school and university students
(whose numbers were swelling), new social movements, and community-based
groups. Examples abound of this process throughout the region.

In Costa Rica, public-sector workers established several multisectoral alliances in the midst of the Combo protests against electricity and telecommunications privatization. In El Salvador, the Movimiento de la Sociedad Civil contra la Privatización (MSCP) and the Alianza Ciudadana Contra la Privatización
(ACCP) held together a variety groups to fend off health care privatization and

later to control the price of basic medicines. In Guatemala, the MICSP galvanized the largest mobilizations in decades against CAFTA and other measures. In Honduras, the CNRP maintained a rural-urban alliance of dozens of the most prominent civil society organizations and labor confederations for seven years until the military coup of 2009. In the aftermath of Hurricane Mitch in Nicaragua, activists and local development workers assembled the Coordinadora Civil—a collection of NGOs, rural organizations, environmental associations, and community groups leading local mobilizations in the 2000s in dozens of municipalities against privatization (in water and energy), structural adjustment agreements, and CAFTA. After 2004, the Coordinadora Social played a similar role in Nicaragua. In the aftermath of Panama's successful campaign against water privatization in late 1998, labor unions, public-sector teachers and health care workers, and students would form the FRENADESSO to prevent the privatization and restructuring of one of Latin America's most extensive public health care and pension systems. All of these multisectoral coalitions and their allies continue to serve as the vanguard of civil society opposition to neoliberalism in the new millennium. From these empirical lessons, we would expect large-scale campaigns to emerge where a multisectoral alliance is already in existence or for campaigns to be much weaker or absent where broad coalitions fail to materialize.

Strategic experience also allowed the popular protest campaigners to learn where to organize and which tactics to employ. In the major campaigns against privatization in Costa Rica, El Salvador, Nicaragua, and Panama, past local protest participation against economic liberalization measures was more common in regions resisting such policies in the present.[3] Prior engagement in anti-neoliberal campaigns significantly reduced the costs of future rounds of mobilization by retaining collective memories and organizational practices of coordination within a community.

The campaigns in all six countries also took advantage of state and community infrastructures enduring from the prior period of state-led development. The Pan-American Highway, constructed at the height of state-led development in the late 1950s and early 1960s, sought to integrate national economies and to assist commercial trade between neighboring countries via the Central American Common Market (CACM). By the early 2000s, the Pan-American Highway (along with other major transportation routes) acted as a strategic location for opposition coalitions to apply disruption and resist economic liberalization policies. In nearly every major campaign highway roadblocks were a crucial tactic. At the subnational level, localities transected by a major highway were much more likely to experience collective action than those lacking transportation arteries, including the latest antineoliberal campaigns erupting in Panama and Guatemala in late 2012 (see chapter 1). By the mid-2000s, several governments enacted legislation that made obstructing roads, bridges, and highways a serious criminal offense with heavy legal penalties.

The opposition coalitions in each country also drew heavily from the sectors that grew at exceptional rates within state institutions during the mid-twentieth century, such as public school teachers associations, public universities, telecommunications, public health, and social security institutes. Public hospitals and public schools provide some of the greatest numbers of state-sector workers in the globalization era. Other institutions tended to be smaller in terms of staff and employees or already privatized, such as electrical power, public works, and water administration. When public health care unions and employee associations are relatively united, they can provide between 20,000 and 30,000 participants to a campaign, and their units (clinics, hospitals, administrative offices) are often distributed in many parts of the country. The public health sector has served (sometimes even at the vanguard) in major anti-globalization campaigns in El Salvador, Costa Rica, Nicaragua, Honduras, and Panama. School teachers associations play a parallel role, but on a greater scale, as even the smallest rural municipality has at least a primary school as a result of state-led development efforts in the 1950s and 1960s. Hence, teachers associations were exceptionally active in campaigns in Costa Rica, Guatemala, Honduras, Nicaragua, and Panama, helping the resistance spread far into the countryside and at times into remote indigenous communities (especially in Guatemala, Panama, and Honduras).

Public universities also enlisted in most of the anti-globalization campaigns. Sometimes that included the participation of not only students and staff but also university rectors. During the Combo protests against electricity and telecommunications privatization in Costa Rica in 2000, several public university campuses canceled classes and replaced them with teach-ins while university administrators called on the general public to participate in the civic resistance to privatization. One of the top leaders to emerge in the anti-CAFTA campaign in Costa Rica was Eugenio Trejos, the rector of Costa Rica's Public Technical University and, between 2006 and 2007, titular head of the Frente Nacional de Apoyo a la Lucha contra el TLC, the coalition of coalitions that surfaced in the peak years of the opposition. Most Central American states maintained only one public university in a single location (usually the capital) on the eve of state-led development in 1940. By 1980, dozens of regional branches of public universities and entire new universities came into existence in a more decentralized fashion as part of economic modernization. These regional campuses coordinated local activities in the protest campaigns in Costa Rica, Panama, Honduras, Nicaragua, and Guatemala.

Beyond the capital cities, opposition movements preferred provincial capitals as a venue for local coalitions to target representatives of the state. Administrative offices are concentrated in provincial capitals. Rural dwellers were familiar with these offices from routine affairs such as applying for licenses and loans, buying and selling in markets, and attending cultural activities. These towns were therefore attractive sites to stage protest activities, especially for those unable to journey to the national capital. Nearly every provincial capital city experienced at least one protest event in the major campaigns covered here.

State-Led Development Legacies in the Era of Global Capital

Even with these commonalities across campaigns and countries, there are notable differences, especially in the composition of multisectoral coalitions. One striking difference between Central American states, which may be changing, is the role of nongovernmental organizations in the opposition coalition. In Guatemala, El Salvador, and Nicaragua, NGOs have played an indispensable role by mobilizing excluded social groups, especially in the countryside. By contrast, in Costa Rica, Honduras, and Panama, NGOs have played smaller roles in protest campaigns.[4] As expected, state-development histories shape these differences. In an earlier period, James Mahoney (2001) observed how structural transformations of liberal reforms in the late-nineteenth-century Central America affected the region's political structures in the twentieth century. The state-led development era now provides the foundations for the patterning of protest campaigns in the current epoch of globalization. In El Salvador, Guatemala, and Nicaragua, opposition movements faced decades of state repression and terror before the recent democratic transitions. Communities were forced to create their own organizations independent of the state, often clandestinely. As the civil wars drew to a close in the late 1980s and early 1990s, many international NGOs began work assisting the victims and refugees of state violence in El Salvador and Guatemala. State exclusion of vast sectors of the population continued at high rates into the twenty-first century; Guatemala and El Salvador rank lowest in the region on indicators of state social spending (Lehoucq 2012: 145–46). In Nicaragua the self-organized popular organizations battling against Somoza's exclusive and repressive rule converted into official state-sponsored associations in the 1980s (detailed in chapter 6), to the point where they were running local governments. As the neoliberal counter-revolution took hold in the 1990s and privatized the national economy, Nicaraguan popular organizations such as the Movimiento Comunal Nicaragüense lost state funding and support, and many former FSLN party organizers, militants, and even ex-soldiers of the Sandinista army turned to NGO development work with the assistance of international cooperation.

Leaders of these NGOs sustain close relationships with popular organizations and opposition political parties. Hence, NGOs maintain high profiles within coalitions battling against privatization and free trade in Guatemala and El Salvador. In Nicaragua, a somewhat similar process took place once the FSLN lost state power in 1990, and many former Sandinista militants threw themselves into NGO-type work.

In Costa Rica, Honduras, and Panama, the state sectors have proven stronger and *relatively* less repressive. The repressive regimes of Nicaragua, El Salvador and Guatemala killed people in the tens of thousands. Although the various Honduran and Panamanian military governments were authoritarian and repressive, their rule did not reach the massive levels of state violence carried out by Somoza's National Guard, and the Salvadoran and Guatemalan security forces notorious for their "death squads," mass graves, and torture techniques. In addition, Costa Rica, Honduras, and Panama have each attempted some level of welfare populism. Costa Rica's tropical welfare state (Edelman 1999) provides resources down to the community level in its DINADECO program (discussed in chapter 3). The program was created in 1968 at the twilight of state-centered development, and the DINADECO-based organizations have played a role in the opposition to free market reforms, including the 1983 IMF price hike and the anti-CAFTA campaign in the 2000s. NGOs in Costa Rica tend to maintain more distance from popular organizations and base many of their activities in the capital (Macdonald 1997; Edelman 1999). This trend is likely changing with the emergence of militant environmental NGOs on the front lines over transnational mining, tourism, and water distribution issues in recent years (Cordero 2014). Even in the 1990s and 2000s, exceptional NGOs like the Red Alforja and FECON carried out important organizing and educational work in the country.

In Panama, the legacy of the populist regime of General Omar Torrijos also provided fewer incentives to form NGOs. Labor unions and public sector employee associations (especially teachers, health care workers, and construction workers) were organized in large enough numbers that they could sustain campaigns without large-scale NGO support. Moreover, the entire organizational architecture of Torrijos's military populism began at the local level, with each *corregimiento* (local administrative unit) represented in the reconstructed National Assembly of the 1970s. These local-level units down to the neighborhood or village were organized as community-development collectives (*juntas comunales*). The state sponsored initiatives within these communal associations supported health care needs and infrastructure development (Priestley 1986).

In Honduras, the legacies of military-directed agrarian reforms and cooperative programs have continued to influence rural organizing, with federations of agricultural cooperatives playing an active role in the larger antineoliberal coalitions of the Bloque Popular, CNRP, and FNRP. The Honduran government has also facilitated local self-organized community associations (*patronatos*) at the neighborhood and village level; these received legal recognition in 2001, after decades of struggle (Sosa and Ortega 2008). Nonetheless, there are important NGOs carrying out organizational work in both Panama and Honduras (increasingly in the spheres of human rights and environmental protection), just not on the scale of El Salvador, Guatemala, and Nicaragua in mobilizing defiant collective action. The effects of these differing state-development histories shed light on current debates within academic and activist circles in the global South as to whether NGOs act as mobilizing or demobilizing agents in popular protest campaigns. NGO participation in protest campaigns partially depends on the national and international *sources* of funding of the nonprofit sector but also on the historical need for non-state-development-type organizations to provide resources where exclusive and repressive governments do not.

Central American democratization since the 1990s has permitted the growth of progressive electoral political parties. The role of opposition political parties also has differed across nation-states. In Nicaragua and El Salvador, two large and nationally organized opposition parties, the FSLN and FMLN, played a leading role in mobilizations. These leftist parties also had an easier time linking with civil society organizations because many of their rank-and-file affiliates maintained overlapping memberships in NGOs, labor unions, and other civil society associations, what has been called social movement partyism (Almeida 2006, 2010b). Indeed, local mobilization against globalization was more likely in those regions where the FMLN of El Salvador or the FSLN of Nicaragua maintained a strong territorial base (see the campaigns discussed in chapters 4 and 6). In addition, countries with small leftist opposition parties (Costa Rica, Guatemala, and Honduras) also actively engaged in street protests and encouraged multisectoral coalition building.

In Costa Rica, Guatemala, and Honduras, left-wing parties may get close to 80,000 votes or more. Even though the majority of these votes are concentrated in the capital, highly motivated party activists are also distributed across the national territory in smaller numbers. The Unidad Nacional Revolucionaria Guatemalteca and Alianza Nueva Nación in Guatemala, the Fuerza Democrática / Frente Amplio in Costa Rica, and Unificación Democrática in Honduras have all assisted protest campaigns by calling up active members to participate in rallies, demonstrations, and roadblocks. Even smaller "new left" and Trotskyist parties have influenced campaigns in Costa Rica and Panama. As we observed in chapter 3, Costa Rica first modeled this relationship between parties and protest campaigns back in the 1930s with the Costa Rican Communist Party and then again in the 1970s and early 1980s with the Pueblo Unido electoral coalition against the first wave of austerity and IMF conditionality, before the Costa Rican left splintered into factions. By the 2000s, a moderate left-of-center opposition party, the Citizen's Action Party (PAC), had emerged in Costa Rica and garnered hundreds of thousands of votes. This new party displaced the decades-old, elite two-party system and came within less than a percentage point of winning the presidential elections in 2006. The PAC would also mobilize against CAFTA and use its resources to assist in coordinating the "No" campaign in the 2007 referendum, with parliamentary representatives and officials even appearing in street protests.

In terms of elections, the FMLN, FSLN, and PAC (representing opposition parties in El Salvador, Nicaragua, and Costa Rica, respectively) seem to have benefited the most in electoral success from their involvement in anti-neoliberal protest campaigns, with victories at the executive level in El Salvador and Nicaragua, and near victory in Costa Rica.[5] In Honduras, a sizable faction of the hundred-year-old Liberal Party split off in 2009 to join the FNRP) and denounce the military coup through street protests and other forms of collective action. Libertad y Refundación (LIBRE), which is made up of the civic organizations in the CNRP, FNRP, and Liberal Party dissidents, is now the second-largest political force after the November 2013 presidential and parliamentary elections, threatening Honduras's long tradition of political hegemony by two elite parties. The FRENADESSO protest coalition (discussed in chapter 5) has converted into a political party in Panama, the Frente Amplio por la Democracia (FAD), and will compete as the left alternative in the 2014 elections, potentially the largest electoral challenge from the left in Panamanian history.

We have observed the importance of state and community infrastructures in supporting the collective opposition to neoliberal forms of capitalism. Therefore, in terms of policy-making suggestions to post-neoliberal governments and reformers in Latin America and the global South, governments should remain aware of how critical it is to maintain a large and geographically extensive state infrastructure in order to fend off unwanted changes emanating from more powerful states and actors in the world economy. Without protected spaces for critical inquiry, such as public universities, schools, and state employee associations that often open their doors and work sites to the general public for gatherings, deliberations, and educational events, it will be difficult to garner a sufficient mass of citizens concerned with the neoliberalization of the national economy and resist the erosion of social citizenship rights. Private and commercial market forces will likely continue colonizing the public sphere, making anti-neoliberal campaigns even more difficult to launch. States should continue to invest heavily in their education, health, and social security systems, as well as other crucial components of the national infrastructure, such as public utilities, providing low-cost access to vital social services. Moreover, recent empirical work is accumulating on the positive outcomes for employment and reducing poverty through strategic social investments in the global South by post-neoliberal and socially reform-minded governments (Flores-Macías 2012; Evans and Sewell 2013), especially in education, universal health care, and job training, even if it means increasing short- and medium-term debt (Cohn 2012; Huber and Stephens 2012). Protecting the state infrastructure along many dimensions ought to be a high priority of both civil society activists and policy makers searching for alternatives to neoliberalism in the twenty-first century.

Notes

CHAPTER ONE: Introduction

1. A campaign may also be abruptly ended by police or governmental repression. This scenario was more common for anti-neoliberal campaigns in nondemocratic regimes during the 1980s.

2. The first major campaign against natural gas exportations and privatization in Bolivia in 2003 (the so-called gas war) ended with the deaths of over 40 indigenous protesters and one soldier when security forces cracked down on protests and roadblocks (Postero 2007). Some of the anti-neoliberal protests in Argentina have also turned violent with the looting of supermarkets, but most of the globalization-induced contention in Latin America has remained relatively less violent.

CHAPTER TWO: A Theory of Local Opposition to Globalization

1. For an important exception, see Walton and Seddon (1994).

CHAPTER THREE: Costa Rica

1. "Los comunistas en la municipalidad," *Trabajo*, Jan. 7, 1933, p. 1.

2. "Los trabajadores del Atlántico, bajo la dirección del Partido Comunista, libran su batalla huelguística contra la United Fruit, contra los finqueros particulares, por alzas del salario, mejoras de trabajo y por condiciones más llevaderas de vida," *Trabajo*, Aug. 12, 1934, p. 1.

3. The PVP won 12 of 45 parliamentary seats in the 1948 elections (Edelman 1999).

4. The party maximized the democratic space that was conceded by various governments between 1931 and 1948. It used its newspaper (*Trabajo*), affiliated labor associations, and city council and parliament members to launch multiple organizing initiatives addressing pressing social issues such as inflation, consumer electricity rates, mass unemployment, low-income housing, rural labor conditions, and labor union rights. This gave the party much more political influence than one would expect for a small opposition political party that never received more than 14,000 votes in national elections, or 16% of the total vote (Molina Jiménez 1999). The party's impact is consistent with Tilly's (1978) assertion that once a government opens up the electoral process to multiple groups, those same groups can use the democratic opening for a range of organizing purposes beyond elections.

5. The PVP-influenced labor confederation CCTRN was also banned in 1951.

6. Interview with the secretary-general of the Asociación Nacional de Empleados Publicos (1985–1990), Jan. 30, 2009, San José.

7. The CTRN and CCTD were social democratic labor unions that broke into smaller groupings of moderate labor unions.

8. UNA later opened regional campuses in Nicoya, Sarapiquí, and Corredores.

9. Consejo Nacional de Rectores 1978. By 1982, the beginning of the foreign debt crisis, public university enrollment neared 50,000.

10. "Movilización nacional contra la ALCOA," *Libertad*, Mar. 21, 1970, p. 1 and 4.

11. "Diputados de ALCOA o diputados de Costa Rica," *Libertad*, Apr. 4, 1970, p. 2.

12. "Unídad Nacional en la lucha contra ALCOA," *Libertad*, Apr. 4, 1970, p. 2.

13. "Diputados de ALCOA o diputados de Costa Rica," p. 2.

14. "24 de Abril de 1970," *Libertad*, May 1, 1970, pp. 4–5.

15. "¡Fuera la ALCOA! Es el grito de todo el pueblo costarricense," *Libertad*, May 1, 1970, pp. 1, 4, and 5.

16. "39 diputados contra el país," *Libertad*, Apr. 25, 1970, pp. 1 and 4.

17. "1 de Mayo de 1970," *Libertad*, Apr. 4, 1970, p. 9. This is an advertisement to join the May Day march in San José to denounce the ALCOA mining contract among other demands. A multi-secotral coalition organizing the event, the Comité Nacional Unitario, included COCC, CGTC, FEUCR, the Asociacion de Empleados del Seguro Social (AESS), Catholic Working-Class Youth (JOC), and the National Federation of Juntas Progresistas neighborhood associations. The May Day march was also organized to take place in 11 regions outside the capital, including Limón, Fortuna, Turrialba, Villa Neily, Golfito, Puerto Cortes, Quepos, Liberia, San Vito de Java, and Siquirres. Citizens living near the municipalities of Heredia, Puntarenas, Cartago, and Alajuela were to gather in San José. For information about these individual May Day marches, see "1 de May en todo el país: celebrada de manera entusiasta y combativa," *Libertad*, May 16, 1970, p. 6.

18. "Nuestros candidatos son los mejores," *Libertad*, Feb. 3–9, 1978, pp. 13–15.

19. "Regidores de Pueblo Unido darán la pelea en 22 municipalidades," *Libertad*, Mar. 31–Apr. 6, 1978, p. 5.

20. The Federación Nacional de Trabajadores Públicos (FENATRAP) was formed in 1975 by the pro-PLN labor confederation CCTD. It was rapidly taken over by groups sympathetic to leftist opposition political parties (Peña Martínez 1982).

21. Several mobilizations by small farmers also took place in the early 1980s that were linked to economomic liberalization. These protests were largely contained in the agricultural sector alone (Edelman 1999).

22. "Bajarán las tarifas eléctricas," *La nación*, June 10, 1983, p. 4a.

23. "Gobierno revisará actitud ante problemas nacionales," *La prensa libre*, June 10, 1983.

24. For example, the more radical faction of the PVP (led by Humberto Vargas Carbonell and Arnoldo Ferreto) led a militant banana workers' strike in the southern Pacific region in July and August 1984. The usual solidarity strikes by Atlantic coast unions and public-sector employees in the cities never materialized because of the internal PVP divisions, and the strike subsequently failed. The radical faction blamed Manuel Mora Verde's moderate faction for not allowing the solidarity actions. See "Trabajadores decidieron levantar la huelga," *Libertad revolucionaria*, Sept. 21–28, 1984, p. 3.

25. Another factor for demobilization in the 1980s was the rise of the *solidarista* movement, which replaced labor unions in many of the banana worker strongholds and in maquiladora production.

26. Teachers won back some of the these benefits during a month-long strike in 2003.

27. "Agricultores de cartago plantean peticiones a gobierno" and "Poder judicial amenaza con huelga," *La nación*, July 18, 1995, p. 6A. Other major peasant organizations such as Mesa Campesina and UPANACIONAL also announced during the strike that they supported the government's pension reform program and would not support the teachers (Menjívar Ochoa 1999).

28. A national poll taken during the first week of the strike reported that 51% of Costa Ricans felt that the demands of the teachers were justified, but nearly 80% of respondents disagreed with the tactics of a labor strike and street protests. In this same survey, 46% of respondents did not think other labor leaders (i.e., the CCN) should mix other grievances related to the Figueres-Calderón Pact, while only 28% thought the demands should be unified. In another public opinion poll reported near the end of the strike in August, 48% supported the strike and 43% were against it. In this same survey, 56% of respondents favored the new pension law, while only 26% felt that it should revert back to the original program favored by teachers. See "Apoyo a reclamo de educadores," *La nación*, July 21, 1995, p. 5A, and "El paro en números," *La nación*, Aug. 17, 1995, p. 5A.

29. Emilia Mora and María Isabel Solís, "Semana crucial para huelga," *La nación*, July 24, 1995. See also "Huelga se estancó," *La nación*, July 25, 1995, p. 4A.

30. Other labor union leaders reported in interviews with the author that in the mid-1990s the main teachers associations' leadership and some labor union leaders maintained strong ties to the party in power, the PLN. These ties worked against calls in the movement's base and in other public-sector unions to continue the mobilizations and move toward a general strike.

31. Interview with leader of the ANEP, June 4, 2007, San José.

32. The law was titled "Ley para el Mejoramiento de los Servicios Públicos de Electricidad y Telecomunicaciones y de la Participación del Estado."

33. The government established the Instituto Costarricense de Electricidad in 1949 after several decades of struggle by the Liga Cívica and Asociación para la Defensa del Consumidor Eléctrico for the state to take over power distribution from foreign management. Telecommunications were added to the ICE in 1963. By 1988, 13 out of every 100 Costa Ricans had telephones in their home, about three times higher than the average for Latin America (Trejos 1988).

34. Interview with leader of the ANEP, June 4, 2007, San José.

35. For example, on March 19, 1999, a mass street demonstration of thousands of workers took place in San José condemning the notion of opening up the ICE to international investors. See "Retiro de directiz y planes de ICE sindicatos presionan a gobierno," *La nación*, March 20, 1999.

36. The Costa Rican Catholic Church established its Social Pastoral Program in 1966 in the context of Vatican II to serve the needs of the poor and excluded. It is estimated that about one-third of parishes have some type of participation in this social program. During the Combo protests the social pastoral program played a key role in rural mobilization in Pérez Zeledón, La Cruz, Tilarán, San Carlos, Alajuela, Turrialba, and the cantones in the province of Limón. Interview with representative of the National Pastoral Social Commission, Apr. 30, 2009, Montes de Oca, Costa Rica.

37. Author interview with FEUCR president (2000) and major student leader of Combo protests, July 30, 2002, San José.

38. See Merino (2000) for a discussion of organizing activities against ICE privatization in 1999.

39. Proyecto Estado de la Nación (2000). The nascent coalition began leafleting its propaganda against the ICE privatization in bus stops, movie theatres, farmers markets and workplaces between January and March 2000. Interview with a leader of the Asociación de Empleados del Instituto Costarricense de Electricidad (ASDEICE), June 4, 2007, San José.

40. One leader inside the FIT reported to me the initial difficulty of negotiating a coalition with environmentalists, given that the ICE is a government development agency

responsible for constructing dams, digging tunnels, and other industrial activities that often come into conflict with environmental NGOs. In the end, however, environmentalists concluded that these activities would best be regulated by the government with domestic political accountability than international energy and telecommunications firms and thus joined the opposition coalition. Interview with a leader of ASDEICE, June 4, 2007, San José.

41. "Marcha por ICE," *La república*, Mar. 24, 2000, p. 5A.

42. "Fogoso país," *La nación*, Mar. 23, 2000, p. 5A.

43. Solis (2002). The PLN held 22 of 57 legislative seats at the time, and its support was decisive if the privatization measure passed in a second round of voting.

44. In addition, on April 24, 2000, the chamber of the Supreme Court that oversees legislative procedures (Sala IV) ruled the passage of the privatization law in the first debate as unconstitutional by the manner that in which the dominant parties introduced the impending law into legislative debate (thus annulling it) (Solis 2002).

45. In a 20-day period (March 16 to April 4) *La nación* reported 274 protest events, out of which 103 were roadblocks (37.6%) (Proyecto de la Nación 2000: 216). My analysis used multiple newspaper sources and uncovered 473 protest events.

46. "Diputados son responsables de protestas," *La república*, Mar. 24, 2000, p. 5A.

47. "Ticos piden consulta sobre combo ICE," *La república*, Mar. 29, 2000, p. 5A. Only 13.7% approved of such tactics during the teachers strike in 1995.

48. Article "g" of the final signed accord, mimeograph in possession of the author.

49. Interview with secretary-general of the ANEP, June 4, 2007, San José.

50. In Costa Rica, the percentage vote for left-leaning opposition parties was higher in communities participating against privatization (6.3%) than in nonparticipating ones (4.5%).

51. "Compañero estudiantes colegio diurno de naranjo," Apr. 7, 2000, copy of letter in possession of author.

52. In Spanish, CAFTA is referred to as the Tratado de Libre Comercio (TLC).

53. On March 23, 2000, another mass march of 100,000 people took place against the privatization of telecommunications and electricity.

54. The author served as a certified international electoral observer for the 2007 CAFTA referendum.

55. Interview with Alberto Salom, PAC legislative deputy, June 7, 2007, San José.

CHAPTER FOUR: El Salvador

1. Partido de Conciliación Nacional (PCN); Partido Revolucionario de Unificación Democrática (PRUD).

2. Interview with author, Aug. 11, 2005, Legislative Assembly Office, San Salvador.

3. Interview with principal leader of the Citizen's Alliance against Privatization, May 5, 2003, San Salvador.

4. Interview with Victor Aguilar, coordinator of CLS and MPR-12, Aug. 9, 2005, San Salvador.

5. These events were recorded, geocoded, and mapped using five national Salvadoran newspapers, labor union chronologies, and NGO reports.

6. In a separate measurement of the influence of public universities not reported here, municipalities bordering public universities were also scored as affected by a university's reach. In this alternative measure, almost one-third of municipalities (32%) with a university or bordering a county with one participated in the Salvadoran anti-privatization campaign while only 12% of nonparticipating municipalities had a nearby university.

7. Santiago Leiva, "FMLN exhorta a población apoyar lucha de los trabajadores del Seguro Social," *Diario co latino*, Sept. 21, 2002.

8. Aguilar interview.

9. These events were recorded, geocoded, and mapped using five national Salvadoran newspapers and NGO reports.

10. A massive national day of protest was held on October 12, 2002, against the Free Trade Area of the Americas and Plan Puebla-Panamá. But this action was part of the larger campaign against health care privatization. The first regional meetings about negotiating CAFTA began in January 2003 in Costa Rica.

11. Interview with national director of FMLN election campaign, May 26, 2011, San Salvador; interview with chairman of FMLN electoral campaign in San Salvador department, Feb. 23, 2010, San Salvador.

12. Santiago Leiva, "FMLN exhorta a luchar porque el agua no se convierta en Mercancía," *Diario co latino*, Aug. 29, 2007.

13. Luis Romero Pineda, "Torrente rojo de 300 mil personas," *Diario co latino*, Mar. 9, 2009.

14. New conflicts flared up between President Funes and the FMLN in 2013 over a private-public partnership law that does allow the subcontracting of some vital government services and operations. The FMLN was able to ensure that water, education, and health care would remain exempt.

CHAPTER FIVE: Panama

1. "No a la privatización del IDAAN," *Panamá América*, Jan. 1, 1999.

2. Interview with secretary-general of the medical association AMOACSS in 1984 and leader of COCINA, May 29, 2009, Panama City.

3. Ibid.

4. "CONATO se agita casa por casa preparando la huelga general," *La prensa* (Panama City), Mar. 6, 1986, p. 1.

5. "Aumento paro en sector industrial," *La prensa*, Mar. 12, 1986, p. 1; "Trabajadores chiricanos rechazan las reformas al Código de Trabajo," *La prensa*, Mar. 13, 1986, p. 8A.

6. Barrantes Méndez continues to serve as a martyr for SUNTRACS to this day and his heroism is celebrated in public gatherings, connecting earlier struggles against neoliberalism in the 1980s to current battles.

7. It should be noted that the massive mobilizations against General Manuel Noriega by the Civic Crusade between 1987 and 1989 were organized largely by upper-middle-class groups that had political grievances over the exclusionary style of rule (Nepstad 2011; Beluche 1994).

8. Interview with SUNTRACS secretary-general, May 22, 2009, Panama City.

9. "Comienzan paro contra reformas," *La prensa*, May 23, 1995, p. 1.

10. Rufino Frías instantly bécame another major figure in the SUNTRACS union as a martyr in protest campaigns against neoliberalism.

11. "Un entierro al ritmo de consignas," *La prensa*, Aug. 10, 1995, p. 6A.

12. Interview with CONUSI secretary-general, May 22, 2009, Panama City.

13. In the 2002 survey an additional 112 respondents did not answer the privatization question or did not know an answer. In the 2003 survey an additional 79 respondents did not answer the privatization question or did not know an answer.

14. "Veraguenses crean coordinadora," *La prensa*, Dec. 16, 1998 p. 7A; "Marchas y protestas en el interior del país," *La prensa*, Sept. 13, 2003, p. 8A.

15. "Sacan a Juan Jované, paro en el Seguro Social," *Panamá América*, Sept. 11, 2003, p. 1, A3.

16. Interview with former director of the css, May 29, 2009, Panama City.

17. "Miles marchan hasta la presidencia," *La prensa*, Sept. 13, 2003, p. 1

18. The massive national hospital complex of the css built by the General Torrijos government in the mid-1970s is named after former president Arnulfo Arias Madrid.

19. "Crean frente pro defensa de la css," *La prensa*, Oct. 8, 2003, p. 9A.

20. "Se desploma popularidad de Martín Torrijos," *La prensa*, June 9, 2005, p. 1; "Rechazan aumento en edad de jubilación," *Panamá América*, May 23, 2005, p. 1.

21. "Protestas simultáneas en la capital y provincias," *La prensa*, May 21, 2005, p. 6a, and "Se estanca el diálogo por la caja," *La prensa*, June 13, 2005, p. 1.

22. Even though the negotiations to end the 2005 css strike resulted in preventing the raising of the retirement age, it did allow individual pension accounts and the transference of some funds to private banks in the final Law 51 that was instituted. This weakened the system of solidarity in which the institute was traditionally based (i.e., contributions to the state system based on income, but standardized medical benefits). Interview with former director of the css, May 29, 2009, Panama City.

23. FRENADESSO now stands for the Frente Nacional por la Defensa de los Derechos Económicos y Sociales. The core composition is made up of CONUSI, SUNTRACS, and public school teachers associations.

24. The analysis includes all 75 districts in existence in Panama in 2005 and the Indigenous Comarca San Blas / Kuna Yala.

25. This assertion was independently verified during an interview with one of the historic leaders of FRENADESSO and CONUSI, May 22, 2009, Panama City.

26. In the banana-growing regions of Costa Rica and Panama, Chiquita Brands is known as Mamita Yunai for its earlier corporate name of United Fruit.

CHAPTER SIX: Nicaragua

1. The FSLN won presidential and parliamentary elections in 1984.

2. The FSLN regained the presidency in elections in late 2006.

3. "Nace frente nacional de trabajadores," *Barricada*, May 9, 1990, p. 1.

4. "La nueva asamblea sandinista," *Barricada international*, Aug. 1991, p. 12.

5. In addition to protesting austerity measures, the May Day rallies also called for the complete demobilization of the Contra counter-revolutionary forces.

6. "Victoria de la huelga," *Barricada*, May 17, 1990, pp. 1, 5.

7. *Barricada*, July 10, 1990, p. 4.

8. "Nicaragua Fires Author of Its Economic Plan from Central Bank Post," *Los Angeles Times*, Nov. 1, 1990.

9. There were 145 municipalities in Nicaragua in 1990. No elections were held in the municipality of San Juan del Norte in the department of Río San Juan. Hence, table 5.1 drops this municipality from the analysis, leaving 144 municipalities.

10. "Gremios Unidos ante embates del gobierno," *Barricada*, May 4, 1995, pp. 1–2.

11. One of the first community-level consumer defense groups formed in this new context was in Masaya in October 1999,: the Asociación de Consumidores de Masaya (ACODEMA). Interview with ACODEMA leader April 25, 2009, Masaya.

12. I personally witnessed the early days of the RNDC water campaign in July 2002, during the third Foro Mesoamericano meetings in Managua. I appreciate the access the RNDC granted me to archives and press clippings on their recent activities.

13. "Segovianos amenazan con protestas," *La prensa* (Managua), Apr. 26, 2005; "Diputados, alcaldes y concejales Sandinistas atizan protestas," *La prensa*, Apr. 27, 2005.

CHAPTER SEVEN: Guatemala and Honduras

1. A call-in poll conducted by a Guatemalan newspaper that asked respondents if they supported the national strike on August 1 to oppose the tax hike calculated 5,522 valid responses, with 93% supporting the strike and 7% opposed to it. See "Apoyo a paro nacional," *Prensa libre*, Aug. 1, 2001.

2. The PAN's anti-neoliberal credentials proved weak as it was the previous party in power and initiated several privatization programs (including state telecommunications) under President Alvaro Arzú (1995–1999). It failed to form deep ties with the popular movement, though it did act on its behalf by abstaining from the vote and calling for a popular referendum.

3. "Aprueban el IVA," *Prensa libre*, July 27, 2001.

4. Alberto Ramírez, "Masiva protesta contra gobierno," *Prensa libre*, Aug. 2, 2001.

5. Several other actions to resist the implementation of CAFTA, including marches in the capital and roadblocks by rural indigenous groups, took place in 2003 and early 2004.

6. In 1996, Guatemalan government signed the International Labor Organization (ILO) Convention 169, which provides rights for indigenous people to control the use of natural resources within their territories.

7. Louisa Reynolds, "EL FNL, sus demandas y sus medidas de hecho," *El periódico*, Sept. 17, 2010.

8. For this section on Honduras, I am particularly indebted to sociologists Mario Posas and Eugenio Sosa and the Centro de Documentación de Honduras (CEDOH).

9. One obvious exception is the case of Nicaragua discussed in chapter 5. There, the FNT protest campaigns of 1990 were also in response to government privatization of lands and factories nationalized during the Sandinista revolution in the 1980s. However, privatization protests against the outsourcing of the basic economic infrastructure did not gather steam in Nicaragua until later in the decade and into the 2000s.

10. "Triunfo Hondureño sobre intentos de privatización," *El nuevo diario*, July 6, 1990, p. 3.

11. Interview with member of the UD leadership council, May 7, 2011, Tegucigalpa, San Pedro Sula.

12. "Para un siglo tendrá combustible Honduras," *El Libertador*, Sept. 2008, p. 20–21, and "Tenemos ALBA," *El Libertador*, Nov. 2008, p. 43.

13. Interview with member of the Colectivo de Mujeres de Honduras (CODEMUH) that participated in this event, May 6, 2011, El Progreso, Yoro.

CHAPTER EIGHT: Conclusion

1. The mobilization against the military coup in Honduras between 2009 and 2011 produced even larger rounds of collective action than the anti-neoliberal protest campaigns had. Nonetheless, the organizational basis of this opposition derived directly from the mobilizations in the years immediately preceding the coup. It would be difficult to account for such widespread resistance without the previous buildup of the multisectoral anti-neoliberal coalition between 2000 and 2009.

2. The exception to these outcomes was the relative success of the public health care workers impeding the privatization process with their month-long strike in mid-1990 (see chapter 7).

3. Similar findings would likely be observed in Guatemala and Honduras once systematic protest event data was collected over multiple campaigns.

4. This observation in no way diminishes the crucial development work, training, and technical assistance NGOs provide in these countries. State-led development histories have created relatively less demand for NGOs to enter contentious politics

5. The PAC in Costa Rica was weakened following the narrow defeat of the opposition in the CAFTA referendum in late 2007. However, the opposition party is now poised to win the presidential elections in the second run-off round in April 2014.

Bibliography

Abbreviations

CELA	Centro de Estudios Latinoamericanos "Justo Arosemena"
CEPAS	Centro de Estudios para la Acción Social
CLACSO	Consejo Latinoamericano de Ciencias Sociales
CRIES	Coordinadora Regional de Investigaciones Económicas y Sociales
ENACAL	Empresa Nicaragüense de Acueductos y Alcantarillados
FLACSO	Facultad Latinoamericana de Ciencias Sociales
NACLA	North American Congress on Latin America
OSAL	*Observatorio Social de América Latina*
RIMISP	Centro Latinoamericano para el Desarrollo Rural

Abouharb, M. Rodwan, and David Cingranelli. 2007. *Human Rights and Structural Adjustment*. Cambridge: Cambridge University Press.

Aguilar Guillén, José Victor. 1993. "El proceso de privatización en El Salvador." Documento de Trabajo #30 (Sept.). Fundación Nacional para el Desarrollo (FUNDE), San Salvador, El Salvador.

———. 1995. "Privatización de las telecomunicaciones y de la distribución de energía eléctrica." *Serie alternativas para el desarrollo* 30:17–23.

Aguilar Hernández, Marielos. 1992. "Las libertades sindicales en los ochentas: el caso de las organizaciones bananeras costarricenses." *Ciencias sociales* 58:85–94.

Almeida, Paul D. 2002. "Los movimientos populares contra las políticas de austeridad económica en América Latina entre 1996 y 2001." *Realidad: revista de ciencias sociales y humanidades* 86:177–89.

———. 2003. "Opportunity Organizations and Threat Induced Contention: Protest Waves in Authoritarian Settings." *American Journal of Sociology* 109(2): 345–400.

———. 2005. "Multi-Sectoral Coalitions and Individual Protest Participation." *Research in Social Movements, Conflicts and Change* 26:67–102.

———. 2006. "Social Movement Unionism, Social Movement Partyism, and Policy Outcomes: Health Care Privatization in El Salvador." In Johnston and Almeida (2006), 57–73.

———. 2007. "Defensive Mobilization: Popular Movements against Economic Adjustment Policies in Latin America." *Latin American Perspectives* 34(3): 123–39.

———. 2008a. "The Sequencing of Success: Organizing Templates and Neoliberal Policy Outcomes." *Mobilization* 13(2): 1655–87.

———. 2008b. *Waves of Protest: Popular Struggle in El Salvador, 1925–2005*. Minneapolis: University of Minnesota Press.

————. 2010a. "Globalization and Collective Action." In Kevin Leicht and J. Craig Jenkins, eds., *Handbook of Politics: State and Society in Global Perspective*, 305–26. New York: Springer.

————. 2010b. "Social Movement Partyism: Collective Action and Political Parties." In N. Van Dyke and H. McCammon, eds., *Strategic Alliances: New Studies of Social Movement Coalitions*, 170–96. Minneapolis: University of Minnesota Press.

Almeida, Paul, and Allen Cordero, eds. 2014. *Handbook of Social Movements across Latin America*. New York: Springer.

Almeida Paul D., and Roxana Delgado. 2008. "Gendered Networks and Health Care Privatization." *Advances in Medical Sociology* 10:277–303.

Almeida, Paul D., and Hank Johnston. 2006. "Neoliberal Globalization and Popular Movements in Latin America." In Johnston and Almeida (2006), 3–18.

Almeida, Paul, and Linda Brewster Stearns. 1998. "Political Opportunities and Local Grassroots Environmental Movements: The Case of Minamata." *Social Problems* 48(1): 37–60.

Almeida, Paul D., and Erica Walker. 2007. "El avance de la globalización neoliberal: una comparación de tres campañas de movimientos populares en Centroamérica." *Revista centroamericana de ciencias sociales* 4(1): 51–76.

Alvarado, Raúl. 2001. "Las jornadas de ALCOA." *Revista herencia* 13(1): 117–27.

Alvarenga Venutolo, Patricia. 2005. *De vecinos a ciudadanos: movimientos comunales y luchas cívicas en la historia contemporánea de Costa Rica*. San José: Editorial de la Universidad de Costa Rica.

Amenta, Edwin, and Michael Young. 1999. "Democratic States and Social Movements: Theoretical Arguments and Hypotheses." *Social Problems* 46(2): 153–68.

Aminzade, Ronald. 1995. "Between Movement and Party: The Transformation of Mid-Nineteenth-Century French Republicanism." In Jenkins and Klandermans (1995b), 39–62.

Anderson, Leslie, and Lawrence Dodd. 2005. *Learning Democracy: Citizen Engagement and Electoral Choice in Nicaragua, 1990–2001*. Chicago: University of Chicago Press.

Andrews, Kenneth. 2004. *The Freedom Is a Constant Struggle: The Mississippi Civil Rights Movement and Its Legacy*. Chicago: University of Chicago Press.

Andrews, Kenneth, and Michael Biggs. 2006. "The Dynamics of Protest Diffusion: Movement Organizations, Social Networks, and News Media in the 1960 Sit-Ins." *American Sociological Review* 71:752–77.

Anner, Mark. 1996. "¿Hacia la sindicalización de los sindicatos?" *Estudios centroamericanos* 573–74:599–614.

————. 2011. *Solidarity Transformed: Labor Responses to Globalization and Crises in Latin America*. Ithaca, NY: Cornell University Press.

Arce, Moises. 2008. "The Repoliticization of Collective Action after Neoliberalism in Peru." *Latin American Politics and Society* 50(3): 37–62.

Arce, Moises, and Paul T. Bellinger Jr. 2007. "Low-Intensity Democracy Revisited: The Effects of Economic Liberalization on Political Activity in Latin America." *World Politics* 60:97–121.

Ardón Mejía, Mario. 2005. *El agua como derecho humano y efectos de la privatización en Honduras*. Tegucigalpa: Brot für die Welt.

Arévalo Solórzano, Oscar. 2002. "Análisis político, constitucional y criminológico del cierre de vías públicas como mecanismo de protesta social." Bachelor's thesis, School of Law, Universidad de Costa Rica.

Artiga-González, Alvaró. 2004. *Elitismo competitivo: dos décadas de elecciones en El Salvador (1982–2003)*. San Salvador: UCA Editores.

Auvinen, Juha. 1996. "IMF Intervention and Political Protest in the Third World: A Conventional Wisdom Refined." *Third World Quarterly* 17(3): 377–400.

Auyero, Javier. 2001. "Glocal Riots." *International Sociology* 16(1): 33–53.

———. 2002. *La protesta: retratos de la beligerancia popular en la Argentina democrática*. Buenos Aires: Libros del Rojas (Universidad de Buenos Aires).

———. 2006. "The Moral Politics of Argentine Crowds." In Johnston and Almeida (2006), 147–62.

Babb, Sarah. 2005. "The Social Consequences of Structural Adjustment: Recent Evidence and Current Debates." *Annual Review of Sociology* 31:199–222.

Babones, Salvatore. 2006. "Conducting Global Social Research." In Chase-Dunn and Babones (2006), 8–30.

Baker, Andy. 2009. *The Market and the Masses in Latin America: Policy Reform and Consumption in Liberalizing Economies*. Cambridge: Cambridge University Press.

———. 2014. *Shaping the Developing World: The West, the South, and the Natural World*. Los Angeles: Sage.

Barahona Mejía, Blas Enrique. 2008. "Impacto de las reformas educativas en el movimiento magisterial hondureño." Master's thesis, FLACSO Programa Centroamericano de Postgrado, Guatemala City, Guatemala.

Barrios Jackman, Mariana, and Sonia Wheelock Díaz. 2005. *Movilización social y gestión del agua en Nicaragua*. Managua: RIMISP.

Becker, Mark. 2011. *¡Pachakutik!: Indigenous Movements and Electoral Politics in Ecuador*. Lanham, MD: Rowman & Littlefield.

Beissinger, Mark. 1999. "Event Analysis in Transitional Societies: Protest Mobilization in the Former Soviet Union." In D. Rucht, R. Koopmans, and F. Neidhardt, eds., *Acts of Dissent: New Developments in the Study of Protest*, 284–316. Lanham, MD: Rowman & Littlefield.

———. 2001. *Nationalist Mobilization and the Collapse of the Soviet State: A Tidal Approach to the Study of Nationalism*. Cambridge: Cambridge University Press.

Beluche, Giovanni. 2014. "Panama: Worker, Indigenous, and Popular Uprising in Bocas del Toro." In Almeida and Cordero (2014).

Beluche, Olmedo. 1990. *La FENASEP en el corazón del pueblo panameño*. Mexico City: Editorial Combatiente.

———. 1994. *Diez años de luchas políticas y sociales en Panamá (1980–1990)*. Panama City: CELA.

Bob, Clifford. 2005. *The Marketing of Rebellion: Insurgents, Media, and International Activism*. New York: Cambridge University Press.

Booth, John. 1985. *The End and the Beginning: The Nicaraguan Revolution*. 2nd ed. Boulder, CO: Westview Press.

Booth, John, and Mitchell Seligson. 2009. *The Legitimacy Puzzle in Latin America: Political Support and Democracy in Eight Nations*. New York: Cambridge University Press.

Borchgrevink, Axel. 2006. *A Study of Civil Society in Nicaragua*. Oslo: Norwegian Institute of International Affairs.

Boudreau, Vincent. 1996. "Northern Theory, Southern Protest: Opportunity Structure Analysis in a Cross-National Perspective." *Mobilization* 1:175–89.

Bradshaw, York W., and Mark J. Schafer. 2000. "Urbanization and Development: The Emergence of International Non-Government Organizations amid Declining States." *Sociological Perspectives* 43:97–116.

Brett, Roddy. 2008. *Social Movements, Indigenous Politics, and Democratization in Guatemala, 1985–1996.* Leiden: Brill.

Briceño Jimenez, Roberto. 2010. "Honduras: la dictadura de un bloque de clases y el movimiento de resistencia popular." In I. Medina Nuñez, ed., *Centroamérica: democracia, militarismo, y conflictos sociales en el siglo XXI*, 172–93. Buenos Aires: Bibliografika de Voros.

Broadbent, Jeffrey, and V. Broackman, eds. 2011. *East Asian Social Movements: Power, Protest, and Change in a Dynamic Region.* New York: Springer.

Brockett, Charles. 1998. *Land, Power, and Poverty: Agrarian Transformation and Political Conflict in Central America.* 2nd ed. Boulder, CO: Westview Press.

———. 2005. *Political Movements and Violence in Central America.* Cambridge: Cambridge University Press.

Browning, David. 1971. *El Salvador: Landscape and Society.* Oxford: Clarendon Press.

Buhlungu, Sakhela. 2006. "Upstarts or Bearers of Tradition? The Anti-Privatisation Forum of Gauteng." In R. Ballard, A. Habib, and I. Valodia, eds., *Voices of Protest: Social Movements in Post-Apartheid South Africa*, 67–87. Scottsville, South Africa: University of KwaZulu-Natal Press.

Bull, Benedicte. 2008. *Globalización, estado y privatización: proceso político de las reformas de telecomunicaciones en Centroamérica.* San José, Costa Rica: FLACSO.

Bulmer-Thomas, Victor. 1987. *The Political Economy of Central America since 1920.* Cambridge: Cambridge University Press.

Burell, Jennifer, and Ellen Moodie, eds. 2013. *Central America in the New Millennium: Living Transition and Reimagining Democracy.* New York: Berghahn.

Bush, Ray. 2010. "Food Riots: Poverty, Power and Protest." *Journal of Agrarian Change* 10(1): 119–29.

Calvo Coin, Luis Alberto. 1995. "La política económica neoliberal o neoclásica actual y su aplicación en Costa Rica." *Ciencias sociales* 70:111–21.

Cambra, José. 1994. "Panamá: La búsqueda de una propuesta económica alternativa en un país ocupado." *Revista de Ciencias Sociales* 63: 49–62.

Cardona, Mirna. 2009. "El Salvador: Repression in the Name of Anti-Terrorism." *Cornell International Law Journal* 42:129–55.

Castro Valverde, Carlos. 1995. "Sector público y ajuste estructural en Costa Rica (1983–1992)." In Trevor Evans, ed., *La transformación neoliberal del sector público*, 48–107. Managua: CRIES.

Cedeño Castro, Rogelio. 1996. "La huelga magisterial de Julio–Agosto de 1995: los trabajadores en lucha contra la exclusión y el hambre." *Revista abra* 21–22: 113–26.

Centeno, Miguel, and Joseph Cohen. 2010. *Global Capitalism: A Sociological Perspective.* Cambridge: Polity.

Centro de Competencia en Comunicación para América Latina. 2007. *Se nos rompió el amor: Elecciones y medios de comunicación en América Latina.* Bogotá: Fundación Friedrich Ebert Stiftung.

Centro de Documentación de Honduras. 1991. "Las huelgas de Mayo." *Boletín informativo* 121:9.

———. 1992a. "Todos y nadie contra el ajuste estructural." *Puntos de vista* 6:21–33.

———. 1992b. "Nace la CUTH." *Boletín informativo Honduras* (May): 15.

Cerdas-Cruz, Rodolfo. 1993. *The Communist International in Central America, 1920–1935.* Hampshire, UK: Macmillan.

Chacón Calderón, Iván Gerbacio, Rodil Antonio Iraheta Fuentes, and Esmeralda Arely Villeda. 2008. "Movimiento popular de resistencia doce de Octubre en El Salvador contra las políticas neoliberales y propuestas de lucha hacia la transformación (2003–2007)." Bachelor's thesis, Department of Sociology, University of El Salvador.

Chalmers, Douglas A., Scott B. Martin, and Kerianne Piester. 1997. "Associative Networks: New Structures of Representation for the Popular Sectors?" In Douglas Chalmers et al., eds., *The New Politics of Inequality in Latin America: Rethinking Participation and Representation*, 543–82. Oxford: Oxford University Press.

Chase-Dunn, Christopher. 2006. "Globalization: A World System Perspective." In Chase-Dunn and Babones (2006), 79–105.

Chase-Dunn, Christopher, Nelson Amaro, and Susanne Jonas, eds. 2001 *Globalization on the Ground: Postbellum Guatemalan Democracy and Development*. Lanham, MD: Rowman & Littlefield.

Chase-Dunn, Christopher, and Salvatore J. Babones, eds. 2006. *Global Social Change: Historical and Comparative Perspectives*. Baltimore: Johns Hopkins University Press.

Chen, Xi. 2012. *Social Protest and Contentious Authoritarianism in China*. Cambridge: Cambridge University Press.

Ching, Erik. 2014. *Authoritarian El Salvador: Politics and the Origins of the Military Regimes, 1880–1940*. Notre Dame, IN: University of Notre Dame Press.

Chomsky, Aviva. 1996. *West Indian Workers and the United Fruit Company in Costa Rica, 1870–1940*. Baton Rouge: Louisiana State University Press.

Chong, Alberto, and Florencio López de Silanes. 2005. "The Truth about Privatization in Latin America." In *Privatization in Latin America: Myths and Realities*, 1–65. Stanford: Stanford University Press.

CID/Gallup. 2004. "National Public Opinion Survey: Guatemala #41." Consultoría Interdisciplinaria en Desarrollo, Guatemala City. http://cidgallup.com/Documentos/OP Gua41eng.pdf.

Cohn, Samuel. 2012. *Employment and Development under Globalization: State and Economy in Brazil*. London: Palgrave.

Colegio Médico de El Salvador. 2002. "ENADE 2002: ofensiva privatizadora de la salud de ANEP y ARENA." *Boletín colmed* 4:1–2.

Comisión de Verdad. 2012. *Informe de la Comisión de Verdad: la voz mas autorizada es la de las victimas*. Tegucigalpa: Comisión de Verdad.

Comité Cívico de Lucha. 2000. "Comunicado de prensa no. 1." News bulletin (Mar. 27). Comité Cívico de Lucha en Pro del ICE, Turrialba.

Consejo Nacional de Rectores. 1978. *Estadistica de la Educación Superior 1978*. San José, Costa Rica: Oficina de Planificación de la Educación Superior.

Contreras, Gerardo. 2009. "Arnoldo Ferreto segura y el Partido Comunista de Costa Rica en la lucha por la segunda y auténtica independencia nacional." *Revista estudios* 22, www.estudiosgenerales.ucr.ac.cr/estudios/n022/papers/iisec1.html.

Cook, María Elena. 1996. *Organizing Dissent: Unions, the State, and the Democratic Teachers' Movement in Mexico*. University Park: Pennsylvania State University Press
———. 2006. *The Politics of Labor Reform in Latin America*. University Park: Pennsylvania State University Press.

Cordero, Allen. 2005. "Clases medias y movimientos sociales en Costa Rica." *Revista de ciencias sociales* 3–4 (109–10): 157–66.
———. 2014. "Forest, Water, and Struggle: Environmental Movements in Costa Rica." In Almeida and Cordero (2014).

Cress, Daniel, and David Snow. 2000. "The Outcomes of Homeless Mobilization: The Influence of Organization, Political Mediation, and Framing." *American Journal of Sociology* 105:1063–104.

Cruz, Miguel. 2011. "Government Responses and the Dark Side of Gang Suppression in Central America." In Tom Bruneau, Lucia Dammert, and Elizabeth Skinner, eds., *Government Responses and the Dark Side of Gang Suppression in Central America*, chap. 7. Austin: University of Texas Press.

Diani, Mario. 2003. "'Leaders' or Brokers? Positions and Influence in Social Movement Networks." In M. Diani and D. McAdam, eds., *Social Movements and Networks: Relational Approaches to Collective Action*, 105–22. Oxford: Oxford University Press.

Díaz Arias, David. 2009. "Social Crises and Struggling Memories: Populism, Popular Mobilization, Violence, and Memories of Civil War in Costa Rica, 1940–1948." Ph.D. thesis, Department of History, Indiana University.

Dobles Oropeza, Ignacio, 1995. "La huelga del magisterio." *Cuadernos sindicales* 1(2): 1–8.

Dougherty, Michael. 2011. "The Global Gold Mining Industry, Junior Firms, and Civil Society Resistance in Guatemala." *Bulletin of Latin American Research* 30(4): 403–18.

Drori, Gili, John Meyer, and Hokyu Hwang. 2006. Introduction. *Globalization and Organization*, 1–22. Oxford: Oxford University Press.

Dunkerley, James. 1994. *The Pacification of Central America: Political Change in the Isthmus, 1987–1993*. London: Verso.

Dwyer, Peter, and Louis Zeilig. 2012. *African Struggles Today: Social Movements since Independence*. Chicago: Haymarket Books.

Earl, Jennifer. 2011. "Political Repression: Iron Fists, Velvet Gloves, and Diffuse Control." *Annual Review of Sociology* 37:261–84.

Eckstein, Susan, and Timothy Wickham-Crowley, eds. 2003. *What Justice? Whose Justice? Fighting for Fairness in Latin America*. Berkeley: University of California Press.

Edelman, Marc. 1999. *Peasants against Globalization*. Stanford, CA: Stanford University Press.

Edwards, Bob, and John D. McCarthy. 2004. "Resources and Social Movement Mobilization." In D. Snow, S. Soule, and H. Kriesi, eds., *The Blackwell Companion to Social Movements*, 116–52. Oxford: Blackwell.

El Salvador Information Project. 1994. Privatization report no. 1 (mimeograph).

ENACAL. 2009. *Plan de desarrollo institucional ENACAL, 2008–2012*. Managua: ENACAL. Available at www.enacal.com.ni/informacion/Wc89973b236e289.htm.

Enríquez, Laura. 2000. "The Varying Impact of Structural Adjustment on Nicaragua's Small Farmers." *Revista europea de estudios latinoamericanos y del Caribe* 69:47–68.

———. 2010. *Reactions to the Market: Small Farmers in the Economic Reshaping of Nicaragua, Cuba, Russia, and China*. University Park: Pennsylvania State University Press.

Enríquez, Laura, and Rose Spalding. 1987. "Banking Systems and Revolutionary Change: The Politics of Agricultural Credit in Nicaragua." In Rose J. Spalding, ed., *The Political Economy of Revolutionary Nicaragua*. Winchester, MA: Allen & Unwin.

Evans, Peter, and William Sewell. 2013. "Neoliberalism: Policy Regimes, International Regimes, and Social Effects." In P. Hall and M. Lamont, eds., *Social Resilience in the Neoliberal Era*, 35–68. Cambridge: Cambridge University Press.

Everingham, Mark. 1998. "Neo-liberalism in a New Democracy: Elite Politics and State Reform in Nicaragua." *Journal of Developing Areas* 32(2): 237–64.

———. 2001. "Agricultural Property Rights and Political Change in Nicaragua." *Latin American Politics and Society* 43(3): 61–93.

Figueroa Ibarra, Carlos. 1991. *El Recurso del Miedo: Ensayo sobre el estado y el terror en Guatemala*. San José, CA: EDUCA.

———. 1999. "Paz, neoliberalismo y protesta popular en Guatemala." In M. López Maya, ed., *Lucha popular, democracia, neoliberalismo: protesta popular en América Latina en los años de ajuste*, 129–48. Caracas: Nueva Sociedad.

———. 2004. "Protesta popular y cooptación de masas en Guatemala." *Revista venezolana de economía y ciencias sociales* 10(1): 129–53.

Flores Macías, Gustavo. 2012. *After Neoliberalism? The Left and Economic Reforms in Latin America*. Oxford: Oxford University Press.

Fonseca, Marco. 2003. "Between Reconstruction and Globalization: Civil Society and Democratic Politics in Guatemala." Paper presented at the Latin American Studies Association Meetings, Dallas, TX (Mar.).

Foran, John. 2005. *Taking Power: On the Origins of Third World Revolutions*. Cambridge: Cambridge University Press.

Fourcade-Gourinchas, Marion, and Sarah L. Babb. 2002. "The Rebirth of the Liberal Creed: Paths to Neoliberalism in Four Countries." *American Journal of Sociology* 108(3): 533–79.

Frank, Dana. 2010. "Out of the Past, a New Honduran Culture of Resistance." NACLA *Report on the Americas* 43(3): 6–10.

Freije Rodríguez, Samuel, and Luis Rivas. 2005. "Inequality and Welfare Changes: Evidence from Nicaragua." In John Nellis and Nancy Birdsall, eds., *Reality Check: The Distributional Impact of Privatization in Developing Countries*, 85–122. Washington, DC: Center for Global Development.

Gandásegui, Marco A. 1998. *La democracia en Panamá*. 2nd ed. Panama City: CELA.

———. 2002. "Panamá 2001: las protestas contra la política neoliberal definen las luchas sociales. *OSAL* 2:133–37.

———. 2003. "La batalla por la seguridad social domina los movimientos sociales en Panamá durante el 2003." *OSAL* 4:193–204.

———. 2005. "Panamá 2005: movilización popular en defensa de la seguridad social." *OSAL* 6:201–11.

———. 2011. "Panamá: la batalla de Changuinola y la política de seguridad de Martinelli." *OSAL* 13:179–83.

Ganz, Marshall. 2009. *Why David Sometimes Wins: Leadership, Organization, and Strategy in the California Farm Worker Movement*. Oxford: Oxford University Press.

García Quesada, and George Iván. 2011. "Formación de la Clase Media en Costa Rica: Economía, Sociabilidades y Discursos Políticos (1890–1950)." Master's thesis, Universidad de Costa Rica.

Garrard-Burnett, Virginia. 2010. *Terror in the Land of the Holy Spirit: Guatemala under General Efrain Rios Montt 1982–1983*. Oxford: Oxford University Press.

Garst, Rachel. 1985. "Guatemalan Unrest Shakes Faith in Plan for Democratic Rule." *Globe and Mail*, Sept. 12.

Goldstone, Jack. 2003. "Bridging Institutionalized and Noninstitutionalized Politics." In J. Goldstone, ed., *States, Parties, and Social Movements*, 1–24. Cambridge: Cambridge University Press.

———. 2011. "Understanding the Revolutions of 2011: Weakness and Resilience in Middle Eastern Autocracies." *Foreign Affairs* 90(3): 8–16.

Goldstone, Jack, and Charles Tilly. 2001. "Threat (and Opportunity): Popular Action and State Response in the Dynamic of Contentious Action." In R. Aminzade et al., eds.,

Silence and Voice in the Study of Contentious Politics, 179–94. Cambridge: Cambridge University Press.

Gould, Jefferey, and Lauria-Santiago Aldo. 2008. *To Rise in Darkness: Revolution, Repression, and Memory in El Salvador, 1920–1932.* Durham, NC: Duke University Press.

Grandin, Greg. 2004. *The Last Colonial Massacre: Latin America in the Cold War.* Chicago: University of Chicago Press.

Green, Duncan. 2003. *Silent Revolution: The Rise and Crisis of Market Economics in Latin America.* 2nd ed. London: Latin American Bureau.

Grigsby, William. 2005. "¿Por qué hay tan poca movilización social?" *Revista envío* 280, www.envio.org.ni/articulo/2980.

Gutiérrez, Ana Lucía, Ciska Raventós, and Carlos Sandoval. 1996. *Voces de la huelga.* Ciudad Rodrigo Facio, Costa Rica: Instituto de Investigaciones Sociales.

Haglund, La Dawn. 2010. *Limiting Resources: Market-Led Reform and the Transformation of Public Goods.* University Park: Pennsylvania State University Press.

Hagopian, Frances, and Scott Mainwaring, eds. 2005. *The Third Wave of Democratization in Latin America: Advances and Setbacks.* Cambridge: Cambridge University Press.

Hall, Peter A., and Michèle Lamont. 2013. Introduction. *Social Resilience in the Neoliberal Era*, 1–31. Cambridge: Cambridge University Press.

Harvey, David. 2005. *A Brief History of Neoliberalism.* Oxford: Oxford University Press.

Hernández, Alcides.1992. *Del reformismo al ajuste estructural.* Tegucigalpa: Editorial Guaymuras.

Herrera, Mauricio. 1995. "Crece pugna por huelga." *La nación*, July 19, 1995.

Hipsher, Patricia. 1996. "Democratization and the Decline of Urban Social Movements in Chile and Spain." *Comparative Politics* 28(3): 273–97.

Horton, Lynn. 1998. *Peasants in Arms: War and Peace in the Mountains of Nicaragua, 1979–1994.* Athens: Ohio University Press.

———. 2007. *Grassroots Struggles for Sustainability in Central America.* Boulder: University of Colorado Press.

———. 2013. "From Collectivism to Capitalism: Neoliberalism and Rural Mobilization in Nicaragua." *Latin American Politics and Society* 55(1): 119–40.

Huber, Evelyne, and John Stephens. *Democracy and the Left: Policy and Inequality in Latin America.* Chicago: University of Chicago Press.

Human Rights Everywhere. 2011. "Preliminary Report on Human Rights Violations during the Days of Protest against Mining Reform in Panama, January to March 2011." Human Rights Everywhere, Panama City. Available at www.hrev.org/wp-content/uploads/2011/03/HREV-HHRRreport-ENG.pdf.

Huntington, Samuel P. 1991. *The Third Wave: Democratization in the Late Twentieth Century.* Norman: University of Oklahoma Press.

Inclán, María de la Luz. 2008. "From the ¡*Ya Basta!* to the *Caracoles*: Zapatista Mobilization under Transitional Conditions." *American Journal of Sociology* 113(5): 1316–50.

———. 2009. "Repressive Threats, Procedural Concessions, and the Zapatista Cycle of Protests, 1994–2003." *Journal of Conflict Resolution* 53(5): 794–819.

Inclán, María de la Luz, and Paul D. Almeida. 2013. "Indigenous Peoples and Revolutionary Movements in Mesoamerica." In D. L. Van Cott, A. Lucero, and T. Dale eds., *Oxford Handbook of Indigenous People's Politics.* Oxford: Oxford University Press

Iraheta, Alma Yanira, and Gilda Xiomara Soriano López. 1999. "El neoliberalismo y su aplicación al proceso de privatización de las telecomunicaciones en El Salvador

(1995–1997) (Caso ANTEL)." Thesis in International Relations, University of El Salvador.

Jenkins, J. Craig. 1995. "Social Movements, Political Representation, and the State: An Agenda and Comparative Framework." In Jenkins and Klandermans (1995b), 14–35.

Jenkins, J. Craig, and Bert Klandermans. 1995a. "The Politics of Social Protest." In Jenkins and Klandermans (1995b), 3–13.

———, eds. 1995b. *The Politics of Social Protest: Comparative Perspectives on States and Social Movements*. Minneapolis: University of Minnesota Press.

Jiménez Castro, Wilburg. 2000. *Préstamos y programas de ajuste estructural*. 2nd ed. San José, Costa Rica: Editorial Universidad Estatal a Distancia.

Johnston, Hank. 2011. *States and Social Movements*. London: Polity.

Johnston, Hank, and Paul Almeida, eds. 2006. *Latin American Social Movements: Globalization, Democratization, and Transnational Networks*. Lanham, MD: Rowman & Littlefield.

Johnston, Hank, Enrique Laraña, and Joseph Gusfield. 1994. "Identities, Grievances, and New Social Movements." In E. Laraña, H. Johnston, and J. Gusfield, eds., *New Social Movements: From Ideology to Identity*, 3–35. Philadelphia: Temple University Press.

Johnston, Jake, and Stephan Lefebvre. 2013. *Honduras since the Coup: Economic and Social Outcomes*. Washington DC: Center for Economic and Policy Research.

Jonas, Suzanne, and Christopher Chase-Dunn. 2001. "Guatemalan Development and Democratization: Past, Present, and Future." In C. Chase-Dunn, S. Jonas, and N. Amaro (2001), 3–8.

Kampwirth, Karen. 1997. "Social Policy." In T. W. Walker, ed., *Nicaragua without Illusions: Regime Transition and Structural Adjustment in the 1990s*, 115–30. Wilmington, DE: Scholarly Resources.

Kaufman, Robert, and Joan Nelson. 2004. Introduction. *Crucial Needs, Weak Incentives: Social Sector Reform, Democratization, and Globalization in Latin America*, 1–19. Baltimore: Johns Hopkins University Press.

Keck, Margaret. 1992. *The Workers: Party and Democratization in Brazil*. New Haven, CT: Yale University Press.

———. 2013. "Taking to the Streets." *Mobilizing Ideas* (Aug. 6), http://mobilizingideas .wordpress.com/2013/08/06/taking-to-the-streets/.

Kincaid, Douglas. 1987. "Agrarian Development, Peasant Mobilization and Social Change in Central America: A Comparative Study." Ph.D. thesis, Department of Sociology, Johns Hopkins University.

Klandermans, Bert. 1997. *The Social Psychology of Protest*. Oxford: Blackwell.

Kolb, Felix. 2007. *Protest and Opportunities: The Political Outcomes of Social Movement*. Frankfurt: Campus Verlag.

Kowalchuk, Lisa. 2011. "Mobilizing Resistance to Privatization: Communication Strategies of Salvadoran Health-Care Activists," *Social Movement Studies* 10(2): 151–73.

Kriesi, Hanspeter. 1995. "The Political Opportunity Structure of New Social Movements: Its Impact on Their Mobilization," in J. Craig Jenkins and Bert Klandermans, eds., *The Politics of Social Protest*, 167–98. Minneapolis: University of Minnesota Press.

Lee, Ching Kwan. 2007. *Against the Law: Labor Protests in China's Rustbelt and Sunbelt*. Berkeley: University of California Press.

Lehuoucq, Fabrice. 2012. *The Politics of Modern Central America.* New York: Cambridge University Press.

Levitsky, Steven, and Kenneth Roberts. 2011. "Introduction: Latin America's 'Left Turn': A Framework for Analysis," in *The Resurgence of the Latin American Left,* 1–30. Baltimore: Johns Hopkins University Press.

Lindo-Fuentes, Hector, and Erik Ching. 2012. *Modernizing Minds in El Salvador: Education Reform and the Cold War, 1960–1980.* Albuquerque: University of New Mexico Press.

Lindo-Fuentes, Hector, Erik Ching, and A. Lara-Martinez Rafael. 2007. *Remembering a Massacre in El Salvador: The Insurrection of 1932, Roque Dalton, and the Politics of Historical Memory.* Albuquerque: University of New Mexico Press.

Lobao, Linda, Gregory Hooks, and Ann Tickmayer. 2007. "Introduction: Advancing the Sociology of Spatial Inequality." In *The Sociology of Spatial Inequality,* 1–28. Albany: State University of New York Press.

López Maya, Margarita, ed. 1999. *Lucha popular, democracia, neoliberalismo: protesta popular en América Latina en los años de ajuste.* Caracas: Nueva Sociedad.

Luciak, Ilja. 2001. *After the Revolution: Gender and Democracy in El Salvador, Nicaragua, and Guatemala.* Baltimore: Johns Hopkins University Press.

Macdonald, Laura. 1997. *Supporting Civil Society: The Political Impact of Non-Governmental Assistance to Central America.* New York: St. Martin's.

Macdonald, Laura, and Arne Ruckert. 2009. "Post-Neoliberalism in the Americas: An Introduction." In *Post-Neoliberalism in the Americas,* 1–20. London: Palgrave.

Maguire, Diarmuid. 1995. "Opposition Movements and Opposition Parties." In Jenkins and Klandermans (1995b), 199–228.

Mahon, James E. 1996. *Mobile Capital and Latin American Development.* University Park: Pennsylvania State University Press.

———. 2004. "Causes of Tax Reform in Latin America, 1975–1995." *Latin America Research Review* 39(1): 3–30.

Mahoney, James. 2001. *The Legacies of Liberalism: Path Dependence and Political Regimes in Central America.* Baltimore: Johns Hopkins University Press.

Mann, Michael. 2013. *The Sources of Social Power, vol. 4: Globalizations, 1945–2011.* Cambridge: Cambridge University Press.

Markoff, John. 1996. *Waves of Democracy: Social Movements and Political Change.* Thousand Oaks, CA: Pine Forge Press.

———. 2006. "Globalization and the Future of Democracy." In Chase-Dunn and Babones (2006), 336–61.

Markoff, John, and Verónica Montecinos. 1993. "The Ubiquitous Rise of Economists." *Journal of Public Policy* 13(1): 37–68.

Martín Álvarez, Alberto. 2005. "Redes transnacionales y coaliciones para accion colectiva contra el tratado de libre comercio." *Estudios centroamericanos* 60(683): 827–41.

Martínez Peñate, Oscar, María Eugenia Ochoa, and Edgar Lara López. 2004. *El Salvador: mundo laboral y sindicatos.* 2nd ed. San Salvador: Fundación Friedrich Ebert.

Marti Puig, Salvador. 2011. "The FSLN and Sandinismo." In D. Close. S. Martí-Puig, and S. McConnell, eds., *The Sandinistas and Nicaragua since 1979,* 21–44. Boulder, CO: Lynne Rienner Publishers.

———. 2012. *La revolución enredada.* 2nd ed. Madrid: Los Libros de Catarata.

Mattson, Sean. 2010. "Panamanian President Ricardo Martinelli Reverses Course on Controversial Legislation." *Latin American Data Base,* Nov. 11.

McAdam, Doug. 1988. *Freedom Summer.* Oxford: Oxford University Press.

———. 1996. "Conceptual Origins, Current Problems, Future Directions." In D. Mc-Adam, J. D. McCarthy, and M. Zald, eds., *Comparative Perspectives on Social Movements: Political Opportunities, Mobilizing Structures, and Cultural Framings*, 23–40. Cambridge: Cambridge University Press.

———. 1999. *Political Process and the Development of Black Insurgency.* 2nd ed. Chicago: University of Chicago Press.

———. 2003. "Beyond Structural Analysis: Toward a More Dynamic Understanding of Social Movements." In Mario Diani and Doug McAdam, eds., *Social Movements and Networks: Relational Approaches to Collective Action*, 281–99. Oxford: Oxford University Press.

McAdam, Doug, Sidney G. Tarrow, and Charles Tilly. 2001. *Dynamics of Contention.* New York: Cambridge University Press.

McCammon, Holly. 2001. "Stirring Up Suffrage Sentiment: The Formation of the State Woman Suffrage Organizations, 1866–1914." *Social Forces* 80(2): 449–80.

———. 2003. "'Out of the Parlors and into the Streets': The Changing Tactical Repertoire of the U.S. Women's Suffrage Movement." *Social Forces* 81(3): 787–818.

McCammon, Holly, and Nella Van Dyke. 2010. "Applying Qualitative Comparative Analysis to Empirical Studies of Social Movement Coalition Formation." In N. Van Dyke and H. McCammon, eds., *Strategic Alliances: Coalition Building and Social Movements*, 292–315. Minneapolis: University of Minnesota Press.

McCarthy, John. 1987. "Pro-Life and Pro-Choice Mobilization: Infrastructure Deficits and New Technologies." In Mayer N. Zald and John D. McCarthy, eds., *Social Movements in an Organizational Society*, 49–66. New Brunswick, NJ: Transaction Books.

———. 1996. "Constraints and Opportunities in Adopting, Adapting, and Inventing." In D. McAdam, J. D. McCarthy, and M. Zald, eds., *Comparative Perspectives on Social Movements: Political Opportunities, Mobilizing Structures, and Cultural Framings*, 141–51. Cambridge: Cambridge University Press.

McMichael, Philip. 2012. *Development and Social Change: A Global Perspective.* 5th ed. Los Angeles: Sage.

Menjivar, Cecilia. 2000. *Fragmented Ties: Salvadoran Immigrant Networks in America.* Berkeley: University of California Press.

Menjívar Ochoa, Mauricio. 1999. "La otra sociedad civil: acción política magisterial entre la hegemonía y la alteridad." Master's thesis, Programa de Estudios de Posgrado en Ciencias Políticas, Universidad de Costa Rica, Rodrigo Facio.

Merino, José. 2000. *Informe de minoría.* San José, Costa Rica: Comisión Especial Mixta.

Mesa-Lago, Carmen. 2007. "Social Security in Latin America: Pension and Health Care Reforms in the Last Quarter Century." *Latin American Research Review* 42(2): 81–101.

Meyer, John W., John Boli, George M. Thomas, and Francisco O. Ramírez. 1997. "World Society and the Nation-State." *American Journal of Sociology* 103:144–81.

Meyer, John, Gili Drori, and Hokyu Hwang. 2006. "World Society and the Proliferation of Formal Organization." In G. Drori, J. Meyer, and H. Hwang, eds., *Globalization and Organization*, 25–49. Oxford: Oxford University Press.

Miller, Eugene. 1996. *A Holy Alliance? The Church and the Left in Costa Rica, 1932–1948.* Armonk, NY: M. E. Sharpe.

Ministerio de Economía (El Salvador). 2014. "Reduce el índice de pobreza al nivel más bajo en la historia reciente del país." *Noticias Ciudadano* (Feb. 11).

Ministerio de Fomento, Industria y Comercio. 2002. *Legislación sobre protección de los derechos del consumidor.* 2nd ed. Managua: Ministerio de Fomento, Industria & Comercio.

Modonesi, Massimo, and Julián Rebón, eds. 2011. *Una década en movimiento: luchas populares en América Latina en el amanecer del siglo XXI.* Buenos Aires: CLACSO/Prometeo Libros.

Molina, Ivan, and Steven Palmer. 2007. *Historia de Costa Rica.* San José, Costa Rica: Editorial Universidad de Costa Rica.

Molina Jiménez, Ivan. 1999. "El desempeño electoral del partido comunista de Costa Rica." *Revista parlamentaria* 7(1): 491–521.

Mora Solano, Sindy. 2011. "Las disputas por los sentidos de lo político en Costa Rica: hacia un balance de las luchas populares de la presente década." In Modonesi and Rebón (2011), 275–96.

Moreno, Ismael. 2002. "En el primer año de Maduro el agua encendió el fuego." *Envío* 249 (Dec.).

Morris, Aldon. 1984. *The Origins of the Civil Rights Movement: Black Communities Organizing for Change.* New York: Free Press.

Nepstad, Sharon Erickson. 2011. *Nonviolent Revolutions: Civil Resistance in the Late Twentieth Century.* New York: Oxford University Press.

O'Kane, Trish. 1990a. "El nuevo panorama sindical." *Pensamiento Propio* (Sept.): 34–37.

———.1990b. "Frenado la contrarevolución." *Pensamiento Propio* (Nov.–Dec.): 29–31.

———. 1995. "New Autonomy, New Struggle: Labor Unions in Nicaragua." In Minor Sinclair, ed., *The New Politics of Survival,* 183–207. New York: Monthly Review Press.

Ortiz, David, and Sergio Béjar. 2013. "Participation in IMF-Sponsored Economic Programs and Contentious Collective Action in Latin America, 1980–2007." *Conflict Management and Peace Science* 30(5): 492–515.

Oxhorn, Philip. 1996. "Surviving the Return to 'Normalcy': Social Movements, Democratic Consolidation, and Economic Restructuring." *International Review of Sociology* 6(1): 117–34.

Paige, Jeffery M. 1997. *Coffee and Power: Revolution and the Rise of Democracy in Central America.* Cambridge, MA: Harvard University Press.

Patel, Raj, and Philip McMichael. 2009. "A Political Economy of the Food Riot." *Review* 32(1): 9–35.

Peña Martínez, Judith. 1982. "El movimiento obrero en Costa Rica en los años de 1970–1978 y la coyuntura de la huelga del Instituto Costarricense de Electricidad." Bachelor's thesis, Department of History, Universidad de Costa Rica, San Pedro.

Pérez Baltodano, Andrés. 2012. "Political Culture." In D. Close, S. Martí-Puig, and S. McConnell, eds., *The Sandinistas and Nicaragua since 1979,* 65–90. Boulder, CO: Lynne Rienner Publishers.

Perla, Héctor, and Héctor Cruz-Feliciano. 2013. "The Twenty-First-Century Left in El Salvador and Nicaragua: Understanding Apparent Contradictions and Criticisms." *Latin American Perspectives* 40(3): 83–106.

Perla, Héctor, Marco Mojica, and Jared Bibler. 2013. "From Guerrillas to Government: The Continued Relevance of the Central American Left." In J. Webber and B. Carr, eds., *The New Latin American Left: Cracks in the Empire,* 327–56. Lanham, MD: Rowman & Littlefield.

Petras, James, and Henry Veltmeyer. 2005. *Social Movements and State Power: Argentina, Brazil, Bolivia, Ecuador*. London: Pluto Press.

Phillips Collazos, Sharon. 1991. *Labor and Politics in Panama: The Torrijos Years*. Boulder, CO: Westview Press.

Podobnik, Bruce. 2005. "Resistance to Globalization: Cycles and Trends in the Globalization Protest Movement." In B. Podobnik and T. Reifer, eds., *Transforming Globalization*, 51–68. Leiden: Brill.

Posas, Mario. 1993. "Ajuste: dos caras de la moneda." *Puntos de vista* 7:3–8.

———. 2003. *Situación actual y desafíos del movimiento popular hondureño*. Tegucigalpa: Fundación Friedrich Ebert.

———. 2011. "Actores sociales y procesos políticos en Honduras (1980–2005)." Unpublished MS.

Postero, Nancy. 2007. *Now We Are Citizens: Indigenous Politics in Postmulticultural Bolivia*. Stanford: Stanford University Press.

Priestley, George. 1986. *Military Government and Popular Participation in Panama: The Torrijos Regime, 1968–1975*. Boulder, CO: Westview Press.

Proyecto Estado de la Nación. 2000. *Estado de la nación en desarrollo humano sostenible*. Pavas, Costa Rica: Proyecto Estado de la Nación.

Quirós Víquez, Ana. 2005. *La situación del agua en Nicaragua*. Managua: Brot fur die Welt.

Quintero, Iván. 2003. *Panamá: movimiento obrero y neoliberalismo*. Panama City: CIDPA.

Ramírez Amador, Guadalupe, and Humberto Rojas Corrales. 1981. "Las huelgas en el seguro social." Bachelor's thesis, Facultad de Ciencias Sociales, Instituto de Estudios de Trabajo, Universidad Nacional, Heredia, Costa Rica.

Raventos, Ciska. 1995. *The Construction of an Order: Structural Adjustment in Costa Rica (1985–1995)*. Doctoral Thesis in Political and Social Science. New School for Social Research.

———. 2013. "'My Heart Says No': Political Experiences of the Struggle against CAFTA-DR in Costa Rica." In J. Burrell and E. Moodie, eds., *Central America in the New Millennium: Living Transition and Reimagining Democracy*, 80–95. New York: Berghahn.

Red Nacional de Consumidores. 2002. "Consumidores dispuestos a defender sus derechos." *Los consumidores en acción* 1(1): 1.

Reynolds, Louisa. 2012. "Panama's Indigenous Protestors Block Roads in Dispute to End Mineral Exploration on Their Lands; Clashes Leave One Dead." *Latin American Data Base*, Feb. 23.

Riquelme, Quintín. 2004. "Los conflictos sociales en el contexto de la democracia paraguaya." In J. Seoane, ed., *Movimientos sociales y conflicto en América Latina*, 55–72. Buenos Aires: CLACSO.

Roberts, Kenneth. 2008. "The Mobilization of Opposition to Economic Liberalization." *Annual Review of Political Science* 11:327–49.

———. 2014. *Changing Course: Party Systems in Latin America's Neoliberal Era*. Cambridge: Cambridge University Press.

Robinson, Kevin. 1995. "Panama: Construction and Banana Workers Lead One-day Strike against Reforms in Labor Code." *Latin American Data Base*, June 1.

Robinson, William I. 1996. *Promoting Polyarchy: Globalization, U.S. Intervention, and Hegemony*. Cambridge: Cambridge University Press.

———. 2003. *Transnational Conflicts: Central America, Social Change, and Globalization*. London: Verso.

————. 2004. *A Theory of Global Capitalism*. Baltimore: Johns Hopkins University Press.

————. 2008. *Latin America and Global Capitalism: A Critical Globalization Perspective*. Baltimore: Johns Hopkins University Press.

Rocha, José Luis. 1998. "En la muerte del BANDES (R.I.P.)." *Envío* 192: 15–24.

Rodríguez Molina, María Elena. 2000. "Protesta social y pacto Figueres-Calderón: modalidades discursivas sobre la huelga de educadores en los diarios La nación y La república." Presented at the V Congreso Centroamericano de Historia, San Salvador, El Salvador (July).

Rojas Bolaños, Manuel. 1978. "El desarrollo del movimiento obrero en Costa Rica: un intento de periodización." *Ciencias sociales* 15–16:13–31.

————. 1997. "Costa Rica: fuegos electorales y estancamiento." *Nueva sociedad* 149:16–19.

Romano, Luis Ernesto. 1996. "La privatización de ANTEL y la modernización del estado." *Estudios centroamericanos* 51(5): 484–87.

Romano, Sarah. 2012. "From Protest to Proposal: The Contentious Politics of the Nicaraguan Anti-Water Privatisation Social Movement." *Bulletin of Latin American Research* 31(4): 499–514.

Rucht, Dieter, and Friedhelm Neidhardt. 1999. "Methodological Issues in Collecting Protest Event Data." In D. Rucht, R. Koopmans, and F. Neidhardt, eds., *Acts of Dissent: New Developments in the Study of Protest*, 65–89. Lanham, MD: Rowman & Littlefield.

Ruhl, J. Mark. 2000. "Honduras: Militarism and Democratization in Troubled Waters." In T. Walker and A. Armony, eds., *Repression, Resistance, and Democratic Transition in Central America*, 47–66. Wilmington, DE: Scholarly Resources.

————. 2010. "Honduras Unravels." *Journal of Democracy* 21(2): 93–107.

Salom, Roberto. 1987. *La crisis de la izquierda en Costa Rica*. San José, Costa Rica: Editorial Porvenir.

Sampson, Robert J., Doug McAdam, Heather MacIndoe, and Simón Weffer-Elizondo. 2005. "Civil Society Reconsidered: The Durable Nature and Community Structure of Collective Civic Action." *American Journal of Sociology* 111(3): 673–714.

Sandoval, Miguel Ángel. 2004. "Balance de un paro nacional." *ALAI, América Latina en movimiento*, June 11.

Sandoval, Salvador. 2001. "The Crisis of the Brazilian Labor Movement and the Emergence of Alternative Forms of Working-Class Contention in the 1990s." *Revista psicología política* 1(1): 173–95.

Sandoval Coto, Manuel 1995. "Las lecciones de la huelga de los educadores." *ABRA* 21–22:127–39.

Sassen, Saskia. 2007. *A Sociology of Globalization*. New York: W. W. Norton.

————. 2008. *Territory, Authority, Rights: From Medieval to Global Assemblages*. 2nd ed. Princeton, NJ: Princeton University Press.

Schock, Kurt. 2005. *Unarmed Insurrections: People Power Movements in Nondemocracies*. Minneapolis: University of Minnesota Press.

Schofer, Evan, and John W. Meyer. 2005. "The World-Wide Expansion of Higher Education in the Twentieth Century." *American Sociological Review* 70(6): 898–920.

Schuld, Leslie. 2003. "El Salvador: Who Will Have the Hospitals?" *NACLA Report on the Americas* 36(4): 42–45.

Segovia, Alexander. 2002. *Transformación estructural y reforma económica en El Salvador*. Guatemala City: F & G Editores.

Segura Ballar, Ricardo, and Jorge Coronado Marroquín. 2008. *El Movimiento Social Contra El Tratado De Libre Comercio.* San José, CA: Comisión Nacional de Enlace.

Segura-Ubiergo, Alex. 2007. *The Political Economy of Welfare States in Latin America: Globalization, Democracy, and Development.* Cambridge: Cambridge University Press.

Seligson, Mitchell. 1980. *Peasants of Costa Rica and the Development of Agrarian Capitalism.* Madison: University of Wisconsin Press.

Seligson, Mitchell, and Vincent McElhinny. 1996. "Low Intensity Warfare, High Intensity Death: The Demographic Impact of the Wars in El Salvador and Nicaragua." *Canadian Journal of Latin American and Caribbean Studies* 21:211–41.

Seligson, Mitchell, and Edward Muller. 1987. "Democratic Stability and Economic Crisis: Costa Rica, 1978–1983." *International Studies Quarterly* 31:301–26.

Serra, Luis. 1985. "The Grass-Roots Organizations." In T. Walker, ed., *Nicaragua: The First Five Years*, 91–118. New York: Praeger.

———. 1991. "The Grass-Roots Organizations." In T. Walker, ed., *Revolution and Counter-Revolution in Nicaragua*, 49–75. Boulder: Westview Press.

———. 2006. "Las luchas sociales en Nicaragua en el contexto electoral." OSAL 20: 225–35.

Shefner, Jon, George Pasdirtz, and Cory Blad. 2006. "Austerity Protests and Immiserating Growth in Mexico and Argentina." In H. Johnston and P. Almeida, eds. *Latin American Social Movements: Globalization, Democratization, and Transnational Networks*, 19–42. Lanham, MD: Rowman & Littlefield.

Sibaja Barrante, Emel. 1983. "Ideologia y protesta popular: la huelga bananera de 1934 en Costa Rica." Bachelor's thesis, Department of History, Universidad Nacional Autónoma, Heredia, Costa Rica.

Silber, Irina Carlota. 2011. *Everyday Revolutionaries: Gender, Violence, and Disillusionment in Postwar El Salvador.* New Brunswick, NJ: Rutgers University Press.

Silva, Eduardo. 2009. *Challenges to Neoliberalism in Latin America.* Cambridge: Cambridge University Press.

———, ed. 2013. *Transnational Activism and National Movements in Latin America: Bridging the Divide.* New York: Routledge.

Silver, Beverly. 2003. *Forces of Labor: Workers' Movements and Globalization since 1870.* Cambridge: Cambridge University Press.

Sklair, Leslie. 2006. "Competing Conceptions of Globalization." In Chase-Dunn and Babones (2006), 59–78.

Smith, Jackie. 2008. *Social Movements for Global Democracy.* Baltimore: Johns Hopkins University Press.

Smith, Jackie, and Dawn Wiest. 2012. *Social Movements in the World System: The Politics of Crisis and Transformation.* New York: Russell Sage Foundation.

Smith-Nonini, Sandy. 2010. *Healing the Body Politic: El Salvador's Popular Struggle for Health Rights from Civil War to Neoliberal Peace.* New Brunswick, NJ: Rutgers University Press.

Snow, David, and Danny Trom. 2002. "Case Study and the Study of Social Movements." In B. Klandermans and S. Staggenborg, eds., *Methods of Social Movement Research*, 146–72. Minneapolis: University of Minnesota Press.

Snow, David, Sarah Soule, and Hanspeter Kriesi. 2004. "Mapping the Terrain." In *The Blackwell Companion to Social Movements*, 3–16. Oxford: Blackwell.

Snow, David, and Sarah Soule. 2009. *A Primer on Social Movements.* New York: W. W. Norton.

Solis, Manuel Antonio. 2002. "Entre el cambio y la tradición: el fracaso de la privatización de la energía y las telecomunicaciones en Costa Rica." *Ciencias sociales* 95(1): 33–47.

Sosa, Eugenio. 2010. *La protesta social en Honduras: del ajuste al golpe de estado.* Tegucigalpa: Editorial Guaymuras.

———. 2012. "La protesta social en Honduras, 1990–2005." Master's thesis, FLACSO, Guatemala City.

Sosa, Eugenio, and Ana Ortega. 2008. *Ciudadanía emergente: la experiencia del patronato regional de occidente.* Tegucigalpa: Guaymuras.

Spalding, Rose. 2007. "Civil Society Engagement in Trade Negotiations: CAFTA Opposition Movements in El Salvador." *Latin American Politics and Society* 49(4): 85–114.

Spence, Jack, Mike Lanchin, and Geoff Thale. 2001. *From Elections to Earthquakes: Reform and Participation in Post-War El Salvador.* Cambridge, MA: Hemisphere Initiatives.

Stahler-Sholk, Richard. 1990. "Stabilization, Destabilization, and the Popular Classes in Nicaragua, 1979–1988." *Latin American Research Review* 25(3): 55–88.

———. 1994. "El ajuste neoliberal y sus opciones: la respuesta del movimiento sindical nicaragüense." *Revista mexicana de sociología* 56(3): 59–88.

———. 1995. "The Dog That Didn't Bark: Labor Autonomy and Economic Adjustment in Nicaragua under the Sandinista and UNO Governments." *Comparative Politics* 28(1): 77–102.

———. 1997. "Structural Adjustment and Resistance: The Political Economy of Nicaragua under Chamorro." In Gary Prevost and Harry E. Vanden, eds., *The Undermining of the Sandinista Revolution*, 74–113. London: Macmillan; New York: St. Martin's.

Stahler-Sholk, Richard, Harry E. Vanden, and Glen David Kuecker, eds. 2008. *Latin American Social Movements in the Twenty-first Century: Resistance, Power, and Democracy.* Lanham, MD: Rowman & Littlefield.

Stanley, William. 1996. *The Protection Racket State: Elite Politics, Military Extortion, and Civil War in El Salvador.* Philadelphia: Temple University Press.

Stearns, Linda Brewster, and Paul D. Almeida. 2004. "The Formation of State Actor-Social Movement Coalitions and Favorable Policy Outcomes." *Social Problems* 51(4): 478–504.

Stiglitz, Joseph, Armatya Sen, and Jean-Paul Fitoussi. 2010. *Mis-Measuring Our Lives: Why GDP Doesn't Add Up.* New York: New Press.

Svampa, Maristella, and Sebastián Pereyra. 2003. *Entre la ruta y el barrio: la experiencia de las organizaciones piqueteras.* Buenos Aires: Editorial Biblos.

Tarrow, Sidney. 1989. *Democracy and Disorder: Protest and Politics in Italy, 1965–1975.* Oxford: Oxford University Press.

———. 1994. *Power in Movement.* Cambridge: Cambridge University Press.

———. 2005. *The New Transnational Activism.* Cambridge: Cambridge University Press.

Taylor, Verta, Katrina Kimport, Nella Van Dyke, and Ellen Andersen. 2009. "Culture and Mobilization: Tactical Repertoires, Same-Sex Weddings, and the Impact on Gay Activism." *American Sociological Review* 74(6): 865–90.

Taylor, Verta, and Nella Van Dyke. 2004. "'Get Up, Stand Up': Tactical Repertoires of Social Movements." in D. Snow, S. Soule, and H. Kriesi, eds., *The Blackwell Companion to Social Movements*, 262–93. Oxford: Blackwell.

Tilly, Charles. 1978. *From Mobilization to Revolution*. Reading, MA: Addison-Wesley.

——. 1986. *The Contentious French: Four Centuries of Popular Struggle*. Cambridge, MA: Harvard University Press.

Tilly, Charles, and Lesley Wood. 2012. *Social Movements, 1768–2004*. Boulder, CO: Paradigm.

Trejos, María Eugenia. 1988. *¿Desnacionalización el ICE?* Cuaderno de Estudio no. 9. San José, Costa Rica: CEPAS.

Trejos, María Eugenia, and José Manuel Valverde. 1995. *Las organizaciones del magisterio frente al ajuste*. San José, Costa Rica: FLACSO.

Tyroler, Deborah. 1990. "Panama: 68 Trade Unions Stage 24-hour Walkout to Protest Government Economic Policies." *Latin American Data Base*, Dec. 7.

United Nations. 1993. "From Madness to Hope: The 12-Year War in El Salvador: Report of the Commission on the Truth for El Salvador." United Nations, New York.

Van Cott, Donna Lee. 2005. *From Movements to Parties in Latin America: The Evolution of Ethnic Politics*. Cambridge: Cambridge University Press.

Van Dyke, Nella. 1998. "Hotbeds of Activism: Locations of Student Protest," *Social Problems* 45(2): 205–19.

——. 2003. "Crossing Movement Boundaries: Factors That Facilitate Coalition Protest by American College Students, 1930–1990." *Social Problems* 50(2): 226–50.

Van Dyke, Nella, Mark Dixon, and Helen Carlon. 2007. "Manufacturing Dissent: Labor Revitalization, Union Summer, and Student Protest." *Social Forces* 88(1): 193–214.

Van Dyke, Nella, and Sarah Soule. 2002. "Structural Social Change and the Mobilizing Effect of Threat: Explaining Levels of Patriot and Militia Organizing in the United States." *Social Problems* 49(4): 497–520.

Vargas, Oscar-René. 1999. *El Sandinismo: Veinte años después*. Managua: CNE.

Vásquez, Abarca. 1992. *Los Movimientos Sociales en el Desarrollo Reciente de Cosa Rica*. San José, CA: UNED/UNAD.

Véliz, Rodrigo. 2009. *Capital y luchas: breve análisis de la protesta y el conflicto social actual*. Cuaderno de Debate no. 10. Guatemala City: FLACSO.

——. 2010. "San Marcos y la crisis energética: rastros de una lucha de clases." In S. Yagenova, R. García, R. Véliz, and W. Santa Cruz, eds., *Los movimientos sociales y el poder: concepciones, luchas y construcción de contrahegemonía*, 49–70. Guatemala City: FLACSO.

Vilas, Carlos. 1986. *The Sandinista Revolution: National Liberation and Social Transformation in Central America*. New York: Monthly Review Press.

Viterna, Jocelyn. 2006. "Pulled, Pushed, and Persuaded: Explaining Women's Mobilization into the Salvadoran Guerrilla Army." *American Journal of Sociology* 112(1): 1–45.

——. 2013. *Women in War: The Micro-processes of Mobilization in El Salvador*. Oxford: Oxford University Press.

Von Bulow, Marisa. 2011. *Building Transnational Networks: Civil Society and the Politics of Trade in the Americas*. Cambridge: Cambridge University Press.

Vreeland, James. 2003. *The IMF and Economic Development*. Cambridge: Cambridge University Press.

——. 2007. *The International Monetary Fund: Politics of Conditional Lending*. New York: Routledge.

Walder, Andrew. 2009. "Political Sociology and Social Movements." *Annual Review of Sociology* 35:393–412.

Walton, John. 1987. "Urban Protest and the Global Political Economy: The IMF Riots." In M. P. Smith and J. Feagin, eds., *The Capitalist City: Global Restructuring and Community Politics*, 364–86. Oxford: Basil Blackwell.

———. 1998. "Urban Conflict and Social Movements in Poor Countries: Theory and Evidence of Collective Action." *International Journal of Urban and Regional Research* 22(3): 460–81.

Walton, John, and Charles Ragin. 1990. "Global and National Sources of Political Protest: Third World Responses to the Debt Crisis." *American Sociological Review* 55(6): 876–91.

Walton, John, and David Seddon. 1994. "Food Riots Past and Present." In *Free Markets and Food Riots: The Politics of Global Adjustment*, 23–54. Oxford: Blackwell.

Walton, John, and Jonathan Shefner. 1994. "Latin America: Popular Protest and the State." In J. Walton and D. Seddon, eds., *Free Markets and Food Riots: The Politics of Global Adjustment*, 97–134. Oxford: Blackwell.

Weiss, Merideth, Edward Aspinall, and Mark Thompson. 2012. "Toward a Framework for Understanding Student Activism in Asia." In Meredith L. Weiss and Edward Aspinall, eds., *Student Activism in Asia: Between Protest and Powerlessness*, 1–32. Minneapolis: University of Minnesota Press.

Weyland, Kurt. 2006. *Bounded Rationality and Policy Diffusion: Social Sector Reform in Latin America*. Princeton, NJ: Princeton University Press.

Wickham-Crowley, Timothy. 1989. "Winners, Losers, and Also-Rans: Toward a Comparative Sociology of Latin American Guerrilla Movements." In S. Eckstein, ed., *Power and Popular Protest: Latin American Social Movements*, 132–81. Berkeley: University of California Press.

———. 1992. *Guerrillas and Revolution in Latin America: A Comparative Study of Insurgents and Regimes since 1956*. Princeton, NJ: Princeton University Press.

Williams, Phillip J., and Knut Walter. 1997. *Militarization and Demilitarization in El Salvador's Transition to Democracy*. Pittsburgh, PA: University of Pittsburgh.

Wood, Elisabeth Jean. 2000. *Forging Democracy from Below: Insurgent Transitions in South Africa and El Salvador*. Cambridge: Cambridge University Press.

———. 2003. *Insurgent Collective Action and Civil War in El Salvador*. Cambridge: Cambridge University Press.

———. 2005. "Challenges to Political Democracy in El Salvador." In Hagopian and Mainwaring (2005), 179–201.

Wood, Lesley. 2012. *Direct Action, Deliberation, and Diffusion: Collective Action after the WTO Protests in Seattle*. Cambridge: Cambridge University Press.

Yagenova, Simona Violetta. 2005. "La Guatemala de la resistencia y de la esperanza: las jornadas de lucha contra el CAFTA." *Observatorio social de América Latina* 6(16): 183–92.

Yagenova, Simona, and Rocio Garcia. 2009. "Indigenous People's Struggles against Transnational Mining Companies in Guatemala: The Sipakapa People vs. GoldCorp Mining Company." *Socialism and Democracy* 23(3): 57–166.

Yagenova, Simona, and Rodrigo Véliz. 2011. "Guatemala: una década en transición." In Modonesi and Rebón (2011), 255–74.

Yashar, Deborah. 2005. *Contesting Citizenship in Latin America: The Rise of Indigenous Movements and the Postliberal Challenge*. Cambridge: Cambridge University.

Zald, Mayer. 1992. "Looking Backward to Look Forward: Reflections on the Past and Future of the Resource Mobilization Research Program." In A. D. Morris and C. M. Mueller, eds., *Frontiers of Social Movement Theory*, 326–50. New Haven, CT: Yale University Press.

Zhao, Dingxin. 1998. "Ecologies of Social Movements: Student Mobilization during the 1989 Prodemocracy Movement in Beijing." *American Journal of Sociology* 103(6): 1493–529.

———. 2001. *The Power of Tiananmen: State-Society Relations and the 1989 Beijing Student Movement*. Chicago: University of Chicago Press.

Index

Page numbers in *italics* indicate figures.